THE EAGLE
AND
THE DRAGON

Recent Titles in
Contributions in Military Studies

Military Planning for the Defense of the United Kingdom, 1814-1870
Michael Stephen Partridge

The Hollow Army: How the U.S. Army Is Oversold and Undermanned
William Darryl Henderson

Reevaluating Major Naval Combatants of World War II
James J. Sadkovich, editor

The Culture of War: Invention and Early Development
Richard A. Gabriel

Prisoners, Diplomats, and the Great War: A Study in the Diplomacy
of Captivity
Richard Berry Speed III

Military Crisis Management: U.S. Intervention in the Dominican Republic, 1965
Herbert G. Schoonmaker

The Persian Gulf War: Lessons for Strategy, Law, and Diplomacy
Christopher C. Joyner, editor

Where Eagles Land: Planning and Development of U.S. Army Airfields,
1910-1941
Jerold E. Brown

First Strike Stability: Deterrence after Containment
Stephen J. Cimbala

Legitimacy and Commitment in the Military
Thomas C. Wyatt and Reuven Gal, editors

The Army's Nuclear Power Program: The Evolution of a Support Agency
Lawrence H. Suid

Russian Imperial Military Doctrine and Education, 1832-1914
Carl Van Dyke

THE EAGLE
AND
THE DRAGON

The United States Military in China, 1901–1937

DENNIS L. NOBLE

CONTRIBUTIONS IN MILITARY STUDIES,
NUMBER 102

GREENWOOD PRESS
New York • Westport, Connecticut • London

Library of Congress Cataloging-in-Publication Data

Noble, Dennis L.
   The eagle and the dragon : the United States military in China,
1901-1937 / Dennis L. Noble.
      p.   cm.—(Contributions in military studies, ISSN 0883-6884 ;
no. 102)
   Includes bibliographical references.
   ISBN 0-313-27299-9 (lib. bdg. : alk. paper)
   1. United States—Armed Forces—China—History—20th century.
2. United States—Armed Forces—China—Military life—History—20th
century.   I. Title.   II. Series.
UA26.C58N63   1990
355.1—dc20   90-3146

British Library Cataloguing in Publication Data is available.

Library of Congress Catalog Card Number: 90-3146
ISBN: 0-313-27299-9
ISSN: 0883-6884

First published in 1990

Greenwood Press, 88 Post Road West, Westport, CT 06881
An imprint of Greenwood Publishing Group, Inc.

Printed in the United States of America

The paper used in this book complies with the
Permanent Paper Standard issued by the National
Information Standards Organization (Z39.48-1984).

10 9 8 7 6 5 4 3 2 1

Copyright Acknowledgments

The author and publisher gratefully acknowledge the following sources for granting permission to use personal and copyrighted material:

Kemp Tolley, "Three Piecie and Other Dollars Mex," *Shipmate,* 28, no. 10 (December 1965): 8-10. Courtesy of *Shipmate,* U.S. Naval Academy.

Papers of Henry J. Poy. Courtesy of Henry A. Poy.

Papers of Glenn F. Howell. Courtesy of R. W. Howell.

Papers of Robert C. Giffen. Courtesy of Robert C. Giffen, Jr.

The map, "North China in the 1920s," is courtesy of Kenneth A. Patterson.

The photographs are courtesy of the U.S. Navy, Clem D. Russell, Oliver G. Webb, Arthur G. Gullickson, and Anthony Ingrisano.

Every reasonable effort has been made to trace the owners of copyrighted materials. The publisher will be glad to receive information leading to more complete acknowledgments in subsequent printings and in the meantime extends its apologies for any omissions.

For Truman R. Strobridge

CONTENTS

Illustrations   xi

Preface   xiii

Abbreviations   xxi

1. Introduction: The Eagle and the Dragon   1

2. Soldiers, Sailors, and Marines   43

3. Troop and Stomp: The Duty Day and Routine   85

4. "A Marvelous Existence": Off-Duty Hours   109

5. Among the "Heathen Chinee": American
   Servicemen's Perceptions of China and
   the Chinese   143

6. Going Asiatic: Servicemen Who Remained
   in China   171

7. Land the Landing Party: Incidents
   Requiring a Show of Force   187

8. Taps: Conclusion   209

Selected Bibliography   213

Index   233

ILLUSTRATIONS

Map: North China in the 1920s   193

Photographs: Between pages 157 and 158

TABLES
 1. Permanent U.S. Ground Troops in China,
    1905-1936   32
 2. Officers' Places of Birth   46
 3. Where Officers Were Acquired   47
 4. Where Officers Were Acquired by Rank   48
 5. Officers Attending Military Schools   49
 6. Which Officers Attended Military Schools   50
 7. Average Age by Rank   51
 8. Year of Enlistment   51
 9. Decorations (DSM or Higher)   52
10. Years of Service, Co. E, 1924-1925
    (Enlisted)   56
11. Home of Record, Co. E, 1924-1925 (Enlisted)   58
12. Service of Men in Co. E, 1924-1925
    (Enlisted)   58
13. Year of Enlistment for Sample of
    Enlisted Men, 1929   59
14. Age of Enlisted Men, 1929   59
15. Age at Enlistment for Sample of Enlisted
    Men, 1929   60
16. Place of Birth for Sample of Enlisted Men,
    1929   60
17. Service of Sample of Enlisted Men, 1929   62
18. Length of Service of Navy Enlisted Force,
    1921-1929   65
19. Four Most Common Charges in Summary Courts-
    Martial During 1927 in Fifteenth Infantry   66

xii   Illustrations

20. Navy Enlisted Men Tried by Courts-Martial,
    1909-1937   71
21. Desertion, U.S. Navy, 1901-1937   72

PREFACE

In 1900, troops of the United States, under the command of Maj. Gen. of Volunteers Adna Chafee, cooperated with an international force that crushed an uprising in China. When Chafee withdrew his men, he left behind one reinforced army infantry regiment, which in 1901 was reduced to one rifle company, to act as the legation guard at Peking. This marks the beginning of a sporadic build-up of American military forces until, twenty-seven years later, U.S. servicemen of all branches of the military establishment were stationed at Peking, Tientsin, and Shanghai, and were cruising the coastal waters and some of the river systems of China.

The thousands of men who served on the China Station before World War II have been all but forgotten, except in the mythology of the military. In the sea stories and barracks tales of soldiers, leathernecks, and old salts, China hands have been depicted as swaggering, larger-than-life men. China hands gained repute as the best professional military men and also the best at drinking and womanizing.

Why have these men been overlooked? Part of the reason is that most of the troops served in the peacetime military. Most Americans would probably agree with the British statesman, William Cecil, who wrote: "Soldiers in peace are like chimneys in summer." People in the United States have traditionally thought of the men in the peacetime military as like a summer chimney, as dirty and useless. Anton Myrer has captured the essence of this

feeling in his novel, <u>Once</u> <u>An</u> <u>Eagle</u>. The protagonist, Sam Damon, has decided to enlist in the
pre-World War I army and is confronted with the
outburst of a Civil War veteran: "You don't join
the army in <u>peacetime</u>, to consort with thieves and
drunkards, ignorant moonshiners and the riff-raff
of the cities of the East. . . . Outlaws, and men
without names--that's what the army's filled with
now, boy. . . ."[1] In short, in our society it is
acceptable to do one's bit in wartime, or, perhaps,
even to nip into the service during severe economic
times, but anyone who would willingly enter the
military during prosperity must be suspect.
Indeed, this attitude is even reflected in the
sparse amount of fiction devoted to the American
military during peacetime. Literally hundreds of
novels have been written about the American
military experience during war, but very few have
been penned on the years between the wars.

If novelists have neglected the twentieth-
century peacetime military, so have historians.
One can understand both the fiction and nonfiction
writer's lack of interest in the subject. The
sweep of events during the clash of battle is
momentous and exciting. To study whether men
conform to Ernest Hemingway's "grace under
pressure" during combat seems more interesting than
to read about the mundane, everyday routines of
normal garrison duty in some small, isolated post.
In recent years, however, there has been a growing
awareness among some historians that military
history should include more than battles, tactics,
and strategy. Richard H. Kohn, for example, has
pointed out how little we really know about the men
who served in the U.S. military in the twentieth
century. This relatively newfound interest has
been dubbed the "new" military history. It
embraces the social aspects of the military, rather
than battles. It asks such questions as: What were
the origins and values of the men who served? How
were the men recruited, and what caused them to
enter the military? What are the relationships
between military and civilian society? How were
minorities in the service treated? These and a
host of other questions are now being explored
under the rubric of the "new" military history.

An analysis of the military experience in East
Asia in the early twentieth century offers the
student of American military history the chance to

learn about the people within the ranks, rather
than the large issues of tactical doctrine,
strategy, or even war plans. Naval officer and
former China hand George Van Deurs recalled the day
that the officers of the Jason read the war plan
that detailed their duties in case of an emergency:
"[W]e all got laughing so hard that it was hard to
keep reading. . . it was just like reading the
funny papers. It was completely ridiculous," given
the equipment of the Asiatic Fleet.[2] Since the
numbers of servicemen in East Asia were rather
small (except for brief periods of unrest in China,
when troops were shuttled in and out), China
provides an excellent microcosm of the American
military on overseas station.

It is important to look at the social aspects
of the American military experience in China.
While twentieth-century U.S. military history is
dominated by two World Wars and two "limited" wars,
the services have spent more years in garrison than
on the field of battle. It becomes important,
then, to study the men who would be the cadre for
wartime expansion.

Studies of twentieth-century American military
personnel run up against federal laws prohibiting
the examination of service records for close to one
hundred years. To compensate, I contacted as many
former China hands as possible and questioned them
either in person or through questionnaires. I have
also relied heavily upon oral histories and any
written materials from the China hands. The comments of wives and children of servicemen, an
important part of the story of the American
military in China, provide an additional perspec-
tive. There is, of course, some danger in using
this type of evidence. Mark Twain once remarked:
"I can remember things that never happened."
Memory is fallible. Some people were recalling
events from more than a half century ago. Whenever
possible, I tried to corroborate witnesses'
comments with other documents.

In addition to the problem of federal privacy
law, there are few works on the social aspects of
the peacetime U.S. military. This is especially
true of those forces on foreign stations. In the
main, the literature centers on the Philippine
Islands or Central America, with most of the
emphasis on strictly military or diplomatic
affairs. Furthermore, previous works have usually

concentrated on only one service. This study marks
the first effort to understand how the peacetime
military lived on a foreign station. The federal
laws prohibiting the examination of service
records and the lack of studies on the social
aspects of the American military make many of the
conclusions presented here impressionistic.   It
must be stressed that definitive conclusions must
await further studies on the subject.

The major thrust of this work is on how the
American military men, both officer and enlisted,
lived in China. The men, however, did not live in a
vacuum. It is important to understand the entire
milieu in which the men lived. Therefore, chapter
one gives a short background history of China, the
involvement of the first units of the American
military establishment in East Asia, and, lastly,
the build-up of men during the second decade of the
twentieth-century.   This introduction is followed
by examinations of the men who served in East Asia,
the nature of the duty, their off-duty pursuits,
how the men perceived China and the Chinese, and
why some military men chose to remain in East Asia
instead of returning to the United States. Since
there were periods of intense actions, one chapter
is devoted to how the men reacted to situations of
great danger.

The reader may wonder why, after the first
chapter, there is so little mention of the larger
events in China, for this was a period of great
change in that ancient country. The average
soldier, sailor, or leatherneck, both officer and
enlisted, had little comprehension of the Chinese
domestic scene or, for that matter, little interest
in what was happening. Even the men with cultural
insight seemed blissfully unaware of the
surrounding political scene. Richard McKenna, for
example, who served as a career enlisted sailor in
China and wrote The Sand Pebbles, arguably the best
novel depicting sailors in China, noted many years
later that "I . . . spent nearly ten years in China
. . . without becoming more than vaguely aware that
the unequal treaties existed. . . . I cannot
explain to myself why I did not know. . . . [I]
knew it was all right to curse and kick Coolies in
China, but that you had better not do anything like
it in Japan and the Philippines."[3] In short, this
study reflects both what the men observed and what
they failed to observe.

If any former China hand should read this study and exclaim, "That is not the way it was when I served there!" I can say only that this points out another problem in studying the China station. Much of what a person observed depended upon when and where one was stationed within East Asia. That is, a soldier stationed at Tientsin in 1914 would have a far different view of the city and the duty than an infantryman stationed there during the unrest of the 1920s. Moreover, for those former China hands who recall nothing adventurous about their service, I believe that marine Lt. Gen. James P. Berkeley best summed up the situation when he observed that each generation of China hands thought the previous days were more glamorous.

I have chosen to study the years 1901 to 1937, as this is the period in which all branches of the American armed forces were stationed in China. Prior to 1900, only naval personnel served in East Asia; after 1937, the army was removed to avert any possible conflict with the Japanese that might cause a full-scale American commitment in the Far East. While all branches of the military deployed personnel to China after 1941, their mission was in the context of a general war and thus irrelevant to an understanding of the peacetime military. The same is true of the year 1900, the year of the Boxer Uprising. Thus, it is only during this narrow thirty-six year gap that we can obtain a meaningful understanding of the peacetime military in China.

A word needs to be said about the spelling of Chinese names and places. Over the years, there have been many attempts to Romanize the Chinese language. The capital of China, for example, has been Peiping, Peking, and Beijing. The system now in use in the People's Republic of China, _Pinyin_, may be confusing to most Americans. Most recognize Canton, but would not realize that Guangzhou is now the recognized spelling of the same city. Therefore, in order to prevent undue confusion, I will use the system that is most familiar to Americans, known as the Wade-Giles, with the _Pinyin_ spelling after the word when first used; thus, Canton [Guangzhou], Peking [Beijing], and Mao Tse-tung [Mao Zedong].

This study offers the chance for the student of American military history to gain an impressionistic glimpse of the people serving within the ranks of the U.S. armed forces on the far outposts of its empire. It also allows us the chance to view how the American military reacted to its role as a colonial occupying force and how a very diverse group of people lived within a culture that was completely foreign to anything in their former experiences. Benjamin Franklin Cooling has correctly noted that "Men, not things, still make war," and it is important to understand the men who served in peacetime, so that we may better grasp how they behaved in war.[4] Further, while it has been a tenet that military personnel have remained outside of the mainstream of society, the reader will find that, in the final analysis, the study of the peacetime military in China is also an examination of American values and history.

Where this book has merit, it is because of the advice, encouragement, and assistance received from the people listed below. I am, of course, responsible for the contents of the work.

At Purdue University, Robert E. May, as dissertation director, bore the brunt of many drafts and flights of fancy, and kept the work within bounds. His insightful comments and patience helped me immeasurably. Leonard H.D. Gordon, Gordon R. Mork, and Gunther E. Rothenberg provided much helpful advice, comment, and encouragement.

I received financial assistance from a Purdue University David Ross Summer Research Grant to help defray the costs in locating former "China hands."

Without the help of these China hands, their wives, and their children, this work would have been difficult to complete. All gave freely of their time; rather than single out individuals, I have listed all in the bibliography.

This study could not have been completed without the assistance of dedicated archivists, curators, and librarians. At the Special Collections, Nimitz Library, U.S. Naval Academy, Mary Catalfania helped with locating papers of former China hands. Mr. Paul Stillwell, head of the Oral History Section of the Naval Institute provided valuable transcripts by naval officers. The librarians at the Manuscript Division of the Library of Congress were most helpful, as were the archivists in the Modern Military Records Section of the National Archives. Mr. Richard von Doenhoff of the Naval Records Section of the National Archives provided me with fast, efficient service.

I wish to thank Dr. Dean C. Allard, Director of the U.S. Naval Historical Center, Mr. Bernard F. Cavalcante, Head of the Operational Archives, and Kathleen Rohr and Jean Akers, also of the Naval Historical Center's Operational Archives.

At the U.S. Army Military History Institute's Archives, I wish to thank Dr. Richard Sommers and Pam Cheney for providing much-needed material on the U.S. Army in China.

At the U.S. Marine Corps Historical Center, the reference and library personnel were very helpful. I wish to especially thank J. Michael Miller and Col. James Leon, USMC (Ret) in the Personal Papers Collection and Mr. Benis Frank, Head of the Oral History Section. Mr. Frank spent many hours discussing China and suggesting avenues of research. The Corps and researchers are fortunate to have his strong leadership in oral history.

Bernard C. Nalty of the Office of U.S. Air Force History gave a great deal of encouragement and advice.

The following interlibrary loan librarians provided critically needed books: Ruth Rothenberg of Purdue University Libraries, JoAnne Hughes of Peninsula College, Port Angeles, Washington, and Rose Symonds of the North Olympic Library System, Port Angeles, Washington.

Peggy Brady, Paula Epstein, Loren Noble, and Don Wilson, all of Port Angeles, Washington, and Earl Hess, of Lincoln Memorial University, provided helpful comments. Barbara Evander quickly and efficiently typed the manuscript.

Mr. William Bassman and Mary Parker provided assistance at the National Personnel Records Center.

At Greenwood Press, Mildred Vasan guided the manuscript through its production. Susan Wladaver-Morgan and Alicia Merritt also provided editorial assistance.

This book is dedicated to Truman R. Strobridge, Command Historian, U.S. European Command. While Historian of the U.S. Coast Guard, Mr. Strobridge took time from his busy schedule to undertake the difficult task of teaching a sailor the intricacies and pleasures of historical research. Through all of my never-ending questions, mistakes, and requests for advice, he remained helpful and somehow kept his patience.

NOTES

1. Anton Myrer, Once an Eagle (New York: Rinehart and Winston, 1968), 237.

2. RADM George Van Duers interview by CDR Etta-Belle Kitchen (1974), 236, Oral History Program, Naval Institute (OHNI), Annapolis, MD.

3. Richard McKenna, "Our Own Houses," in New Eyes for Old: Nonfiction Writings by Richard McKenna, eds. Eva Grice McKenna and Shirley Grave Cochrane (Winston-Salem, NC: John F. Blair, 1972), 116.

4. Benjamin Franklin Cooling, "Toward a More Usable Past: A Modest Plea for a Newer Typology of Military History," Military Affairs, 52, no. 1 (January 1988): 31.

ABBREVIATIONS

ARMY/MARINE CORPS

GEN	(Gen.)	General
LGEN	(Lt. Gen.)	Lieutenant General
MGEN	(Maj. Gen.)	Major General
BGEN	(Brig. Gen.)	Brigadier General
COL	(Col.)	Colonel
LCL	(Lt. Col.)	Lieutenant Colonel
MAJ	(Maj.)	Major
CPT	(Capt.)	Captain
1LT		First Lieutenant
2LT		Second Lieutenant
LT	(Lt.)	Lieutenant
Msgt.		Master Sergeant
Sfc.		Sergeant First Class
Sgt.		Sergeant
Corp.		Corporal
Pfc.		Private First Class
Pvt.		Private

NAVY (OFFICER)

ADM	(Adm.)	Admiral
VADM	(VAdm.)	Vice Admiral
RADM	(RAdm.)	Rear Admiral
	(Commo.)	Commodore
CAPT	(Capt.)	Captain
CDR	(Comdr.)	Commander
LCDR	(Lt.Comdr.)	Lieutenant Commander
LT	(Lt.)	Lieutenant
LTJG	(Lt. j.g.)	Lieutenant, Junior Grade

1

INTRODUCTION: THE EAGLE AND THE DRAGON

Until the Age of Discovery, the inhabitants of China had four-thousand years of relative isolation. Then, in the sixteenth century, Portuguese and Spanish explorers and envoys began to arrive in East Asia, followed closely by traders and missionaries. Occurring at almost the same time was the rise of the Manchus and the establishment of the alien Ch'ing dynasty. These two events had many consequences, some of lasting significance.

The Ming dynasty (1368-1644) was supplanted by the Mancus, a Jurched tribe from what is now Manchuria. The Manchus established the Ch'ing dynasty. In order to maintain the goodwill of the Chinese, they absorbed many Chinese traditions, kept the Ming government and social institutions, and assimilated Chinese into their bureaucracy. This does not mean that the Manchus were benevolent. Indeed, the regime ruled with an iron fist and strove to separate Manchu from Chinese. The presence of outsiders was accepted by some Chinese, but the autocratic rule of a foreign element did not sit well with all.

Foreign rule caused an undercurrent of discontent. The unrest helped in the formation of secret societies and nationalistic/racial revolt and revolution. The first anti-Manchu activities were the Ming loyalist movements, which attempted to revive the Ming dynasty. When these failed, resistance was kept alive among such secret societies as the White Lotus Sect. When the Manchus relaxed their grip slightly, as they did from 1736 to 1795, anti-Manchu discontent rose to the surface, leading, for example, to the White Lotus Rebellion (1796-1804). This rebellion was quelled, only to be taken up again by the Taipings from 1850 to 1864.[1]

Until the West came into ascendancy in the world, China remained relatively isolated or could at least dictate the terms upon which the West could engage in trade. Those who wished to enter into commerce could deal with a few selected merchants only at Canton [Guangzhou]. As England's power grew, it desired to expand beyond Canton. Most frustrating of all to the English was the large imbalance of trade against Great Britain. The English imported great amounts of tea and silk, but were not exporting anywhere near enough goods to make up the imbalance. The problem is clearly spelled out in Emperor Ching Lung's [Jian Ling] communication to King George III in 1793. "[T]here is nothing we lack," wrote Emperor Ching. "We have never set much store on strange or ingenious objects, nor do we need any more of your country's manufacturers."[2]   England would need to find something that could provide both a wedge to open China and to redress the imbalance of trade. The wedge was opium.

Beginning in 1819, opium became gold to traders in China. From 1822 to 1830, eighteen-thousand chests of opium passed through Lintin Island, just outside of Canton. (A chest usually weighed 140 pounds.) The trade produced a dramatic reversal in China's economic situation. In the first decade of the nineteenth century, for example, China had gained approximately $26,000,000 in her world balance of payments. From 1826 to 1836, $38,000,000 flowed out of the Celestial Kingdom.[3]

Most of the opium for China came from India, where it was a monopoly of the East India Company. A Chinese imperial edict in 1800 had prohibited the cultivation or importation of the drug. The East India Company ceased transporting the product in its ships, but did not stop either growing opium or selling the drug to any private concern from any nation. Thus, the East India Company continued to reap profits and made the opium trade a bootleg enterprise. The trade, in fact, resembled the illegal drug operations currently being carried out in the United States. Ships carrying opium would use Portuguese Macao [Aomen] as a base or would anchor offshore. Small, fast boats would then be loaded and sent to illegal dealers. The unscrupulous trader would pay for the drug with tea, silk, or silver specie.   Most of the Western maritime nations participated in this traffic, including the United States, but the largest cargoes came aboard English merchantmen.   The influence of the illegal trade reached into government as some officials were bought out by the smugglers.   Addiction ran rampant, especially among the Chinese upper class.   In short, the drug became one of the dominant factors in Chinese life.

Eventually, the Chinese imperial government decided upon strong action.   It appointed Lin Tse-hsu [Lin Zexu] as High Commissioner at Canton to suppress the trade.   Lin was a man of strong character--aggressive, against opium, and anti-foreign. He took seriously his instructions to stamp out the opium trade.

Lin began his crackdown in 1839.   He ordered foreign and Chinese merchants to turn over all opium stocks for destruction.   All foreign merchants were required to post a bond in pledge that their ships would never again bring the drug into Canton.   Those who made the pledge and violated it were to be put to death.   In the meantime, Lin ordered the Canton factory district surrounded by troops and armed boats, and all foreigners were confined to the district.   When the British tried to leave Canton and the Chinese attempted to stop them, it provided the spark for the beginning of the Opium War (1839-41) and the opening of China.[4]

The Opium War was a lopsided conflict.   The Chinese had nothing to match the military power of the West.   The British sent a squadron of ships and a few thousand men to blockade and bombard Canton, which quickly surrendered. The squadron then moved northward toward the Yangtze River [Chang Jiang], taking ports as it went.   Off Nanking [Nanjing] in central China, the British navy prepared to pound the city into submission.   Nanking followed the example of Canton and surrendered.   In 1842, China capitulated and accepted Great Britain's terms. The Treaty of Nanking, concluded on 29 August 1842, and supplemented by the Treaty of the Bogue, concluded 1 October 1843, laid the basis for China's relations with the West for almost a century.

The two treaties provided an indemnity of $21,000,000, which included $6,000,000 as compensation for the opium destroyed by Lin, $12,000,000 for war costs, and $3,000,000 for debts owed to British merchants. The island of Hong Kong [Xiangang] was ceded to Great Britain in perpetuity and the ports of Amoy, Canton, Foochow [Fuzhou], Ningpo, and Shanghai were opened to foreign trade and consular service. China agreed to a uniform tariff fixed at 5 percent ad valorem, to be changed only by mutual agreement. In the Treaty of the Bogue, the full privilege of extraterritoriality (the exemption of foreigners from Chinese legal jurisdiction) was obtained for British subjects, and Britain received most-favored-nation status. This insured that any right, privilege, or concession extended in the future to any other nation would automatically accrue to Great Britain. Furthermore, the Chinese agreed to set aside, in each of the newly opened ports, areas where foreigners could reside. These would eventually constitute foreign cities under foreign governments at all important points throughout China.[5]

Great Britain was the first nation to force China into submission, but it was not the only nation to take advantage of the war. In short order, the United States and the other major powers began to seek advantages. In 1842, after the signing of the Treaty of Nanking, Commo. Lawrence Kearny, commanding a naval squadron sent to the Far East at the outbreak of the war, approached Chinese officials and formally expressed the hope that American merchants would be put on the same basis as those from Great Britain. He received assurances that this would be done, and subsequently the United States received most-favored-nation status. The United States, however, did not force this right. The Chinese granted it. This was a calculated move on the part of the Imperial government, which believed that safety might be found in playing off one Western nation against the other.[6]

The emphasis on trade by Kearny reflects the perceived importance of commerce between the United States and China. One student of early Chinese-American relations has noted that the "China trade was a vital factor in U.S. capital formation during the nineteenth century."[7] Indeed, trading had begun even prior to American independence. John Ledyard, who was a corporal of marines on Capt. James Cook's last voyage to the Pacific in 1776, was one of the first to point out the advantages of dealing with the Far East. Upon his return, he traveled to North America in 1782 and published his account of Cook's voyage. The former marine noted that a triangular trade from New England could return handsome profits. Material from the east coast of the United States would be bartered for the furs of the Pacific Northwest. The furs, in demand in China, would be exchanged for tea and silk, which would reap great profits in New England. Using his fame as an author, Ledyard approached such businessmen as Robert Morris of Philadelphia and others in an attempt to convince them of the chance for riches. Ledyard, however, failed in his efforts.[8]

Shortly thereafter, a group of merchants, led by Morris and Daniel Parker of New York, purchased the 360-ton Empress of China and fitted her out for the China trade. These entrepreneurs, however, decided to trade with the Middle Kingdom without stopping in the Pacific Northwest. Samuel Shaw was selected as supercargo. The merchants chose over forty tons of cargo, consisting of ginseng (which the Chinese held in high esteem as a medicinal herb) and other articles. In February 1784, the ship cleared New York harbor and six months later, after touching at Java and Macao, Empress hove to near Canton. Ten months later, with a large cargo of tea, the ship weighed anchor and was homeward bound, arriving in New York in May with reported profits of some $37,727.[9]

In January 1786, Shaw was appointed the first American Consul at Canton. The same year saw a marked increase in trade between the new nation and the Middle Kingdom. Five merchantmen cleared Canton, and within three years, the numbers had increased to more than twenty. Importation of Chinese tea into the United States increased steadily. In 1790, for example, three million pounds were shipped; within twenty years, the amount rose to eight million pounds. Eventually, merchants awoke to Ledyard's advice. By 1812, the triangular fur trade had produced its first millionaire, John Jacob Astor.[10]

Through the nineteenth century, the China trade was an up-and-down affair. Until the American Civil War, it boomed; following the war, it slowed somewhat, reflecting the United States' preoccupation with internal matters. However, as Nathaniel Peffer has pointed out, the most favored nation status "became one of the fixed points in American foreign policy."[11] In fact, the United States was second only to Great Britain in gaining advantages from the opening of China.   On 3 July 1844, a treaty was signed between the United States and China. The treaty followed the same lines as the one between Great Britain and the Middle Kingdom. Americans could trade at the newly opened ports; the United States enjoyed consular representation, most-favored-nation status, and extra-territorality; its citizens were permitted to reside in areas set aside for them.   The treaty included a stipulation that if American goods were landed at one port and customs duties paid on them, they could be reshipped to another port without payment of additional duties, thus driving a wedge into the Chinese coastal trade.[12]

The drug situation in China after the Opium War was no better than before. Opium traffic continued without check. By 1850, the volume entering China had risen to at least 52,000 chests per year. Another source of friction between China and the West concerned the coolie trade.   Peasants and unskilled urban laborers were being shipped to many parts of the world. Most of the trade was to the West Indies. One of the worse aspects of the trade was the inhumane method of transporting the coolies. Thousands died in airless, overcrowded holds. Like opium, this traffic was too profitable to be stopped.[13]

The continuing opium trade, the coolie trade, humiliation over defeat, and many other grievances led to a continuing high level of unrest in the Celestial Kingdom.   In the American and French treaties with China, a provision had been made for revision in twelve years. As the 1850s approached, Britain also demanded a review. The British wanted additional concessions, not the least of which was the right to navigate the Yangtze River.   The Chinese refused to negotiate. Again, West and East were close to war.

In 1856, the incident needed to spark violence occurred in Canton. A Chinese ship under British registery, the _Arrow_, was accused by Chinese authorities of harboring pirates. The ship was boarded, twelve crewmen were taken prisoner, and the British flag was hauled down. Britain demanded an apology and the release of the imprisoned crewmen. The men were eventually returned, but Viceroy Yeh Ming-Chien [Ye Mingchen] refused to

apologize.   The British consul, Harry Parkes,
called for the Royal Navy.   The ships began a
bombardment of the Canton forts, and Yeh called
upon the Chinese to crush the British.   A second
war was on.   But in the Arrow War (1856-58), the
British had the support of the French, who were
incensed about the torture and killing of a French
missionary in Kwangsi [Guangxi] Province.[14]

The Arrow War, like the Opium War, was a lopsided contest.   Canton soon fell to the Anglo-
French alliance.   The allies then demanded negotations at Peking [Beijing]. In the meanwhile, the
European nations had been joined by representatives
of Russia and the United States in their demands.
As usual, the emperor told the negotiators to deal
with the officials in Canton.   This time, the
Western powers refused this arrangement, and an
expedition started toward the capital.   An Anglo-
French force took Shanghai and then moved to the
port of Tientsin [Tianjin], the gateway to Peking.
After the capture of the port, negotiations took
place, with treaties   signed by all four powers in
June 1858.   This did not end the hostilities.
Ratification was to take place in Peking, but
difficulties ensued.   For example, the American
minister, John E. Ward, indignantly left Peking
when he was required to perform the kowtow.   In
1860, in retaliation for the imprisonment and
killing of a British and French delegation at
Peking, a strong Anglo-French expedition burned and
looted the Imperial Summer Palace.   At last, the
Chinese were forced to submit.[15]

Britain, France, Russia, and the United States
won the right to maintain diplomatic representation in Peking. Citizens of the four powers could
now travel anywhere in the interior of China, under
the protection of extraterritoriality; ten more
ports were opened along the coast and up the
Yangtze River to Hankow [Hangzhou], and foreign
ships were permitted to navigate the Yangtze River.
Opium was legalized, and the right of missionaries
to preach Christianity and to own property anywhere
in the interior was recognized.   While foreigners
could travel to the interior, only missionaries
could reside there.[16]

During Arrow War, China was also racked by the
domestic uprising known as the Taiping Rebellion.
The rebellion was a major watershed in modern
Chinese history and cost the lives of millions of

Chinese.   In fact, the uprising had an effect on
the Arrow War and events in later Chinese history.
The Taiping Rebellion was basically an uprising of
peasants who were converts to their own forms of
Christianity.   The revolt was a mixture of anti-
Manchu revolution and a religious crusade.

The immediate cause of the rebellion may be laid
to a declining empire.   Beginning with the rule of
Chia-Ch'ing (1796-1820), the quality of the Manchu
rulers declined.   At nearly the same time, the
emperors were beset by a number of problems that
would have been difficult for even first-rate
rulers to handle.   One of the largest problems, as
we have seen, was how to deal with the inroads of
the West.   The dissipation of the rulers had contributed to China's defeat in the Opium War.
Simultaneously, the Middle Kingdom was stricken by
devastating crop failures and economic depression.
In short, by the 1850s, the combination of traditional unrest against the Manchus and a disin-
tegrating empire made for an unstable country.[17]

The leader of the rebellion, Hung Hisu-chuan
[Hung Xinchuan], was a Christian convert, but had
his own idea of Christianity.   He founded a new
trinity: God the Father, Jesus the Elder Brother,
and himself the Younger Brother.   He received
visions that instructed him to conquer for the new
faith.   Because Western missionaries and traders
seemed to the Chinese to have so much power, it is
not   surprising   that   a   strange   admixture   of
Christianity,   wizardry,   and   superstition   should
emerge.   In 1850, he began his crusade against
Buddhist and Taoist temples in Kwangsi Province.
Eventually, the movement touched sixteen of the
eighteen provinces in China and lasted for eleven
years. Ssu-Yu Teng, however, believes that the
primary causes were opposition to Manchu rule and
the economic depression brought on by the Manchus.

When the rebellion broke out, many Westerners
looked favorably upon the rebels.   Indeed, the
movement proclaimed some rather radical ideas for
China. The stated aims of the rebellion encouraged
monogamy,   prohibited   footbinding,   allowed   female
suffrage,   and   tried   to   simplify   the   Chinese
language.   As the years passed, however, many
Westerners began to have second thoughts.   One of
reasons for their change of mind was the rebels'
religious fanaticism.

Furthermore, many from the West were uneasy with

the rebellion's nationalism. Formally, the Western powers adopted a neutral stance toward the Taiping Rebellion. Neutrality, however, was mainly for home consumption. Great Britain used the uprising to make further inroads into China. When the rebels did not receive help from the British and other Western powers, the Manchus did not have to worry about the intervention of outside forces; the Manchus were thus indebted to the West. The Western powers knew a divided China was not good for trade. They preferred a strong, centralized government that could stand by its part of the treaties. Near the end of the rebellion, the Western powers gave arms, naval support, and advice to the Manchus. Of course, the support came with strings attached, in the form of greater demands for more influence in China.

Western influence upon the uprising affected the outcome of the rebellion, but the primary cause of its failure was weakness from within. Internal dissension caused many of those who had supported the uprising to lose faith and give up their support of the rebels. As the years wore on, many of the new leaders of the rebellion began to betray their peasant origins. In the end, the rebellion "resembled more a traditional Chinese 'peasant' insurrection than a modern revolution."[18]

The Taiping Rebellion was an important event in modern Chinese history. The effects of the rebellion were huge. It changed the political situation in the Middle Kingdom by weakening the central government. It caused a "shift in control of the military and political power from the central government to local governments."[19] It had an important influence on China's modernization. Many thoughtful Chinese could see the problems arising from Western intervention during the rebellion. These Chinese began to try to rely on themselves. One of the projects they undertook was the modernization of their army and navy. "There is no doubt that the Taiping Rebellion greatly stimulated China's westernization."[20]

Toward the end of the nineteenth century, many Chinese were frustrated, and the focus of their frustration eventually centered upon the foreigner. The reasons behind the anti-foreign feelings can be broadly grouped into several categories: anti-Christianity, resentment of foreign economic domination, anger over imperialism, and the effects of

natural disasters.   All of the frustrations eventually boiled over and became a part of the Boxer
Uprising of 1900.[21]

The Treaties of Tientsin (1858) allowed missionaries to move into the interior of China and to
purchase or rent land for the construction of
churches.   If they could not gain enough converts,
the missionaries often offered money and protection
to those Chinese who entered the church.   When
converts became involved in disputes with local
officials, missionaries rushed to their aid, thus
establishing a new favored class.   The gentry, as
the guardians of Confucian ways, resented the
inroads into their power by any foreign religion.

Most Chinese blamed the foreigners for their
economic difficulties.   The influx of foreign
imports depressed the economy.   After the Taiping
Rebellion, the expansion of foreign trade further
dominated China.   In 1899, for example, China had
a trade deficit of 69 million taels and a government budgetary imbalance of 12 million taels; a
tael, at that period, equaled $1.63.   To counter
this shortfall, the court increased taxes, which
fell most heavily upon the peasants.   This added
burden drove many to banditry and secret societies.
By the end of the nineteenth century, the country
was faced with the bankruptcy of village
industries, rising unemployment, and general
economic hardship. All of these problems were laid
at the door of the foreigner.

Along with the man-made difficulties, nature
added to the problems of the Chinese.   Both floods
and drought affected millions of people.   The
superstitious blamed outsiders for offending the
spirits by bringing in an alien religion.   Many
experienced a feeling of approaching extinction.
The more enlightened members of Chinese society
proposed institutional reform, but the radicals
and many peasants thought the best reform would
be the killing of the foreigners.

By the beginning of the twentieth-century, all
of these forces provided a volatile mixture that
needed very little to cause an explosion.   The
spark that finally led to bloodshed was provided in
1900 by a secret society called the I-ho ch'uan, or
the "Righteous and Harmonious Fists," after their
method of calisthenics.   In the West, they were
known as the "Boxers," and the Boxer Uprising of
1900 eventually led the United States to station

troops of all branches of the American armed forces in China.

The Boxers began as an anti-Ch'ing secret society and helped in the White Lotus Rebellion. By the late 1890s, the anti-dynastic secret society had become xenophobic, vowing to kill foreigners and their collaborators. The Boxers appealed to the superstitious with their practice of magic. They claimed that, after one hundred days of work with their society, they were immune to bullets and that, after four hundred days, they were able to fly. They used incantations, charms, and other devices to invoke supernatural powers. The Boxers, being anti-foreign, believed that the use of guns was not correct and preferred the traditional weapons of swords and lances.

By 1900, the Boxers had gained favor in the Imperial Court. The dowager empress, Tzu Hsi [Zi Xi], had the leader of the secret society summoned to Peking to demonstrate his invulnerability to bullets. The immunity was "proved," and the dowager ordered court attendants to learn boxing. Half of the government's troops joined the Boxers. Westerners looked on uneasily as rising anti-foreignism, coupled with the Boxer craze, stirred an undercurrent of unrest throughout most of the areas where non-Chinese resided. The growing concern caused Western diplomats to request guards for their legations in Peking. The Boxers, finding encouragement from the court, cut the railway line between Tientsin and Peking, thus isolating the capital city. Foreign diplomats feared a blood bath was about to begin. The British minister, Sir Claude MacDonald, sent out an urgent call for help, and an international naval force began to assemble off Taku. The events of the Boxer Uprising were set into motion.[22]

In the nineteenth century, vessels of the U.S. Navy represented the only American military force in China. Between 1800 and 1839, there were nine separate American naval deployments to Asia. On the sixth cruise, in 1835, the senior officer present was authorized to fly the broad pennant of a commodore. The establishment of the East India Squadron dates from this period, although it was not until 1845 that the squadron was organized in conventional form.[23]

The purpose of the East India Squadron was to protect American lives, property, and commerce.

The squadron was also to assist in increasing American commercial interests in China and providing training for the officers and men of the navy. The geographical expanse of the squadron's responsibilities was huge: from a line stretching from the Bering Sea in the north, through the Hawaiian Islands, to the Antarctic in the south, and thence westward to the east coast of Africa. This immense area was patrolled by only a few ships. In the early years, the squadron consisted of two or three units. The flagship was usually a frigate of fifty-four guns or a sloop-of-war mounting eighteen guns. The squadron increased greatly during Commo. Matthew C. Perry's mission to Japan (1853-54), but then reverted to normal size after the mission.

The squadron existed more on paper, for administrative purposes, than in a tactical sense. Its ships made individual cruises, and it was unusual for all to be in one port together. The vessels logged countless nautical miles and visited innumerable ports. In 1854, for example, Macao, Canton, Hong Kong, Amoy, Ningpo, Shanghai, Shimoda, Hakodate, Manila, and Singapore were visited. In addition, navy craft penetrated some of China's river system. The <u>Susquehanna</u>, for example, sailed up part of the Yangtze River in 1854 and founded the Yangtze River Patrol. Other squadron units performed hydrographic surveys. Administrative duties, the bane of many later commanding officers, were light. Discipline and relations with consuls and foreign squadrons made up the bulk of the responsibilities of the officers in charge.[24]

The commanding officers of the ships in Asia enjoyed a degree of independence not seen in most commands. Transit from New York to Hong Kong normally took 120 days. A reply to a communication could take upwards of six months to reach the commander. Naval officers were "guided in their . . . actions by ideas of national honor."[25] Navy Department regulations allowed the commodore to act as he saw fit in the case of hostilities involving American lives or interests, and he was allowed to protect European as well as American lives. In the event of trouble, diplomatic representatives applied directly to the commanding officer of a ship for help. They could only request help, for the responsibility for direct action rested in the hands of the navy.[26]

The East India Squadron served three groups: merchants, missionaries, and diplomats. Throughout the nineteenth century, however, the navy had too few ships on station to offer much protection for the merchants. In addition, before the Opium War, the Chinese made no allowance for warships, and merchants were not inclined to encourage military units in fear that it would upset their relations with the Chinese. It was only after China was forced open that business began to welcome the presence of naval units.[27]

A lack of sufficient numbers of ships also caused the navy to be of very little use to missionaries in China prior to 1900. Furthermore, the missionaries who were in the Middle Kingdom in the nineteenth century tended to reside in the same locations as businessmen and, thus, in areas where Chinese did not welcome warships. But toward the end of the 1800s, and into the twentieth century, the number of American missionaries rose dramatically. The squadron would find itself increasingly enmeshed with this group.

The navy in nineteenth-century China best served diplomats. Diplomatic relations opened ports, which allowed the navy's ships to move freely along the coasts and rivers. Charles T. Hanson, Jr., has pointed out that "movement is the key word in discussing the naval-diplomatic association."[28] Warships provided diplomats with independent mobility in China and, in fact, provided an outward sign of style and dignity appropriate to their rank. In other words, it was more impressive for an official to arrive in a warship than a mere merchantman. Further, navy ships usually were the means of transportation for diplomatic personnel from the United States to East Asia. "Navy vessels probably rendered their greatest service as floating legations."[29]

The officers of the U.S. Navy did play a role in Chinese-American relations prior to the Boxer Uprising. We have already seen how Commo. Kearny helped gain a most-favored-nation treaty for the United States. During the same period, the Chinese hired an American lieutenant from the Constellation to demonstrate explosives. Kearny and his officers demonstrated the art of Western shipbuilding and armament. The navy also played a role in trying to suppress the coolie trade. In one action, for example, a navy ship intercepted and freed 423

Chinese aboard an American merchantman.   James M.
Merrill, however, has written that the "customary
attitude of American officers, who looked upon
Orientals as inferior beings, whose territory could
be used with impunity by their men-of-war whenever
the situation warranted" canceled many of the
chances for gaining goodwill and respect.[30]

Officially, the East India Squadron remained
neutral during the Opium and Arrow Wars and the
long years of the Taiping Rebellion.   Commo.
Cornelius K. Stribling, when ordering a ship to
Foochow in 1860 to protect American interests,
informed the captain: "In all your intercourse with
the Chinese you are to act with kindness.   Force
must not be resorted to except upon being satisfied
no other means at your command will be effectual.
[I]t is of utmost importance that we should in our
intercourse with the allies and Chinese evince our
neutral position with perfect impartiality."[31]   In
reality, however, "perfect impartiality" was almost
impossible, given the racial attitudes then exist-
ing.   Probably the best example of how American
forces could become involved in the hostilities in
China occurred during the British and French bomb-
bardment of the Taku forts, near Tientsin, in 1858.
The allied gunboats could make little headway
against a strong current and stood in danger of
receiving heavy casualties.   Commo. Josiah Tattnal,
the American East India Squadron Commander, ordered
a rented vessel to tow the gunboats out of range.
"Blood is thicker than water!" was the traditional
reply given by the commodore for his actions.   One
of his lieutenants also recorded that the commodore
remarked that "he'd be damned if he'd stand by and
see white men butchered before his eyes."[32]   Apparently, Washington felt that Tattnal was correct,
for he received no reprimand. All in all, for a
neutral power, American naval forces kept busy in
matters concerning force.   The U.S. Marine Corps,
for instance, recorded a total of twenty-two
landings, from 1854 to 1899, in China.   A total of
twelve sailors and marines were killed during the
operations, and twenty-nine were wounded.[33]

The navy played a small role in the Taiping
Rebellion.   During the early years of the uprising,
Commo. Perry's sympathies were on the side of the
rebels.   For example, when merchants and Commissioner Humphrey Marshall requested additional help
in protecting American businesses from the rebels,

the commodore replied that no command of his would be used against "an organized revolutionary army gallantly fighting for a more liberal and enlightened religious and political position."[34] It is important to realize, however, that to Perry, his most important duty was in Japan and that "his determination not to permit any interference with it" helped to govern his actions toward China.[35] As the years passed, the Taiping Rebellion had less diplomatic importance than the treaty revision with the Manchus. Hanson has observed that by the end of 1854, the "navy was obliged to operate within the framework" of State Department policy regarding the Chinese civil war; this policy, as noted, was one of neutrality. As Hanson has shown, the "squadron commanders did this without complaint, despite their obvious sympathies for the Taiping cause."[36] Lastly, the squadron simply could not muster enough ships to play a very large role, even if it had wanted to, in the affairs of the rebellion.

The American Civil War marked a major change for the East India Squadron, as well as for the U.S. Navy in general. The federal blockade of Southern ports required the navy to recall as many ships as possible from foreign stations. By September 1862, only a pair of ships remained in the Far East. After the war, the navy began to return units back to the foreign stations and simultaneously renamed all the distant stations. The East India Squadron became the Asiatic Squadron in 1865.[37]

After the Civil War the navy was allowed to degenerate. Dudley W. Knox has aptly labeled the period from after the Civil War to the late 1800s as "the maritime eclipse of the United States," and naval historians recognize the period as the nadir of the navy.[38] Instead of carrying out the innovations in steam and armament introduced in the Civil War, the service actually regressed. Rather than joining the other world powers in converting to steel and steam warships, the United States clung tenaciously to wood and sail. Following traditional practice in the United States, the navy shrank rapidly after the cessation of hostilities. During the Civil War, for example, the Federal Navy mustered 58,296 officers and men. By 1889, only 1,902 men were carried on the active list. The ship statistics for the Asiatic Squadron graphically demonstrate the cutbacks. In 1876, the squadron consisted of thirteen ships, but twenty-two years later, in 1889, there remained only three units, little better than when the squadron was first formed.[39]

The navy continued with wooden ships and sail for a number of reasons. The nation was isolationist and had no desire to compete with Europeans. Most policy-makers felt that the Atlantic and Pacific Oceans protected the United States from any invasion and that traditional role of the navy, that of single-ship commerce-raiding and coastal defense, was sufficient. Single-ship commerce-raiding required distant stations to protect American shipping, and this had led to the establishment of such stations prior to the Civil War. If the United States shifted to a steel and steam navy, it would need overseas coaling stations, which the country did not possess. In other words, the United States needed sailing ships to maintain distant stations. Policy-makers, as already noted, did not care to become involved with European affairs and instead shifted their interests to the Latin American and Asian areas. In these areas, even obsolete U.S. ships were better armed than those of the surrounding areas. Lastly, line officers, led by Adm. David D. Porter, fought with engineering officers to keep navy ships in sail. In short, national policy and a conflict within the navy combined to cause the U.S. Navy to become obsolete.

Nearing the end of the nineteenth century, the navy made a complete reversal to become a world-class force. The "Naval Revolution," from the late 1800s to the Spanish-American War, saw the demise of the "Old Navy" and the advent of steel and steam ship force, with first-class battleships. The genesis of this revolution is attributed to national policy and changes from within the navy.[40]

Samuel Flagg Bemis notes that prior to the Spanish-American War and the acquisition of the Philippines, which he describes as a "great national blunder," the United States had committed no serious mistakes and made few errors in international relations. This was due largely to the European concern for a balance of power in Europe and Asia and the United States' isolated position. The main foreign policy objectives of this country were freedom, peace, and fair trade, all of which were compatible with its national

security. The blunder of the Spanish-American War,
according to Bemis, led to increasing involvement
in the political affairs of Europe and Asia and to
a "long row of further diplomatic blunders."[41]
  Revisionist historians, however, believe economic forces are the key to understanding the commercial and territorial expansion of the United
States. William A. Williams, for example, points
out that as early as 1860 agricultural interests
were convinced that their economic welfare depended
upon overseas expansion. Farmers became advocates
of an expansionist policy, and it was their urging
and support that helped to produce a strong navy to
help in overseas expansion.[42]
  Walter LaFeber also favors an economic interpretation of American diplomacy in the late
nineteenth century. LaFeber notes that by the
1890s the industrial sector of the United States
had produced a large surplus of goods, as well as a
severe depression and growing labor unrest. With
the economic panic and following depression of
1893, American decision-makers felt the only way
out of the current domestic problem was through the
establishment of an overseas commercial empire,
which again called for the building of a strong
navy.[43]
  No matter which explanation one chooses to
support, the changing emphasis of national policy
meshed with internal naval developments. Young
officers lobbied for modernization and, beginning
in 1882, under sympathetic secretaries of the navy
and presidents, the service began to rebuild. Most
naval historians recognize the large role two men
played in forming the "new navy."
  Capt. Alfred Thayer Mahan, son of army officer
Dennis Mahan, who was a professor of Engineering at
the U.S. Military Academy, entered the Naval
Academy against his father's wishes in 1859. His
career was uneventful for the next twenty-five
years, although he soon found that he cared little
for the sea and wished to make his mark in
intellectual pursuits. In 1884, after writing a
history of the Civil War navy, Alfred Mahan was
invited to lecture on naval tactics and history at
the newly established Naval War College, Newport,
Rhode Island. His lectures evolved into the two
works for which he is most noted, The Influence of
Sea Power Upon History, 1660-1793 (1890) and The
Influence of Sea Power Upon the French Revolution

and Empire, 1793-1812 (2 volumes, 1892).   In
addition, he published a number of articles and
essays on sea power.   His writings earned him
worldwide fame.

Mahan concluded that England had become a great
power by controlling the seas and the commerce they
bore.   He laid out a number of the elements of sea
power, based upon England's experience, that the
United States needed to achieve to gain greatness.
He wanted the United States to abandon its isolationist (continentalist) policy and to pursue an
aggressive competition for world trade, which
required a strong merchant marine, colonies, and a
large navy.   The merchant marine would carry
foreign trade and help keep navalism in the
public's mind, while colonies would provide raw
materials, markets, and naval bases.   Mahan felt
that the annexation of Hawaii would provide a
steppingstone to Asia and, should the United States
acquire a canal in Central America, Hawaii would be
the Pacific bastion to help protect the waterway.
Mahan believed that colonies would extend Western
civilization.   He was convinced that the navy
should gain command of the sea by defeating the
enemy's fleet in a decisive battle and that only
battleships could fight such engagements.[44]

At the same time that Mahan began to publish
his books, Benjamin F. Tracy began his tenure as
Secretary of the Navy (1889-93).   Tracy has been
credited as one of the leaders in the building of
the new navy by some historians, while others
believe that he was highly influenced by Mahan.
Indeed, many of their thoughts are closely related.
Tracy believed that the sea was the prime
ingredient of empire and that the United States
should rule the sea.   To do so, America needed
overseas bases and a large navy.   Instead of
single-ship raiding and coastal defense, he advo-
cated command of the sea based upon battleships
capable of destroying an enemy's fleet in mid-
ocean.   Between 1890 and 1896, the United States
departed from her traditional naval policy and,
although balking at times, Congress authorized the
building of nine battleships.   Tracy also brought
about a "squadron of evolution" in 1889, which was
the precursor of a concentrated battle fleet.   The
squadron practiced steaming and tactical formations
in large groups.   By 1897, the squadron was merged
into the North Atlantic Squadron and developed into

a fighting fleet.[45]

By the end of the nineteenth century, the United States and her navy had made fundamental changes that would affect the American military experience in China. Until the beginning of the twentieth century, the navy was the only American military force in the Middle Kingdom. The primary duty of the service, since 1839, had been the protection of American lives and interests. Commanders of the Asiatic Squadron, because of the great distances involved, enjoyed a degree of freedom from the higher echelons of command rare in the military. The only guide for officers seemed to be their sense of national honor. Beginning in 1900, however, events in China, combined with military reorganization, changes in technology, and an altered perception of national interest, would spell the end of naval preeminence and the independence of the officer corps. The beginning of the twentieth century would see all branches of the American military in China.

The U.S. command structure, mission, and troop strength in China during the first three decades of the twentieth century reflected the unstable conditions in East Asia. The period was marked by sudden increases in troop strength to meet perceived threats to American nationals and their property. As the various crises passed, the number of military men would be reduced, but by 1930, there were more American armed forces in China than at the turn of the century. With all branches of the armed forces in East Asia, disagreements over command structure broke out between the navy, war, and state departments. As the Chinese began to take more control over their own affairs, the mission of the American military began to change.

On 21 June 1900, the Boxers began to besiege the legations in Peking. An international relief force, which included marines, soldiers, and sailors of the U.S. military, was cobbled together and struck out for the capital city. By 16 August, this force was victorious. In charge of American ground forces was Maj. Gen. of Volunteers Adna Chafee. The quick but decisive victory led to the Boxer Protocols, which caused many more Chinese concessions to the West.[46]

When U.S. ground forces were withdrawn from Peking, Chafee left behind a legation guard of one U.S. Army reinforced regiment. By the spring of

1901, this had been reduced to one rifle company. In 1905, due largely to the efforts of the American Minister to China, W. W. Rockhill, the army force was replaced by marines, and thereafter leathernecks furnished the legation guard. Louis Morton and Allan R. Millett have noted that the reasons for this switch "are not clear." Rockhill apparently thought the marines presented a better military appearance, were better disciplined, trained for legation duty, and could be reinforced quickly, without command squabbles, from ships of the Asiatic Fleet or from the marine force in the Philippine Islands. Millett has pointed out that the use of marines was "attractive to the State Department," because they were "politically safe," having performed landing duties "throughout the world with few casualties." Furthermore, marines landed from ships of the Asiatic Fleet would cause little stir from the newspapers in the United States. The sight of troops boarding ships in America for service in a far-off country might possibly cause loud outcries from the press. Lastly, with the exception of the legation guards, any marines who were landed in China were "not bound by the Boxer Protocol to cooperate with foreign troops."[47]

The navy in the Pacific underwent major changes in 1907. The Asiatic Fleet and Pacific Squadrons were consolidated into the Pacific Fleet, with headquarters at San Francisco. The new fleet consisted of three squadrons and two torpedo flotillas. Two squadrons and one flotilla were stationed in the Orient. The navy withdrew all battleships from the former Asiatic Squadron and replaced them with four armored cruisers. A vessel was maintained at Shanghai, and three gunboats cruised the Yangtze River. In 1910, the Navy Department once again reorganized its forces in the Pacific by reestablishing the Asiatic Fleet.[48]

In 1911, the simplified chain of command envisioned by Rockhill was broken, due to the overthrow of the Manchus. At first, diplomatic observers either did not appreciate the importance of the revolution or saw no danger to foreigners. On 17 October 1911, for example, the American Charge d'Affaires informed the State Department that the rebellion was in no way anti-foreign. Less than one month later, however, foreign observers were becoming alarmed. American Minister

W. J. Calhoun wired the State Department inquiring as to whether the United States planned on cooperating with the British in occupying the rail line between Peking and Tientsin should conditions require it. Secretary of State Frank Knox, on 10 November, replied that if such action became necessary, "this Government will participate in protection of the railway . . . under the protocol of 1901."[49] Eleven days later, on 21 November, Calhoun reported that, due to increased lawlessness and rumors of attacks upon foreigners, he had ordered all Americans to depart the interior. On 25 November, he reported that the foreign ministers in Peking had decided to recommend to their representative governments a quiet increase of legation guards to the maximum strength allowable under the Protocols. Three days later, Knox wired Calhoun that he should inform the various ministers that the United States "recognizes the obligation imposed by the rights under the protocol of 1901 and will hold at Manila in constant readiness from 500 to 2500 men for dispatch on short notice." When Knox asked for Calhoun's estimate of the number of troops needed, the minister replied that the "British Minister . . . advises a regiment. I would not recommend more at present." This time, the army, not the marine corps, received the orders. Again, the reasoning behind this move is not known at the present time.

The request for a regiment was pared down to 500 men because the conditions along the railroad had become "less acute," and the Chinese government promised to keep the road open. On 10 January 1912, the Commanding General of the Philippines Division, ordered one battalion of the Fifteenth Infantry, under the command of Maj. James M. Arrasmith, to proceed immediately to China. The troops landed at Chinwangtao [Qinhuangdao], the seaport closest to the Peking-Mukden [Shenyang] Railroad, approximately 150 miles northeast of Tientsin, on 18 January. Major Arrasmith received instructions from Calhoun as to the mission of his command. Arrasmith was to relieve British troops guarding the rail line between Tongshan [Tangshan] and Lanchow [Lanzhou] Station, some seventy-five miles from Tientsin. In addition, the major was to detail a detachment of one officer and forty men to Tongshan. The American officer was informed that "Chinese Imperial and Revolutionist troops are at the liberty to utilize the railway line. . . and will not be interfered with." It was clearly stated, however, that the Chinese would in no case be allowed to interfere with the railway and would not be permitted to damage it. Acknowledging the difficulties in this assignment, the instructions cautioned that: "Officers commanding posts and patrols should be informed of the conditions and told to do their best, with the forces at their disposal."

By 2 March 1912, Calhoun was again informing Washington of the unrest in China. In his message to the State Department, he noted that houses had been burned, including some missions. No doubt to help his case, the minister also wrote that several foreigners had been reported killed. Communications had been interrupted, because the telegraph wire had been cut. Calhoun then went on to state that "in view of prevailing anarchy, decided to bring 1,000 troops from Tientsin for restraining effect. English, French, Germans, Japanese, and Russians will participate. I have applied to Arrasmith for 200 men." The next day, the men were on their way to Peking. The army, however, was quickly relieved by marines from the U.S.S. Abrarenda and from Taku on 11 March. The legation guard had now ballooned to battalion size.

Even before troops arrived in Peking, Calhoun claimed more soldiers were needed elsewhere in China and he continued to report on disturbances. The State Department, on 4 March, informed Calhoun that he could, "without awaiting further instructions, communicate with the Commanding General, Philippine Islands, informing him that you need additional troops. He has instructions from the War Department to send you . . . the remainder of the 1200 men already provided for." Two days later, on 6 March, Calhoun requested the additional troops. On 20 March, the Fifteenth Infantry was raised to its statutory strength when the Second Battalion was organized from the troops already present. In his annual report of 1912, Maj. Gen. J. F. Bell, commanding the Department of the Philippines, reported to the Chief of Staff of the Army that six "companies of the China contingent are now at Tientsin, and two are scattered along the railroad in detachments, varying in size from 20 to 115 men."

Even though conditions stabilized somewhat in

China between 1913 and 1920, army troop strength increased. In 1914, the outbreak of World War I caused the withdrawal of most of the European forces in East Asia. The Japanese requested the United States to assume responsibility for the former German zone along the railways, and in September 1914, the remaining battalion of the Fifteenth Infantry was transferred from Manila to Tientsin.

The 1920s were filled with unrest in China, which brought about large changes in U.S. forces in China. The first change entailed the gunboats on the Yangtze River. Navy gunboats had plied the river since 1854, but it was not until 21 March 1921 that the patrol force was organized as part of the Asiatic Fleet. Capt. D. M. Wood was appointed first commander and had five gunboats under his command. On 12 October, the first flag officer, RAdm. W. H. G. Bullard, boarded his flagship, the Isabel, a converted yacht. In September of the same year, the army requested and the State Department approved the removal of one battalion of the Fifteenth Infantry from Tientsin to Manila. On the other hand, within two years in 1923, the navy requested Congress to authorize funds for the construction of six new gunboats to replace the aging Yangtze patrol craft. The navy cited "appeals from American citizens and organizations as the result of the political turmoil in China."[50]

The period from 1923 to 1928 marks an era of constant unrest in China, with a great number of American troop movements into the country. Marine officer Robert O. Bare has recalled that there were several wars occurring in 1926. There was "one down in the Shantung Province, there was one up around the Peking area. There were all sorts of warlords . . . . [A] lot of people got killed, and the poor peasants were taxed to death, their farms were run over. There was a lot killing and beheading."[51] The major unrest came from Chiang Kai-shek's drive to unite China. As Chiang moved into the Yangtze River valley, the key to the foreign positions was Shanghai. One third of the city's 3 million people lived in the International Settlement that occupied 5,500 acres of land. The perceived threat to the Settlement alarmed the foreign powers, especially Great Britain, which quickly announced that it would send a full division to Shanghai. President Calvin Coolidge stated that, because the United States owned no concessions in the city, he would not send troops. However, Adm. Clarence S. Williams, Commander-in-Chief of the Asiatic Fleet, along with the Department of State, convinced Coolidge that troops should be dispatched to protect American lives and property.

The Fourth United States Marine Corps Regiment, fresh from duties guarding the U.S. mail west of the Missouri River, received orders on 28 January 1927 to embark at San Diego for expeditionary duty in China. The marines sailed on 3 February, aboard the navy transport Chaumont, with Headquarters and Service Companies, First and Third Battalions, totaling 66 officers and 1,162 enlisted men. The Second Battalion remained in the United States to complete mail guard duties.[52]

The Chaumont moored at the Standard Oil Company's docks in Shanghai on 24 February, and there Col. Charles S. Hill and his command received an unpleasant surprise. Coolidge rejected American Minister John V. A. MacMurry's recommendations to have the leathernecks immediately join the Shanghai Defense Force. Instead, the marines would remain aboard the troop ship until there was a direct threat to American lives and property. Except for a brief march through the Settlement on 5 March for exercise, the men remained penned up on the ship for over three weeks. Morale rapidly deteriorated. Marine officer Omar T. Pfeiffer recalled the low state of the men's morale as evidenced by the number of absent without leave offenses.[53]

By 21 March 1927, Chiang's Nationalist army was moving inexorably towards Shanghai, and the city's municipal council declared a state of emergency. At last, the marines were ordered off the Chaumount to assist in the defense of the Settlement. Coolidge, however, wished to avoid contact with the Chinese armies. MacMurry was informed, in very plain language, that "it must be definitely understood that this force is present for the purpose of protecting American life and property at Shanghai. The Government is not prepared to use its naval force at Shanghai for the purpose of protecting the integrity of the Settlement." Due to these political considerations, the marines were assigned internal security in the International Settlement. On 25 March, Brig. Gen. Smedley D. Butler arrived in Shanghai to take command of all marines ashore.

At first designated the Marine Corps Expeditionary Force, Asiatic Fleet, Butler's command was renamed the Third Marine Brigade on 4 April.[54]
If Coolidge wanted a low profile from the marines in China, then the choice of Butler was a strange one.   The   officer was one of the most colorful senior officers to serve in China.   Born of Quaker parents, he chose the profession of arms. His father was a congressman for thirty-one years and Chairman of the House Naval Affairs Committee during the Harding and Coolidge administrations. Some of Butler's critics have suggested that this helped the marine's career.   Butler began his career by falsifying his age, becoming a sixteen-year-old officer in the Spanish-American War. He saw no   combat during the war.   A glance at a photograph of the young Butler reveals an almost gaunt,   clerkish-looking   man,   far   from   the recruiting picture of a stalwart marine officer. For almost two decades, however, this man had almost constant field service in what today would be considered counter-guerrilla warfare in the Orient, Central America, and the Caribbean.   He first served in China during the Boxer Uprising, where he won a brevet to captain for rescuing an enlisted man while under heavy fire.   An incident in Nicaragua in 1912, when Butler was feverish and his eyes bloodshot, earned him one of his colorful nicknames -- "Old Gimlet Eye."   Lowell Thomas once described Butler as the "ideal" marine.   He was a disciplinarian and an outstanding leader.   He was also very outspoken about his views, even when they clashed with those of his superiors.   No one has ever disputed his bravery.   He is one of only three marines to have twice won the Congressional Medal of Honor--the nation's highest military award.[55]
Upon assuming command, Butler decided to write daily secret memorandums to his friend, Maj. Gen. John A. Lejeune, the Commandant of the Marine Corps, about any difficulties that he might encounter with Admiral Williams.   While Butler was certainly outspoken, he was also canny enough to know that if trouble between him and the navy developed, then he would need all the help he could muster on his side.   Butler's correspondence reveals two ambitious men, each of whom was extremely proud of his respective service.   On his first meeting with Williams, the leatherneck officer felt he was "entering an icebox."   Butler

claimed the first words that were spoken to him were in the "nature of a complaint" about the admiral not being informed, or consulted, as to the marine's orders. Williams also felt that there were entirely too many marines in the brigade, but perhaps that was because Butler was an officer "who wants to build a big job for himself and get a promotion." The leatherneck then fired back that he was not one of the "Gimmie Family," that it did not "make a damn bit of difference whether you have one marine [here] or ten million, my record is secure," and that he did not care if he was promoted or not. Then he told Williams that if "you don't care to take my advice and some Americans are murdered in this town and you sit quietly here with half the Marines available guarding coal piles, you will be held responsible." Eventually, after much sparring, Butler and Williams developed an understanding, although the relationship could never be called a warm one.[56]

The dispatch of Butler to China caused The New York Times to publish a full-page spread under the title "Butler of the Marines Goes to War." The otherwise staid Times labeled the leatherneck the "Premier 'Fighting Devil' among 'Devil Dogs.'" Time magazine featured Butler on its cover and noted that he "takes trouble by the whiskers." The magazine also wrote that his adventures had a "dime novel" flavor. With this much ballyhoo, the general public and the press must have expected exciting headlines from China. What happened instead, in the words of Butler's biographer, was "masterful peacekeeping rather than belligerency." Butler realized that the military did "not [have] sufficient armed men in the United States, let along here in China, to send off [troops], into the interior . . . and protect the lives and property of Americans living way off in the bushes." Furthermore, the "question of protection of property comes up everyday and we reply, 'that property can be replaced, but lives cannot.'" Butler repeated the orders not to man perimeter posts or to assume responsibility for preserving the integrity of the Settlement. The marines, however, were to support the frontline defenses if it were necessary to prevent a breakthrough. The "Devil Dog's" final report on his actions in China shows that he was as much a peacekeeper as a warrior. Butler wrote that it was his policy "to use every means to dissuade the Chinese from troubling our citizens and would certainly not fire one shot until convinced that every possible peaceful endeavor to prevent a clash had failed." Indeed, the endorsement made by Adm. Mark L. Bristol noted that the marine, "whose experience in the past had, in general, been that of the military offense," had learned to be a diplomat. Butler had earlier written to Lejeune that he was "hanging hard to the theory that the Chinamen must settle among themselves their own form of Government and their own rules. But . . . they must not molest our citizens." When the great confrontation did occur, it took place in Nanking. Conditions in Shanghai slowly began to return to normal. By April 1927, the Fourth Marine Regiment was performing normal garrison duties.[57]

In May 1927, attention shifted to North China. Fearing threats to foreign life and property, Adm. Williams and Minister MacMurry proposed the establishment of a strong point on or near the North China coast where Americans could be gathered behind a defensive perimeter if necessary. Tientsin was selected as the site. Adm. Williams would move the recently arrived Sixth Marine Regiment, plus another 1,500 marines to be sent from the United States, to the city. General Butler, on 21 June, shifted his headquarters to Tientsin. Again, the confrontation never material-ized. The largest battles the marines engaged in were barroom brawls with the Army's Fifteenth Infantry and foreign troops during their off-duty hours.

Adm. Mark L. Bristol relieved Williams on 9 September 1927. Bristol was uneasy about the stationing of the bulk of the Third Brigade at Tientsin, where it could not be supported by the ships of the fleet. Americans seeking shelter there could easily be cut off. Shanghai, on the other hand, offered none of these disadvantages. The largest ships could navigate the Whangpoo [Huangpu] River to the city and then provide covering fire and marines for a possible withdrawal or landing. Therefore, Bristol recommended the reduction of the marines to just the Fourth Regiment at Shanghai. Butler, however, recommended just the opposite. Part of Butler's reasoning may be glimpsed from marine officer James L. Underhill's comment that Butler "never got along well with the Navy" and "didn't like being so close under the thumb of an admiral. So he decided to pull out and go up to Tientsin."[58] MacMurray recommended that all of the leathernecks remain. The State and Navy Departments approved Bristol's recommendations. In September 1928, the movement of leathernecks out of China began. The Third Brigade was disbanded on 13 January 1929, and the last marines in Tientsin left ten days later. This marks the end of the large-scale troop increases of the 1920s. Still, as the decade drew to an end, the U.S. Marine Corps had gained a new overseas post: Shanghai Marines would become part of the Corps' mythology.[59]

The presence of two land forces, marine and army, under separate commands and each completely independent of the other, led inevitably to interservice disagreements. These difficulties were exacerbated by the insistence, by every Secretary of State from John Hay on, that the military forces in China were there "solely to assist and support the American minister to discharge his responsibilities." This, of course, meant that the troops were under the control of the State Department. No reinforcements or withdrawals could be undertaken by the War Department without the consent of the Secretary of State.[60]

The first move to change this arrangement was undertaken in the summer of 1921 by John W. Weeks, Secretary of War, who recommended a single command under the Navy Department, with the army removing its troops from China. The State Department, while it had no objection to a single command, did not agree on the removal of the Fifteenth Infantry, because the force was in "China for political, not military reasons, and by its presence alone might avert a repetition of the Boxer Uprising." One year later, the War Department began to explore the possibility of either withdrawing the forces in China or placing them under a single command. The first course of action was abandoned. American troops were needed in China "to maintain the prestige of the United States in the Far East, to meet its commitments to the other Western powers, and, most important, to check Japanese aggression."

The second alternative, that of establishing a unified command, was considered the best course of action, given the State Department's insistence upon keeping troops in China. In October 1922, the General Staff decided to back a plan put forth by

Brig. Gen. William D. Connor, Assistant Chief of Staff, G-4. Instead of a single command composed of army and marine corps forces, Connor proposed that the army command be made an independent command under a brigadier general, reporting directly to the War Department rather than to the Philippine Department Commander. This would make the army commander the senior ground commander, who could then deal on a more equal basis with the American Minister and without reference to the Navy or State Departments. The separate command would be designated "American Forces in China." The name would provide for the marines and any other American force that might be added.

On 1 April 1923, the War Department published a General Order establishing the new command and designated Connor as its first commander. The navy, not too surprisingly, objected. Also not surprisingly, objections were raised by the army commander of the Philippine Department. He pointed out that the primary reason for American troops in China was to protect the legation and keep the railway line to the sea open. This might be beyond the capabilities of an independent China command. Reinforcements for the command would have to come from the Philippines, and separate commands might complicate the problem. The army, however, proceeded with the plan, but came to a halt when comments of Secretary of State Charles E. Hughes were received. While Hughes was all for a stream-lined command, he wished Weeks to understand clearly that whenever differences arose, the final word must be the American Minister's. American forces were in China to protect the legation at Peking, and no separate status except "as an organization ancillary to the legation" would be accepted.

Connor, after waiting a year at his new post, began to request the establishment of a unified command. The War Department, although in favor of the move, dragged its feet. In the meantime, the Navy Department continued its opposition to the unified command. Again, the most important stumbling block was the State Department. The American Minister would not recommend a merger of the two commands. By April 1924, two years after arriving in China, Connor was no closer to his goal. Even the title, "American Forces in China," remained in question. With no settlement on the unified command in sight, in May 1924, army planners

decided that the name was no longer appropriate and
recommended that the command be redesignated "U.S.
Army Forces in China." Furthermore, there would be
no changes in the strength, status, or command of
army or marine forces in China.   Army planners
realized that, while a unified command would
simplify matters, it was impossible to obtain such
a goal without the approval of the State Department, and this was not forthcoming.   On 2 June
1927, a General Order was published officially
redesignating the army troops as "U.S. Army Forces
in China."

It was not until the Japanese puppet state of
Manchukuo was established in September 1931, that
the State Department began to consider seriously
the withdrawal of troops from East Asia.   In 1932,
additional troops from the army's Thirty-first
Infantry were sent to assist the marines in manning
the barricades in Shanghai's International Settlement.   As the Sino-Japanese war heated up,
diplomats and others began to worry about a real or
imagined incident provoking a confrontation between
Japan and the United States.   Charles W. Thomas,
writing in 1937, pointed out how easy it would be
for "some drunken American soldiers to come in
contact with Japanese soldiers" and start a riot.[61]
This thought was further expanded upon by a student
at the Army War College. Maj. John T. Zellers wrote
that maintaining the Fifteenth Infantry in China
was "not worth the risks and cost involved."
Zellers believed, as did many others, that the
United States' best course of action in East Asia
was the "instrument of diplomacy, in the promotion
of . . .[its] interests."[62] Arguments such as
these apparently helped to convince Washington, for
in 1938, the Fifteenth Infantry was ordered to
leave China.   The withdrawal of the army from
Tientsin marks the beginning of the end of the old
military China hands' way of life.

The mission of the U.S. military forces in China
changed over the first thirty-seven years of the
twentieth century.   Dating from the end of the
nineteenth century, the armed forces in East Asia
served to protect American lives and property, and
to help in the promotion of commerce.   By the early
twentieth century, the military was also expected
to help keep open the railroad between Peking and
Tientsin, maintain American prestige in China, and,
somehow stop Japanese expansion in East Asia.   As

the Chinese began to assert more and more control
over their own affairs, beginning in the 1920s, the
mission of the American forces began to change.   In
the U.S. sector of the railroad, for example,
troops were withdrawn in 1928.   Furthermore,
International Trains, long used for keeping
communications open to the sea, were discontinued
in 1925.   The train guards usually had only a first
lieutenant and twelve enlisted men.   Any determined
attempt by a large number of armed Chinese could
easily overwhelm the detachment.   Former Fifteenth
Infantry officer Paul L. Freeman recalled that
there was such fear of an incident that the troops
could not handle "that we were even required to
disarm our train guards so there wouldn't be any
danger of shooting. . . . [W]e put the regimental
boxing team on as train guards. We felt . . . sure
that they could take care of themselves."[63]   One
student of early Chinese-American military
relations has noted: "Obviously, the trains were
able to operate only as long as the Chinese did not
call the bluff."   This is the prime reason that
guards were not used aboard the trains after
1925.[64]

Brig. Gen. Connor, before being relieved by
Brig. Gen. J.   C. Castner in 1926, noted that to
keep troops in China that could be easily over-
whelmed was to invite disaster.   If the troops
attempted to fight, they would be annihilated; if
they merely stood by in a confrontation, the United
States would suffer a loss of prestige.   Connor was
convinced that the best course of action would be
to withdraw the army forces and rely upon the
Asiatic Fleet to assist in any difficulties.

Castner quickly echoed Connor's observations and
recommendations. The newly arrived general believed
that the original mission of the army in China was
outdated and requested a new set of instructions.
The War and State Departments disagreed, even
though the American Minister noted in 1928 that the
mission to keep the opening to the sea was "neither
surrendered nor waived, [but] is virtually in abey-
ance." The army's mission had thus been reduced to
somehow protecting American lives and property in
the Tientsin area.   Roy K. Flint has succinctly
summed up the Fifteenth Infantry's job in China by
the end of the 1920s: it was there for "a political
purpose and [had] little military value."[65]

The mission of the navy also changed over the

Table 1
Permanent U.S. Ground Troops in China, 1905-1936

Fiscal Year	USMC[1]	USA
1905	102[2]	
1906	125	
1907	125	
1908	125	
1909	125	
1910	125	
1911	125	
1912	221[3]	1,292[3]
1913	221	1,252
1914	221	849
1915	221	1,404[4]
1916	221	1,274
1917	221	1,355
1918	221	NA
1919	221	NA
1920	221	1,497
1921	221	1,198
1922	221	671
1923	221	987
1924	339[5]	977
1925	640	982
1926	430	1,015
1927	4,639[6]	1,090[6]

Year		
1928	4,542	979
1929	2,740	1,012
1930	1,746	1,008
1931	1,220	954
1932	2,164	766
1933	2,400[7]	758[8]
1934	2,313	722
1935	1,573	754
1936	1,543	841

Sources: U.S. Army Center for Military History, Washington, DC.; Reference Branch, Marine Corps Historical Center, Washington, DC.
Note: NA = not available.

1 Does not include marines aboard ships of Asiatic Fleet.
2 Establishment of U.S. Marine Corps unit at Peking.
3 Build-up of troops due to overthrow of the Manchus.
4 Reflects build-up of troops because of U.S. manning German concession during World War I.
5 Increase reflects concerns of West as Chiang Kai-shek began efforts to unite China.
6 Perceived threat to Shanghai as Chiang moved northward.
7 Reflects crisis at Shanghai as Japanese approached.
8 Does not include the 31st Infantry's service in Shanghai from 5 February to 30 June 1932.

years.   Although the service recognized the
increasing strength of the Chinese, its largest
interest lay with Japan.   Indeed, as Bernard D.
Cole has pointed out, the Commander-in-Chief of the
Asiatic Fleet during the 1920s, "considered [the
fleet's] main mission to be to prepare for a
large-scale naval war.   The mission of protecting
and furthering American interests in China was
considered secondary."[66] Further, even the mission
of protecting lives and property changed.   As shown
in Shanghai in 1927, the mission informally adopted
by naval units was the rescue of Americans, but not
the protection of property.   Butler's colorful
description of helping Americans in the "bushes"
will be recalled.   The marine officer also averred
that keeping a large force at Tientsin was "futile
from the pure military standpoint of 'guaranteed
safety' to our nationals." Like the army, the navy
was faced with insufficient manpower to protect
both lives and property.   The best-trained men for
landing parties from ships came from the marine
corps.   In 1925, the Corps consisted of only 1,298
officers and 18,000 enlisted men, many of whom were
already engaged in Nicaragua and Haiti.   Furthermore, the marines who were posted in the Far East
were scattered at stations in Peking, Shanghai,
Guam, and the Philippines, in addition to small
detachments aboard the various ships of the fleet.
It is not surprising, then, that while the official
mission of the navy during the 1920s was the protection of American lives and property, the number
of men available made the unofficial policy of protecting lives the only viable course of action.[67]
Table 1 illustrates the number of U.S. military
ground troops in China during the period under
study. The statistics show very clearly that Butler
was correct in pointing out the inability of the
military to guarantee the safety of Americans in
China.
     By 1937,the U.S. military forces in China had
expanded.   From a few cruising ships, the number of
units had grown until the marine corps had detachments at Peking and Shanghai by the end of 1920s.
The navy had units on the Yangtze River and cruising China's coastal waters, while the army had the
Fifteenth Infantry stationed at Tientsin.   With so
many different units in East Asia, the military
attempted to form a single command structure.   This
was thwarted, however, by the insistence of the

Secretary of State that the military forces in China were there to assist and support the American Minister.   In other words, except for administration and discipline, the troops were under the control of the State Department. This arrangement continued throughout the 1920s.   The 1920s saw great unrest in China, which led to periodic increases in troop strength to meet perceived threats to American lives and interests.   As the Chinese began to assert themselves, the American military's mission began to change.   Most American commanders realized that they did not have sufficient men, either in China or in the entire military establishment, to hold out against a determined Chinese attack against any of the American points of interest.   Eventually, the unofficial mission of the U.S. military in China became only the protection of American lives, although Washington continued to state otherwise. Smedley D. Butler probably summed up the views of the China commanders best when he wrote that the Chinese "must settle, among themselves, their own form of government and their own rules. But . . . they must not molest our citizens."   With the Japanese push into China, the last phase of the confusing military mission took place.   Fearing what might be sparked by an accidental incident between the troops of Japan and the United States, the Fifteenth Infantry was finally ordered to leave China.   This marked the beginning of the end of the old China duty for the American military.

NOTES
    1. Material on modern Chinese history comes from: John King Fairbank, The United States and China, 4th ed. Cambridge, MA: Harvard University Press, 1979); John King Fairbank, ed., The Cambridge History of China, vol. X, Late Ch'ing, 1800-1911, part 1 (New York: Cambridge University Press, 1978); John King Fairbank and Kwang-ching Liu, eds., The Cambridge History of China, vol. XI, Late Ch'ing, 1800-1911, part 2 (New York: Cambridge University Press, 1978); Immanuel Hsu, The Rise of Modern China, 3rd ed. (New York: Oxford University Press, 1983).   For the White Lotus Rebellion, see: Susan Mann Jones, "Dynastic Decline and the Roots of Rebellion," in Fairbank, Cambridge History, X, 107-162.
    2. Ssu-Yu Teng and John K. Fairbank, eds.,

*China's Response to the West: A Documentary Survey,
1839-1923* (Cambridge, MA: Harvard University Press,
1979), 19.

3. Material on the Opium War comes from Edgar
Holt, *The Opium Wars in China* (London: Dufors,
1964); Peter Ward Fay, *The Opium Wars in China,
1840-1842: Barbarians in the Celestial Empire in
the Early Part of the Nineteenth Century and the
War By Which They Forced Her Gates Ajar* (Chapel
Hill, NC: University of North Carolina Press,
1975); Nathaniel Peffer, *The Far East: A Modern
History* (Ann Arbor, MI: University of Michigan
Press, 1958), 55; Frederick Wakeman, Jr., "The
Canton Trade and the Opium War," in Fairbank,
Cambridge History, X, 173.

4. Lin was dismissed in 1841 and sentenced to
exile in Ile, near the Russian border in Central
Asia. He was recalled in 1845 and died of natural
causes. Hsin-pao Chang, *Commissoner Lin and the
Opium War* (New York: Norton, 1970).

5. Hsu, *Modern China*, 190.

6. Dudley W. Knox, *A History of the United
States Navy* (New York: Putnam 1948), 161-65; Earl
Swisher, *China's Management of the American
Barbarians: A Study of Sino-American Relations,
1841-1861, With Documents* (New York: Octagon
Books, 1972), 56-58; Carroll Storrs Alden,
Lawrence Kearny: Sailor Diplomat (Princeton, NJ:
Princeton University Press, 1936).

7. Frank A. Kierman, Jr., "Ironies of Chinese-
American Military Conflict," in *The American
Military and the Far East: Proceedings of the
Ninth Military History Symposium, United States
Air Force Academy, 1-3 October 1980*, ed. Joe C.
Dixon (Washington: Government Printing Office,
1980), 183.

8. Ibid., 183-84.

9. Charles C. Chadbourn, III, "Sailors and
Diplomats: U.S. Naval Operations in China,
1865-1877" (Ph.D. diss., University of Washington,
1976), 14.

10. Kierman, "Chinese-American Conflict," 184;
U.S., Bureau of the Census, *Historical Abstracts of
the United States, Colonial Times to 1957* (Washington: Government Printing Office, 1960), 549.

11. Peffer, *Far East*, 63.

12. Ibid., 64. For works on trade: Robert G.
Albion, Robert G. Albion, William A. Baker, and
Benjamin Woods Labaree, *New England and the Sea*

(Middleton CT: Wesleyan University Press, 1972); Foster   Dulles,   The   Old   China   Trade   (Boston: Houghton Mifflin, 1930); John King Fairbank, Trade and Diplomacy on the China Coast: The Opening of The   Treaty   Ports,   1842-1854   (Palo   Alto,   CA: Stanford   University Press, 1969).

13. Peffer, Far East, 67-68.

14. Ibid., 60-70.

15. David   Hurd,   The   Arrow   War: An   Anglo-Chinese   Confusion,   1857-1861   (New   York: Mac-millian, 1968); Peffer, Far East, 71-73.

16. Hsu, Modern China, 209-19.

17. The   best   single   source   on   the   Taiping Rebellion is: Ssu-Yu Teng, The Taiping Rebellion and   the   Western   Powers: A   Comprehensive   Survey (London: Oxford University Press, 1971).

18. Ibid., 413.

19. Ibid., 391.

20. Ibid., 390.

21. Hsu, Modern China, 387-90.

22. Ibid., 392-93. For the best source on the Boxer Uprising from Chinese sources, see: Chester C. Tan, The Boxer Catastrophe (New York: Columbia University Press, 1955).   Good popular accounts are in: Peter Fleming, The Seige at Peking (New York: Harper   and   Brothers,   1959),   48-59;   Richard O'Connor, Spirit Soldiers: A Historical Narrative of the Boxer Rebellion (New York: Putnam, 1973), 7-70.

23. For works on distant stations and the East India/Asiatic   Squadron,   see: Robert   Greenhalgh Albion,   "Distant   Stations,"   U.S.   Naval   Institute Proceedings,   80   (March 1954):   265-73;   Chadbourn, "Sailors   and   Diplomats;"   Charles   T.   Henson,   Jr., Commissioners   and   Commodores: The   East   Indian Squadron   and   American   Diplomacy   in   China (University,   AL: University   of   Alabama   Press, 1982);   Edwin   P.   Hoyt,   The   Lonely   Ships: The   Life and   Death   of   the   U.S.   Asiatic   Fleet   (New   York: David McKay , 1976); James M. Merrill, "The Asiatic Squadron: 1835-1907,"   American   Neptune,   29   (April 1969):   106-17;   E.   Mowbray   Tate,   "American   Merchant and   Naval   Contacts   with   China,   1784-1850," American Neptune, 30 (July 1971); 171-91.

24. For a deeper analysis and insight into the navy's   purpose   in   China,   see: Peter   Karsten, The Naval Aristocracy: The Golden Age of Annapolis and   the   Emergence   of   Modern   Navalism   (New   York: Free Press, 1972), 140-50, 250-68; Albion, "Distant

Stations," 268; Henson, Commissioners and Commodores, 15; Merrill, "Asiatic Squadron," 108-09; Kemp Tolley, Yangtze Patrol: The U.S. Navy in China (Annapolis, MD: Naval   Institute   Press,   1971; reprint, 1984), 16, 18 (page references are to reprint edition).

25. Merrill, "Asiatic Squadron," 109.   See also: Tyler Dennett, Americans in Eastern Asia: A Critical Study of the Policy of the United States With Reference to China, Japan, and Korea in the 19th Century (New York: Barnes and Noble, 1941); Charles O. Paulin, Diplomatic Negotations of American Naval Officers, 1778-1883 (Baltimore: Johns Hopkins University Press, 1912).

26. Merrill, "Asiatic Squadron," 109.

27. Henson, Commissioners and Commodores, iv.

28. Ibid., v.

29. Ibid.

30. Merrill, "Asiatic Squadron," 110.

31. Quoted in ibid., 112.

32. Edgar   Stanton   Maclay,   Reminiscences   of the Old Navy: From the Journals and Private Papers of   Captain   Edward   Trenchard   and   Rear-Admiral Stephen Decatur Trenchard (New York: Putnam, 1898), 83. See also: E. R. Curtis, "Blood is Thicker Than Water," American Neptune, 27 (July 1967): 157-76.

33. Harry   Allansen   Ellsworth,   One   Hundred Eighty Landings of United States Marines, 1800-1934 (Washington: History and Museum Division, Headquarters, U.S. Marine Corps, 1935; reprint 1974), 21-23 (page references are to reprint edition); Milton Offutt, The Protection of Citizens Abroad by the Armed Forces of the United States (Baltimore: Johns Hopkins University Press, 1928), 28-31, 38-39, 41, 77-79.

34. Quoted in Charles T. Hanson, Jr., "The U.S. Navy in the Taiping Rebellion, "American Neptune, 38 (January 1978): 31.

35. Ibid., 30.

36. Ibid., 40.

37. Albion, "Distant Stations," 269-70.

38. Knox, United States Navy, 318.

39. Ibid., 317.

40. The United States Navy did have property for a coaling station at Yokohama, Japan, but had "overlooked the fact" until the Pacific Mail Company requested to sublease the land in 1899. The property had been on perpetual lease since 1864. Steward W. Livermore, "American Naval Base

Policy in   the   Far   East,   1850-1914," Pacific
Historical Review, 13 (June 1944): 114-15, 120-21;
Chadbourn, "Sailors and Diplomats," 200-01.; Knox,
United States Navy, 131-58; Kenneth J. Hagan,
American Gunboat Diplomacy and the Old Navy, 1877-
1899 (Westport, CT: Greenwood Press, 1973).
    41. Samuel Flagg Bemis, A Diplomatic History
of the United States, 5th ed. (New York: Holt,
Rinehart, and Winston, 1965), 474, 482, 1004.
    42. William A. Williams, The Roots of the Mod-
ern American Empire: A Study of Growth and Shaping
of Social Consciousness in a Marketplace Society
(New York: Random House, 1969), 30, 319-48, 351-81,
440-45, 449-50.
    43. Walter LaFeber, The New Empire: An Inter-
pretation of American Expansion, 1860-1897 (Ithaca,
NY: Cornell University Press, 1963), 60. See also:
Thomas J. McCormick, China Market: America's Quest
for Informal Empire, 1893-1901 (Chicago: Quadrangle
Books, 1967).
    44. Robert   Seager   II,   Alfred   Thayer   Mahan
(Annapolis, MD: Naval Institute Press, 1977).
    45. Benjamin   Franklin   Cooling,   Benjamin
Franklin Tracy: Father of the Modern American
Fighting Navy (Hamden, CT: Archon Books, 1979);
George T. Davis, A Navy Second to None: The De-
velopment of Modern Naval Policy (Westport, CT:
Greenwood Press, 1971); Walter R. Herrick, Jr.,
The American Naval Revolution (Baton Rouge, LA:
Louisiana State University Press, 1966); Harold
Sprout and Margaret Sprout, The Rise of American
Naval Power, 1776-1918 (Princeton, NJ: Princeton
University Press, 1939).
    46. For   the   best   source   on   army   operations
during the Boxer Uprising, see: Annual Report of
the War Department for the Fiscal Year Ended June
30, 1900, Part 7, Report of the Lieutenant-General
Commanding   the   Army   (Washington: Government
Printing Office, 1901), 433-546; for the U.S.
Marine Corps, see Robert Winslow Glickert, "The
Role of the U.S. Marine Corps in the Boxer
Rebellion". (M.A.   thesis, American University,
1962); for the U.S. Navy, see: William R. Braisted,
The United States Navy in the Pacific, 1897-1909
(Austin, TX: University of Texas, 1958), 75-112.
    47. Allen   R.   Millett,   Semper   Fidelis: The
History   of   The   United   States   Marine Corps (New
York: Macmillan, 1980), 21, 216; Louis Morton,
"Army and Marines on the China Station: A Study in

Military and Political Rivalry," Pacific Historical Review, 29 (February 1960): 53.

48. The various changes in the Asiatic Fleet are covered well in: Robert E. Johnson, Thence Round Cape Horn: The Story of the United States Naval Forces on Pacific Station (Annapolis, MD: Naval Institute Press, 1963); Robert E. Johnson, Far China Station: The U.S. Navy in Asian Waters, 1800-1898 (Annapolis, MD: Naval Institute Press, 1979); Hoyt, Lonely Ships.

49. Unless otherwise noted, all quoted material dealing with the background and arrival of army troops in China will be found in: Charles W. Thomas, "The United States Army Troops in China, 1912-1937," (History Term paper, Stanford University, June 1937); U.S., Department of State, Papers Relating to the Foreign Relations of the United States, 1901 and 1912 (Washington: Government Printing Office, 1920).

50. Kemp Tolley, Yangtze Patrol, 16, 97.

51. LGEN Robert O. Bare interview by Benis M. Frank (1968), 50, U.S. Marine Corps Oral History Program (MCOH), U.S. Marine Corps Historical Center (hereafter MCHC), Washington, DC.

52. Kenneth W. Condit and Edwin T. Turnbladh, Hold High the Torch: A History of the 4th Marines (Washington: Historical Branch, U.S. Marine Corps, 1960), 119-20. For material on the Chinese military during the 1920s, see: F. F. Liu, A Military History of Modern China, 1924-1949 (Princeton, NJ: Princeton University Press, 1956).

53. Condit and Turnbladh, Hold High the Torch, 127-28; MGEN Omar T. Pfeiffer interview by MAJ Lloyd E. Tatem (1968), 70-71, MCOH.

54. Quoted in Condit and Turnbladh, Hold High The Torch, 127.

55. Only two major works have been written on Butler: Lowell Thomas, Old Gimlet Eye: The Adventures of Smedley D. Butler (New York: Farrar & Rinehart, 1933), and Hans Schmidt, Maverick Marine: General Smedley D. Butler and the Contradictions of American Military History Lexington: University of Kentucky Press, 1987).

56. Letters from Smedley D. Butler to John Lejeune, 1 April and 4 April 1927, "1926-1929," Smedley D. Butler Papers, collection P.C. 54, Personal Papers Collection, MCHC.

57. The New York Times, 13 March 1927, p. 7; Time, 9 (20 June 1927): cover; Butler Papers;

Marine Corps 3rd Brigade Under Smedley D. Butler, USMC, Subject File: 1911-1927, "ZK" File, box 799, (ZK file), Record Group (RG) 45; Naval Records Collection, Office of Naval Records and Library, National Archives, Washington, DC.

58. LGEN James L. Underhill interview by Benis M. Frank (1968), 65, MCOH.

59. Millett, Semper Fidelis, 225.

60. The most succinct account of the complex effort to gain a single command in China is found in Morton, "Army and Marines on the China Station." I have relied heavily upon this work, and, unless otherwise noted, all quoted material on the subject is from this work.

61. Thomas, "Army Troops in China," 49. The Thirty-first Infantry served in Shanghai from 5 February to 30 June 1932. For a detailed account of the defense of Shanghai: William Francis Nolan, "America's Participation in the Military Defense of Shanghai, 1931-1941," (Ph.D. diss., Saint Louis University, 1978).

62. Major John T. Zeller, "The Maintenance of United States Army Forces in China," 15 April 1938, Course at the Army War College, Archives, U.S. Military History Institute (A, USMHI), Carlisle, PA.

63. GEN Paul L. Freeman interview by COL James N. Ellis, Senior Officer Debriefing Program (SODP), U.S. Army War College (AWC), 29 and 30 November 1973, p. 21, Paul L. Freeman Papers, A, USMHI.

64. Thomas, "Army Troops in China," 36.

65. Ibid., 24; Roy K. Flint, "The United States Army on the Pacific Frontier, 1899-1939" in The American Military and the Far East, 159.

66. Bernard D. Cole, Gunboats and Marines: The United States Navy in China, 1925-1928 (Newark, DE: University of Delaware Press, 1983), 27.

67. Marine Corps 3rd Brigade, ZK File; Cole, Gunboats and Marines, 50-51.

2

SOLDIERS, SAILORS, AND MARINES

The old China Station has become an integral part of the mythology of the U.S. military. Indeed, the stories told by soldiers, sailors, and marines are so intertwined with the truth that it is difficult at times to discern the dividing line between myth and reality. Most of the fictional tales have described strict but fair officers with unblemished records. The myth further endows them with the leadership qualities that made men follow in combat, but these officers also possessed the graces that allowed them entry into the better social circles. To continue the myth, enlisted men were long-service men, who cared for little except a good time and desired to retire in East Asia. The surest way to chastise a ranker was to threaten him with an early return to the United States. This chapter seeks to assess whether the myth of the old China hand reflects historical reality.[1]

Many obstacles confront scholars seeking a clear picture of the American soldiers, sailors, and marines who served in China. Foremost is a federal law that prohibits the examination of personnel records for seventy-five to one hundred years. Without actual service files, any type of group biography necessarily lacks crucial documentation. Other problems include a lack of personal papers due to constant transfers and, in the case of en-listed men, often a lack of education that prevent-ed diary entries. Further, some men in the ranks faced a stigma if they did attempt to keep journals. Two soldiers of the Fifteenth Infantry, for example, published portions of their diaries in the regimental newspaper. In the next issue, another soldier replied, not altogether tongue-in-cheek: "what two full grown men [would] want with a diary is to [sic] deep for my under-standing."[2]

The difficulties, then, of obtaining a sharp image of the men serving in China prior to World War II are many. Some of the problems, however, can be mitigated. Edward M. Coffman and Peter F. Herrly have pointed out, for example, that it is possible to obtain personal information about officers from the Army Register. Navy and marine corps officer information likewise may be gleaned from the Navy Register. While the information from the registers is certainly not complete, it does invite deductions about the officer corps.[3]

Data about enlisted men are more difficult to obtain, since there are no registers. There are, however, a number of other options. Frederick S. Harrod has noted that newspapers and magazines aimed at enlisted men can provide information on the rank and file.[4] The use of periodicals, however, can also present a false picture. Beginning in 1928, The Sentinel, the Fifteenth Infantry's newspaper, for example, ran a series on the outstanding enlisted men of the regiment. We are thus able to obtain insight into the backgrounds of some of the men. Since the editor was looking for exemplary cases, however, it is unclear whether these individuals were representa-tive. The traditional method of perusing officers' diaries for entries concerning the men also entails some pitfalls, due mainly to the large gap between the two groups. Many officers simply bought the stereotype of the ranker; others condescended to the men, while still others simply ignored them. In fact, reading some officers' diaries or memoirs, one would never know that there were enlisted men in the service: Glenn Howell, a navy officer and prolific diarist, devoted only 5 pages in one 267-page journal to the white hats on the ship he commanded.[5] Don Rickey, Jr., offers yet another way to obtain information about enlisted men: locate and interview, either in person or by question-naire, men who served in the military during a specific period of history. The difficulty here is that memory can play tricks.[6] In short, obtaining detailed, accurate information on the men who served in China from 1901 to 1937 is a problem too

great to overcome fully without access to service
records. By using a combination of all the methods
discussed above, however, and knowing their fail-
ings, we may obtain a beginning understanding of
these men. Because studies on officers are more
numerous and enlisted men are relatively unknown,
the focus of the narrative in this chapter will be
on the men in the ranks.[7]

The reasons that men entered the officer corps
are as varied as the men themselves. Joseph
Stilwell was advised to enter the army to obtain
needed discipline. Charles J. Wheeler, from
Mobile, Alabama, enjoyed the sight of navy ships
visiting the city; a friend failed to qualify for
Annapolis, but the process made Wheeler interested
and he decided to try for an appointment. William
D. Irvin's father was a furniture dealer and
undertaker in a small mining town; he recalled that
his family was all for a naval career, "as long as
it was supported by somebody else." Matthew
Ridgway's father was a regular army officer and
West Point graduate, but Ridgway remembered, his
father never pressed him to enter the army.
Patriotism caused some to sign up: Smedley
Darlington Butler lied about his age to enter the
marine corps during the Spanish-American War. The
possibility of being drafted during World War I
inspired others to enter the ranks of the officer
corps.[8]

To gain a first look at the officers serving
in China, I used information obtained from service
registers for 1929. This year was selected because
all branches of the American military were then
stationed in China, and the large shuttling of
troops to China during the restless 1920s was
completed. In other words, this year should best
represent a peacetime cross section of the U.S.
armed forces in China.

It has long been accepted that men from the
South dominated the officer corps prior to World
War I. The Great War caused a large influx of
temporary officers into the American military,
which in turn produced a heterogeneous cadre of
leaders. Coffman and Herrly found in their study
that men from the Midwest seemed to dominate the
army officer corps between the wars.[9] Army and
navy officers serving in China in 1929, however,
most frequently came from the South, with the
Midwest ranking second. The majority of men

serving in the marine corps, on the other hand, were apt to have listed the heartland as home. When the totals are added together for all the branches of the armed forces in China, the South is the region that most officers claimed as their place of birth. The margin is not, however, over-whelming--only 8 percent separates Southerners from those from the Midwest--indicating that there has indeed been some mixing of the officer corps. (See Table 2)

Table 2
Officers' Places of Birth (In percentages)

	USA N=43	USN N=301	USMC N=135
Northeast	9	12	7
Mid.Atlantic	19	19	17
Midwest	23	25	36
South	40	35	27
West	--	8	11
Foreign	7	1	2

Source: Officer Registers, 1929.
Northeast: Maine, New Hampshire, Vermont, Massachu-setts, Rhode Island, and Connecticut.
Middle Atlantic: New York, New Jersey, and Penn-sylvania.
Midwest: Minnesota, Iowa, Missouri, North and South Dakota, Nebraska, Kansas, Wisconsin, Illinois, Michigan, Ohio, and Indiana.
South: Delaware, Maryland, Virginia, West Virginia, North and South Carolina, Georgia, Florida, Dis-trict of Columbia, Kentucky, Tennessee, Alabama, Mississippi, Arkansas, Louisiana, Oklahoma, and Texas.
West: Montana, Idaho, Wyoming, Colorado, New Mexi-co, Arizona, Utah, Nevada, Washington, Oregon, and California.

a. Geographical divisions after Coffman and Herrly
b. In this and other tables concerning officers, only line officers are used.
c. There is some discrepancy due to rounding.

Chief of Staff of the Army Douglas MacArthur wrote: "Officers are commissioned from many sources of which the Military Academy is only one."[10] MacArthur went on to argue that the officer corps in the army should be comprised of at least 50 percent West Point graduates. Peter Karsten, on the other hand, has shown that the navy was largely officered by naval academy graduates.[11] In China, the men serving as gold stripers in the navy were predominantly from Annapolis. In the army, the majority of officers had signed aboard from civilian sources, such as colleges. The marine corps, on the other hand, had more men from the ranks as leaders than any of the military services (Table 3).

Table 3
Where Officers Were Acquired (In percentages)

	USA N=43	USN N=301	USMC N=135
Academy	26	89	13
Civilian	40	6	35
Enlisted	33	5	52

Source: Officer Registers, 1929.
Note: There is some discrepancy due to rounding.

Table 4 further breaks down the source of procurement of officers by rank. This indicates whether an officer's background affected his chance for promotion. By comparing Tables 3 and 4 we learn that an officer's background did in fact determine how far he could be promoted. This is most prominent in the marine corps. A majority of leatherneck officers in China (52 percent) came from the ranks. All of these men served only at company grade; not a single officer from the ranks was above the rank of captain.

The army obtained 30 percent of its officers from the ranks and, like the corps, none of these men were above company grade. Only 5 percent of navy line officers were former white hats and, likewise, none of these men rose above the grade of lieutenant (captain in the army and the marine corps).

Table 4
Where Officers Were Acquired by Rank
(In percentages)

USA N=43	COL, LCL, MAJ	CPT, 1LT, 2LT
Academy	5	21
Civilian	2	37
Enlisted	--	33

USN N=301	ADM, CAPT, CDR, LCDR	LT, LTJG, ENS
Academy	18	72
Civilian	2	4
Enlisted	--	4

USMC N=135	BGEN, COL, LCL, MAJ	CPT, 1LT, 2LT
Academy	--	13
Civilian	11	24
Enlisted	--	52

Source: Officer Registers, 1929.
Note: There is some discrepancy due to rounding.

Men from civilian sources made up the largest portion of army officers (44 percent), were the second largest group in the marine corps (35 percent), and a very small portion in the navy (6 percent. However, men obtained for the officer cadres in this category could and did advance above the company-grade level. The marine corps appears to have offered the best chance of promotion for the men who fell into this group, with potential for advancement to general officer.

The navy, as Karsten has pointed out, was the most homogeneous of all the American armed forces.[12] A very large 89 percent of the naval officers in China were Annapolis graduates, while only 13 percent of marine officers had trained at the same academy. West Pointers made up 26 percent of the Fifteenth Infantry's officers. Not surprisingly, a full 90 percent of the officers who graduated from the naval academy were able to be promoted above the rank of lieutenant. It is

interesting to note, however, that of the 10 percent of the officers from civilian sources serving
in the navy above the grade of lieutenant in China,
none commanded a capital ship. The most these
officers could expect in the way of command was an
auxiliary or perhaps an executive officer's billet
aboard a larger unit. In other words, command at
sea of a major unit was the domain of Annapolis
graduates.

Duty with troops has an interesting set of
figures for the Fifteenth Infantry. At the company
grade, there is very little separation between all
of the categories, with military academy graduates
being in the minority. (21 percent) This reflects
the large infusion of men into the army during
World War I.

Lt. Gen. John W. Leonard recalled that "the
schools are what saved the Army before World War
II. If it hadn't been for the educational system
in the Army, we never would have been able to
expand like we did."[13] The prestige schools, the
Army Staff and Command School and the Naval and War
Colleges, were of great help to the career of an
officer. Furthermore, since most officers could
not obtain field training in an era of government
fiscal restraint, theoretical instruction became a
vital component of their military education. Army
personnel in China had received the most classroom
military education, while navy men had the least.
This is understandable, for junior naval officers
were expected to learn their trade mainly aboard
ship, with training continuing as an officer was
transferred to various classes of ships.

Table 5
Officers Attending Military Schools
(In percentages)

	USA N=43	USN N=301	USMC N=135
Prestige	7	4	5
Additional Schools	47	28	18

Source: Officer Registers, 1929.

An officer's background largely dictated whether he would obtain the necessary additional instruction to help his career. No navy ex-enlisted man was ordered to a prestige school, but 4 percent of the army and 2 percent of the marine corps' former rankers had attended, and the men from civilian sources in both the army and marine corps were in the majority for the higher education. Not surprisingly, Annapolis graduates were most likely to attend the Naval War College.

Table 6
Which Officers Attended Military Schools
(In percentages)

	USA N=43	USN N=301	USMC N=145
Academy	5	88	1
Civilian	13	7	12
Enlisted	4	--	2

Source: Officer Registers, 1929.

With the ending of World War I and demobilization, the army was drastically cut back. Most of the officers who had held temporary commissions found themselves either out of the service or at their lower permanent rank. Jens A. Doe, serving in the Fifteenth Infantry in 1929, for example, was a West Point graduate, class of 1914. By 1916, he was a first lieutenant, and one year later had obtained his captaincy. By 1920, Doe had risen to the rank of major, but in 1922, he was reduced to captain; by 1927, he was again a major.[14] This up-and-down promotion pattern tended to produce an elderly officer corps. This especially holds true for the men who came up through the ranks. As shown in Table 4, most former enlisted men were not promoted above company grade; one would thus expect the officers in the marine corps and army at this grade to be much older than naval officers. Table 7 confirms this.

Lastly, one sign of distinction for promotion purposes was the type of decoration a military officer had received. American officers serving in China in 1929 who received awards equal to or

Table 7
Average Age by Rank

	USA N=43	USN N=301	USMC N=35
2LT(ENS)	26	25	27
1LT(LTjg)	34	27	34
CPT(LT)	38	33	39
MAJ(LCDR)	39	38	49
LTC(CDR)	46	43	49
COL(CAPT)	58	51	52

Source: Officer Registers, 1929.

Table 8
Year of Enlistment (In percentages)

	USA N=43	USN N=301	USMC N=135
Prior to 1917	26	40	40
1917-1918	52	8	21
After 1918	21	52	39

Source: Officer Registers, 1929.

higher than the Distinguished Service (DSM), the fifth highest medal a military man could receive, are shown in Table 9. There are no real surprises in this set of data. The army, having the largest number of troops in combat, would be expected to receive the most decorations, with the marine corps following second, and the navy third. Two members of the marine corps serving in China received the Medal of Honor, the highest military award of the United States.

Did members of the officer corps actively seek assignment to China? Without examining every request for assignment to duty, this question can

Table 9
Decorations (DSM or Higher) (In percentages)

USA N=43	USN N=301	USMC N=135
17	4	11

Source: Officer Registers, 1929.

not be accurately answered. The available evidence, however, suggests that many simply took the assignment to East Asia as just another tour of duty in a long career. Charles Bolte needed command duty and wanted foreign duty in the Philippines, but instead was ordered to Tientsin. Others actively sought assignment to China. Ridgway recalled that requesting duty with the Fifteenth Infantry was one of the key personal decisions in his career. Paul L. Freeman also sought assignment to Tientsin. The officer had heard his parents recalling "wonderful trips from the Philippines to China," so he decided to see the country first-hand. A 1925 letter of George C. Marshall indicates that his service in China with the Fifteenth Infantry was more than fortuitous. He related that he was "more and more pleased with my choice of station and duty. It suits me perfectly."[15]

There is evidence that some officers did not care for duty in the Middle Kingdom. (This will be discussed in more detail in Chapter 4.) Glenn Howell's comment that, despite his finding Yangtze River duty pleasant, he was ready to move on to another station was probably typical of most career officers.[16]

Were the officers in China, as the myth suggests, the best? Again, without access to many service records, this is patently impossible to determine accurately. There is no doubt that many of the officers were in fact very talented. Marine corps legend, Smedley D. Butler, served two tours of duty in the Middle Kingdom, once during the Boxer Uprising and later as the commander of the Third Marine Brigade in 1927-29. Of the fifty-seven officers serving in the Fifteenth Infantry during 1927, one was promoted to General of the

Army (George C. Marshall) and twenty-four reached general officer. Furthermore, six future Commandants of the Marine Corps served in China.[17] While there is no doubt that talented officers did serve in the Middle Kingdom, it is improbable that only men with the finest records were assigned to that location. For example, Joseph Felder recalled that he requested China duty simply because it was time for an overseas tour, and he and his wife thought the Middle Kingdom would be an interesting location to visit. This demonstrates that many officers thought that China duty would be a different type of foreign tour and requested the station for that reason. With many requests for service in China, the War Department had a sizable pool of men to chose from, but these candidates were not necessarily the premier personnel in the service. Certainly the War Department did not actively seek out the best officers, as has been implied by some.[18]

Some of the officers serving in China did not think too highly of their brother officers, which gives some hint as to the quality of men on the station. Navy doctor Charles S. Stevenson, for instance, noted that most of the marines he served with never read a worthwhile book, and "far too many know all the bars and other places in a city and little about people in a foreign country." The Chief of Staff of the Third Marine Brigade in Tientsin, according to the doctor, was a "Prince (prick--I mean). One would not like to think of him . . . at the tiller in a first class war."[19] While some of the doctor's comments may be attributed to careerism or to the natural friction between navy and marine corps officers, examination of the backgrounds of the military leaders who served in China indicates that the officers there were no better than those serving at other locations.

A broad picture of the U.S. military leaders serving in China in 1929 can thus be painted from the limited amount of data available. An officer serving as a company commander in the Fifteenth Infantry at Tientsin was most apt to speak with a Southern drawl and would have entered the army from civilian life during World War I. He would have been between the ages of thirty-four and thirty-eight, and have attended at least one army school. He had a very slight chance of promotion above company grade. A marine corps officer at company grade, serving in Peking, Shanghai, or Tientsin, would have entered the service prior to 1917 and have begun his career as an enlisted leatherneck. He would speak with a Midwestern twang and be between thirty-four and thirty-nine years of age. It is very unlikely that he would be promoted beyond the company-grade level or that he would have a chance to attend a service school. A naval officer serving in China, either in the Asiatic Fleet or in one of the river gunboats, would most likely have been a graduate of Annapolis. This gold striper, serving in the rank of lieutenant or lieutenant (junior grade), would be twenty-seven to thirty-three years of age and have entered the navy after 1918. This man would probably have attended at least one additional service school. Of all the American officers serving in the Middle Kingdom in 1929, the naval officer was most likely to be promoted above the rank of lieutenant (captain in the army and marine corps).

Who were the men who served in the enlisted ranks in China? Samuel B. Griffith II has written that career leathernecks prior to World War II were "perennial privates with disciplinary records a yard long." They had fought in the "banana wars" and with soldiers and sailors of every nation in "every bar in Shanghai, Manila, Tsingtao [Qingdao], Tientsin, and Peking."[20] Naval officer Henri Smith-Hutton recalled that the men serving in the navy on the China Station during 1922 were "professional" sailors who liked the Orient, as well as liquor and women. Very few had been to high school, but all wanted to remain in the navy, and they especially wished to continue serving in the Asiatic Fleet or in the gunboats. They were "very good petty officers, not necessarily educated men, but good, solid, old-fashioned sailor types."[21] Freeman recalled that any soldier with ten or fifteen years of service who was soldiering in China "could qualify as a command sergeant major in our Army today."[22]

At present, the most accessible information on enlisted men in the army in China is found in the Fifteenth Infantry's newspaper, The Sentinel. In 1924-25, the periodical also published a yearbook that included company photographs and some biographical material. Company E forwarded a great deal of information, while other companies provided only a bare minimum of data. Beginning in 1928,

the newspaper ran a series of articles entitled
"Outstanding Men of the Regiment." Using these
materials, we can gain insight, if not a definitive
portrait, into the type of men serving in the
Fifteenth Infantry through at least 1929.[23]

Most accounts, either in barracks stories or
by the few serious researchers on the army in
China, stress the fact that enlisted men serving in
the Fifteenth Infantry had requested duty in the
Middle Kingdom and were long-service men. Indeed,
The Sentinel reported that only second-enlistment
men could request duty in East Asia.[24] Former
soldiers who had served in China echoed the
newspaper's statement, adding that the need for a
good record was an additional prerequisite.[25] An
examination of the few available reminiscences of
the men who actually soldiered during this period
in Tientsin, combined with the 1924-25 Company E
data and articles in the regimental newspaper,
however, reveal a somewhat different picture.
Robert Smith joined the army in 1914 at Indianapolis, Indiana, and underwent his processing
into the service at Columbus, Ohio. After a few
weeks in Ohio, Smith, along with a large group of
men, was assigned directly to Tientsin. Charles G.
Finney, who wanted to escape the railroad workshops
of the Midwest, joined in 1922. Because he wanted
to be as far away from his former environment as
possible, the new recruit wanted duty in Hawaii.
The recruiting corporal, however, suggested that
perhaps China would be the best station for a man
with a high school education. Finney, realizing
that this was even farther than Hawaii, followed
the corporal's suggestion.[26]

Based on information from the 1924-25 yearbook,
Table 10 shows that a majority of men in Company E
(56 percent) had four years or less of service.
Note that the largest number of men had served only
two years. Thus, based on the small amount of data
provided and from reminiscences of the men themselves, the commonly-held belief that army China
hands were long-service men can be questioned.
These figures should not be too surprising, however, when one realizes the combination of events
occurring in China and in the U.S. military during
the 1920s. The Middle Kingdom had been in a state
of continual unrest from the beginning of the
twentieth century, and the unsettled conditions
became even more acute during the middle of the

Table 10
Years of Service, Co. E., 1924-1925 (Enlisted)
(In percentages)

N= 78 Years of Service		Years of Service	
1	4	13	3
2	18	14	--
3	17	15	3
4	17	16	1
5	17	17	1
6	8	18	--
7	13	19	--
8	4	20	--
9	1	21	--
10	5	22	--
11	1	23	--
12	--		

Source: 15th Infantry Annual, 1924-1925.
Note: There is some discrepancy due to rounding.

1920s. At the same time, the U.S. military had been
reduced drastically after the end of the Great War.
Further, the American armed forces, except for the
World War I period, remained a volunteer force. In
the early 1920s, economic conditions were such that
recruiters had difficulties in obtaining enough men
to fill the ranks.   Thus, these circumstances limited the Fifteenth Infantry's pool of experienced
men.   By necessity, the Fifteenth Infantry would
have to accept first enlistment men, some no more
than raw recruits.   Indeed, the old military adage
about "the needs of the service" holds true for the
1920s in China.   That is, when men are badly needed
in one location, any type will be taken until the
need is satisfied, no matter what the normal requirements are.
     Even though the information gathered from the
Company E yearbook indicates that the majority of
men, up to 1929, were on their first enlistment, a
few items from The Sentinel give us a picture of
some of the long-service men.   In 1921, for
instance, the oldest man in the Medical Detachment

was a Corp. William Dorsay who had twenty-two years
of service, with six discharges all of which stated
that his character was "excellent."   Corp. Dorsay
had begun his career with Troop F, First Cavalry,
in 1894.   Five years later, as a corporal, he was
transferred to the Eleventh Cavalry.   Prior to the
Spanish-American War, he had served at frontier
posts, and during the war served in both Cuba and
the Philippine Islands.   In 1901, he transferred to
the Hospital Corps.   Also serving in the Fifteenth
Infantry in 1921 was Msgt. Thomas Lynett, of
supply.   Lynett's twenty-two years of service were
all in the Fifteenth Infantry, with "at least one
period in Monterey, California."   Lynett entered
the army on 25 November 1898.   Msgt. Lynett's
discharges all reported his character as "good,"
and in 1921 he retired and returned to the United
States.[27]   Norman B. Howes, although serving as a
sergeant, had held a commission during World War I
and had reached the rank of major.   He served with
the Second Division and was recommended three times
for the Distinguished Service Cross. Howes retained
his major's rank in the Officer's Reserve
Corps.[28]   Msgt. Lawrence H. Thomas, of the Service
Company, was another long-service soldier and is
probably one of the best representatives of the
career enlisted man prior to World War II.   Thomas
entered the army at the age of twenty-one on 1
February 1901 and served in the Philippines with
the Twenty-sixth and Twenty-seventh Infantry.   He
then returned to the Zone of the Interior, as the
United States was referred to by the army, to serve
in the Twelfth Infantry.   In 1917, he was
commissioned and rose to captain.   During the war,
he served in the Eighth Infantry and was cited in
orders seven times. He was discharged as a captain
on 30 November 1920, and reenlisted as a master
sergeant.   He had two additional tours of duty with
the Fifteenth and one more with the Twenty-fifth
Field Artillery.   By 1924, he had twenty-three
years of service and had not mentioned retirement.[29]

The more complete data from the 1929 Sentinel
shows a shift in the make-up of the enlisted men in
the Fifteenth Infantry.   By the end of the 1920s,
for example, long-service men were in the majority,
with only 19 percent of the soldiers having five
years or less of service (Table 13). Furthermore,
the majority of the men were between thirty-five

Table 11
Home of Record, Co. E, 1924–1925 (Enlisted)
(In percentages)

N=78

Northeast	14
Middle Atlantic	24
Middle West	28
South	21
West	13

Source: 15th Infantry Annual, 1924–1925.
Note: Geographical locations after Coffman
and Herrly.

Table 12
Service of Men in Co. E, 1924–1925 (Enlisted)
(In percentages)

N=78

World War I	18	Former service	4
Decorations	4	in another branch of armed forces	

Source: 15th Infantry Annual, 1924–1925.

and thirty-nine years of age, with the next largest
grouping between thirty and thirty-four (Table 14).
Most of the men had joined the army between the
ages of twenty and twenty-two, with the next largest group between fifteen--the youngest--and eight-
teen. This would seem to indicate that the men who
served in China in 1929 were, in most cases, old
enough to have finished secondary school, but not
college. Many of the men may indeed have finished
high school, but the editor did not seem to think
this was an important item, and it was only sporadically recorded. One man was awarded a bachelor's
degree, earned during his off-duty hours.

Table 13
Year of Enlistment for Sample of Enlisted Men,
1929 (In percentages)

N=47

Prior to 1900	--	1918	4
1901-1915	43	1919	6
1916	2	1920-1924	19
1917	6	After 1924	19

Source: The Sentinel, 1929.
Note: There is some discrepancy due to rounding.

Table 14
Age of Enlisted Men, 1929 (In percentages)

N=47

20-23	3	35-39	31
24-29	34	40-49	10
30-34	17	50+	3

Source: The Sentinel, 1929.
Note: There is some discrepancy due to rounding.

This major shift in the make-up of the men is again explainable by events both in the Middle Kingdom and the United States.   By the end of the 1920s, China had become more stable, thus spelling an end to the need to rush troops there.   Furthermore, the beginnings of bad economic times in the United States had, no doubt, caused many soldiers to remain in the army.   Indeed, now the service could concentrate on having more experienced men serving in the Middle Kingdom.

The majority of men in the ranks serving in the Middle Kingdom in 1929 (36 percent) were from the Midwest.   By this time, however, the geographical region with the largest number of men was the South (19 percent), with the Middle Atlantic states and West following close behind (Table 16).   Note

Table 15
Age at Enlistment for Sample of Enlisted Men,
1929 (In percentages)

N=47

Age	%	Age	%
Below 16	3	22	12
16	27	23	9
17	--	24	--
18	--	25	6
19	6	26	3
20	15	27	--
21	15	28	3

Source: The Sentinel, 1929.
Note: There is some discrepancy due to rounding.

Table 16
Place of Birth for Sample of Enlisted Men,
1929 (In percentages)

N=47

Region	%	Region	%
Northeast	2	South	19
Middle Atlantic	15	West	15
Middle West	36	Foreign	13

Source: The Sentinel, 1929.
Note: Geographical divisions based upon Coffman
and Herrly.

that 13 percent of the men were listed as being
from a foreign country. As early as February 1927,
the Adjutant General's Office had recognized the
number of foreigners serving in the Fifteenth
Infantry and had attempted to stop this practice.
This figure and the Adjutant General's actions show
that many of the men serving in the American military in China were born outside of the United
States. In 1921, for example, one soldier insisted,

tongue-in-cheek, that he was in an outfit "where the details were written in five languages," while Company E, in 1924, listed fourteen foreign-born soldiers out of the seventy-eight assigned.   By 1928, the Infantry Journal reported that of the 800 members of the Fifteenth, 115 spoke more than one language, with German most predominant.[30]

Table 17 illustrates the wide variety of military experiences enlisted men of the Fifteenth Infantry had encountered.   Certain data in this table deserve comment.   Unlike the officers of the regiment, a large percentage of the men (42 percent) had left the army at one time for civilian pursuits and then returned.   The shortest period of time that these men spent outside of the army was two months, the longest was nine years.   (This leaving and then returning to military service is known as broken service.)

Not too surprisingly, given the fact that long-service men were beginning to form the majority in the regiment, a quarter of the soldiers had served in World War I.   Eleven percent had received commissions during the war; 4 percent had combat experience in areas other than Europe, especially in the Philippines and in Siberia.

Two groups of figures in Table 17 are particularly interesting.   The army of the 1920s was largely a continental one, with only five stations other than China outside the Zone of the Interior. Yet, in this sample, 39 percent of the soldiers had spent time outside of the contiguous United States, with the largest number having served in the Philippines or having had more than one tour of duty in China.   Moreover, at least 18 percent of the men had either purchased their discharges in order to enlist for duty in the Middle Kingdom or had voluntarily taken a reduction in rank in order to serve with the Fifteenth Infantry. In the interwar army, when promotions were glacially slow, for men to give up their rank seems to be an excellent indicator that the China Station was perceived as good duty.

The men who made up the army rank and file in 1929, then, were a diverse group.   The reasons they entered the military were varied.   However, the motivations may be divided into four broad groups: economic or other dissatisfaction with their lives; desire for adventure or travel; patriotism;   and a desire for a military career.   Pfc. Richard Boles,

Table 17
Service of Sample of Enlisted Men, 1929
(In percentages)

N=47

Broken Service	42	Served in Alaska	18
Prior Service	7	Hawaii, Panama	
Service in WWI	26		
Wounded/POW	5	Served in China,	
Mexican Border	5	Philippine Islands	21
Philippines (combat)	2		
Decorated	4	Purchased discharge	
Served as Officer	6	or took reduction	
Siberia (combat)	2	to serve in China	18

Source: The Sentinel, 1929.

for example, seems to have looked upon the army as a way to further his "desire to see the world." Born 21 September 1901 in Hilham, Tennessee, he graduated from high school at the age of seventeen and went to work for an oil company.   Boles' employment took him to Argentina, and while in South America, he visited Paraguay, Uruguay, and Peru.   He returned to the United States in 1923 and, in order to see Alaska, enlisted in the army for the Seventh Infantry.   He was discharged in 1926 and remained a civilian for one year before reenlisting on 1 July 1927 for China.[31] Sgt. Cecil C. Moore, Company F, Fifteenth Infantry, seems to have been a man who strongly desired a military career.   Moore was badly wounded during the Meuse-Argonne Offensive on 8 October 1918 and was medically retired.   As soon as possible, however, the soldier requested a reexamination and gave up his pension to return to active duty.   Sgt. Gordon D. Harrison is probably one of the best examples of a man who wanted to actively pursue the military life.   Harrison, born in Georgia, spent five years in the French Foreign Legion in Morocco and then enlisted in the U.S. Army.   He had served with the Eighth Infantry in Germany and, by 1928, had spent six years in China.[32]

There is very little information about the marines and sailors who served in the Middle Kingdom in the 1920s.   The very sketchy details, however, imply that, in the main, these men were probably much like their fellow enlisteds in the Fifteenth Infantry. That is, they entered for the same four reasons. For example, Howell records the background of a sailor identified only as "Ski." This white hat was born near Pittsburgh of Polish parents, and his father died when the baby was one month old.   The mother gave the child to an orphanage when he reached the age of two.   Ski spent the next twelve years at this institution. At the age of six, he ran away for the first time. He was finally released when he was fifteen.   He worked at various odd jobs and finally secured a steady position as a bellhop in a Pittsburgh hotel. His mother relocated him and, because he had employment, demanded that he support her and his stepfather.   Ski refused and ran away to enlist in the navy at around sixteen years of age.   He first came to East Asia in the South Dakota in 1919 and by 1921 was serving in the gunboat Palos.[33]

Patriotism also motivated enlisted personnel in the naval services.   Julius Isaacson recalled that he entered the navy because of patriotic feelings after the United States declared war on Germany in 1917.   The desire for travel also entered into the picture.   In 1927, George H. Cloud, for example, who had taken college courses and was employed, walked to the train depot to mail a letter.   While performing this task, he saw a train with China-bound marines stopped at a siding.   After talking to the leathernecks, Cloud thought, "What a place to go!"   The following week the young man found himself unemployed and decided to sign aboard the marine corps for duty in China as an enlisted man.[34]

Even with the small amount of information available about the enlisted men, we are able to see just how short-handed the American military was after the Great War.   Naval officer Wheeler recalled that in 1919 the South Dakota, later the Huron, was so short of its proper complement that it could not sail from New York to join the Asiatic Fleet.   Recruiters were forced to send almost all of their recruits to the ship without the benefit of training.   "They came on board," said Wheeler, "in civilian clothes, in Army uniforms, in rags, and everything else."   Such a   motley crew was bound to cause problems. En route to Panama, many of the new recruits decided that some aspects of navy life, such as scrubbing your own clothes and slinging hammocks, were not attractive, so they began to throw their uniforms and hammocks over the side. Once the South Dakota arrived in the Canal Zone, over fifty men deserted, and Wheeler noted that "we wished more had."[35]

In 1922, the periodical, Fleet Review, further illustrated the inexperience of the navy during the early 1920s. The magazine noted that close to 78 percent of the sailors had less than four years of service. This is shown in Table 18.[36] As the 1920s progressed, the personnel situation did not improve. In a 1927 letter to the commanding officer of the Submarine Division of the Asiatic Fleet, for example, the Bureau of Navigation, which was responsible for matters concerning personnel, noted that the Appropriation Act for 1928 had cut the number of men for the navy from 86,000 to 83,250. This would require "radical reductions in practically all ships." The submarine tender Canopus' completment, for instance, was reduced by fourteen. This shortage of experienced crews was bound to have caused administrative difficulties and disciplinary problems.[37]

One of the persistent stereotypes about the enlisted men in China is that of men constantly in trouble. Indeed, a perusal of the most readily available material seems to reinforce this view. In 1923, for example, the Fifteenth Infantry convicted 296 men for court-martial offenses, with one man sent to the Federal Prison at McNeil Island, Washington, and ten sent to the Disciplinary Barracks, Alcatraz Island, California.[38]

A 1924 letter to the Adjutant General's office discussed the "increasing number of American Army deserters who have appeared [in Shanghai]."[39] Marshall, in 1925, recorded 249 convictions, while one year later, the regiment reported 246, with eleven men sent to Alcatraz.[40]

The marine corps also had its problems. Marine Officer Adolf B. Miller noted in his diary in 1927 that the leathernecks under his command had been restricted to their quarters due to the number of men being absent without leave (AWOL) or drunk.[41] Butler, because he felt the marines were getting restless and the regimental commanders were not doing enough to keep them in line, had his chief of staff, Ellis Bell Miller, take disciplinary powers

Table 18
Length of Service of Navy Enlisted Force, 1921–
1929 (In percentages)

Years Fiscal Year	Under 4	4–8	8–12	12–16	16–20	Over 20
1921	83.4	7.4	4.6	3.0	1.2	0.4
1922	77.5	10.3	5.8	4.2	1.8	0.4
1923	77.3	12.5	5.9	3.0	1.1	0.2
1924	77.0	12.7	5.9	3.1	1.1	0.2
1925	72.1	16.3	6.4	3.5	1.3	0.4
1926	57.5	25.2	9.5	5.8	1.7	0.3
1927	57.5	23.4	11.1	6.1	1.7	0.2
1928	54.8	21.5	15.7	5.8	1.9	0.3
1929	56.3	17.7	17.3	6.2	2.2	0.3

Source: Annual Report of the Chief of the Bureau of Navigation.

away from the commanders and formed a star chamber summary court at brigade headquarters. This seems to have produced the desired results.[42]

During the period under study, the military system of justice recognized two types of infractions: criminal and military. The former consisted of cases that would be punished by prison terms and were the same as under civilian law, including murder, assault, theft, and the like. Military offenses, on the other hand, had no parallel in civilian courts. These included disobedience to orders, desertion, and similar offenses. There were three types of major courts-martial a serviceman could receive. In descending order of the severity of punishment, they were general, summary, and special. There were also non-judicial punishments given by local commanders. Men who received this punishment could be confined to the command for short periods of time.[43]

Statistics indicating that enlisted men were constantly in trouble must be used with caution. In 1927, for instance, the Fifteenth Infantry reported forty-five special courts-martial. Table 19 lists the four most common charges in these proceedings. As shown, the most frequently cited infraction was drunkenness.[44] In short, while the

Table 19
Four Most Common Charges in Summary Courts-Martial
During 1927 in Fifteenth Infantry

N=45

AWOL	10[*]
Drunk	7
Failure to appear on time	7[+]
Disrespect	5

Source: 15th Infantry, "Courts-Martials," National
Archives
[*]   8 cases of drunkenness, as secondary charge.
[+]   4 cases of drunkenness, as secondary charge.

offenses were unlawful, none of them would be
considered serious in a civilian court of law.   In
fact, in today's military, the men would probably
be given alcohol counseling instead of a sentence.
This does not, however, mean that all charges were
not serious. As noted above, in 1923, eleven men
were sent to prison.   Still the preponderance of
cases covered minor offenses. Often, court-martial
proceedings were used simply to keep men in line.
This is illustrated well by the case of marine Pvt.
R. B. Brightman.   While serving aboard the Helena
in 1911, the private received five days of solitary
confinement on bread and water for "willful
inefficiency."[45]
     Many officers saw the men in the ranks as little
more than the dregs of society and felt that
courts-martial were the best way to restrain the
men.   In 1903, for example, Capt. Eugene H. C.
Leutz wrote that because the navy did not "get the
best elements of the male population," it followed
that those who entered the service were men of
"poorer . . . roving and adventurous dispositions.
These have never know restraint, so that the
discipline and routine work of the Navy is irksome
to them."[46] This became a circular argument: the
undesirable type of men in the service required
many courts-martial, and the large number of
courts-martial proved that the men were
undesirable.
     The tensions between officers and enlisted men
as shown in courts-martial are shown well by naval

officer Howell.   In 1925, he confided to his
journal that one of the "greatest responsibilities
of a naval officer is that of punishment of men."
The lieutenant commander felt that sailors are "a
peculiarly irresponsible group" in their conduct
ashore, and that the only difference between a
young sailor and a grammar schoolboy "is that the
latter wears knickerbockers."   Howell then noted
that since one could not turn a bluejacket over
one's knee and spank him, one used courts-martial.
At first, the young officer felt that brig time was
the best dose of medicine for the men, until a
visit to the Bilibid Prison at Manila led him to
ponder how confinement sapped a man's self-respect.
He also believed that slapping a sailor in the
ship's brig on bread and water was ludicrous,
because it so resembled "shutting little Willie
in the closet without any supper."   On the other
hand, Howell did not look forward to what he
believed was coming--the end to this sort of
punishment--because he felt that "carefully used it
is very useful for discipline."   In fact, four
years earlier, while commanding the Palos, Howell
recorded that he had used this punishment five or
six times and, while he was "never keen about
using" it, the confinement had produced "excellent
results."   It straightened out two men, made
another more careful and scared a fourth into
"temporary good behavior."[47]

Officer corps indiscretions in China, unlike
those of enlisted personnel, have received little
attention in military lore.   One has to do a
great deal of digging to find that those that wore
the gold also committed civilian and military
offenses.   Marine officer Omar T. Pfeiffer's oral
history includes a number of references to marine
or navy leaders in trouble because of instances of
theft and alcoholism.[48]   Another marine officer
related that when he first arrived in Peking, many
of the officers were at best incompetent.   They
were soon sent home.[49]   This treatment highlights
another major difference in how the military
justice system worked.   Unless an officer had
committed a criminal offense, he was required to
resign from the service rather than receive a
sentence.   In short, the men in the ranks in China
have been accused of being constantly in trouble,
and courts-martial statistics are usually used to
prove this point.   There are, however, indications

that officers, in proportion to their smaller numbers, were as apt to be in trouble as the men. Furthermore, because most legends about service in China come from tales passed on by the gold stripers, it is not surprising that there have been few accounts of leaders' faults. There have been, however, just enough officers who are willing to tell both sides of the story to show that both groups committed indiscretions.

The stereotype of the China hand constantly running afoul of the law is correct up to a point. Court-martial statistics may be used to confirm this impression. Still, one should interpret such data in relationship to statistics for the entire service. In 1929, for example, there were five soldiers convicted of general court-martial offenses on the China station, which was fewer than any other area in the army. Even the Military Academy had more men convicted. Furthermore, as will be discussed below, the largest number of problems came prior to 1930; after that date, the numbers began to decline.[50]

The present evidence indicates that the 1930s marked a major change in the composition of the American troops in China. The largest single reason for this change was the Great Depression. Robert K. Griffith, Jr., has correctly stated that mass unemployment became a "bonanza" for the regular army, as well as for the other armed forces.[51]

A brief sampling of the men who served during the 1930s, however, still shows a mixture of reasons for joining the service. Edwin C. Schierhorst entered the army because he did not care to be a grocery clerk. Eugene F. Horrall, who served in the navy, entered the service "to get a start." Former marine Albert Tidwell thought he was "too big to be at home," and the Corps "seemed the proper thing to do for survival." Glenn M. Hargrave recalled that he enlisted in the marine corps "to escape farm work." Howard L. Povey wanted a seaman's career and felt the navy was the best place to find it. Malcolm P. Stimmers stated he had been a hobo and entered the navy for "security."[52]

The changing nature of the military in China during the 1930s is graphically shown by a quick glance at the seniority list of the non-commissioned officers serving in Peking and at Tientsin.

Of twenty-five leathernecks in the non-commissioned grades in 1936, only five had a date of rank from before 1930, with the oldest dating from 1924.   In the Fifteenth Infantry, the picture was much the same, with the oldest non-commissioned officer's date of rank listed as 1919 and with the majority in the years 1934-35.[53] Thus, the senior enlisted grades appear to have been filled by younger men, indicating better chances for promotion.

The marine corps at Peking apparently continued to accept many foreigners into its ranks.   In 1931, for instance, the legation guard reported fifty-six men who were not native-born Americans.   Sfc. Charles Hennrick was born in Danzig, enlisted in the army in 1921, and then reenlisted in the marine corps.   By 1935, he had served in Nicaragua and had two tours of duty in China.   Marine officer James P. Berkeley reported that the leathernecks at Peking had more Italians "than the Italian Marines had in their . . . guard."[54]

One of the most interesting aspects of this changing enlisted force concerns the education level of the men.   A 1936 article in the American Embassy Guard News reported that the numbers of college marines were increasing service-wide.   Of the men, 92 percent had higher than an elementary education, while 3,043 recruits out of a total of 3,713 had either attended or graduated from high school.   Furthermore, some 256 had attended college, but not graduated, while nineteen had obtained at least a bachelor's degree.[55]

The better-educated enlisted men no doubt pleased both recruiters and many officers.   This change, however, led to some friction among the men in the ranks that has not been adequately explored.   Richard McKenna, before his untimely death, was beginning work on this subject in his unfinished novel, The Sons of Martha, which takes place aboard a navy ship at Guam in the 1930s.[56] Undoubtedly, the pre-1930s sailors, soldiers, and marines resented many of the better-educated men filling the ranks, for they feared that the new-comers would make promotions faster.   When marine officer George H. Cloud first enlisted in the marine corps, for example, the recruiter tried to talk him out of signing aboard, because he did not think an educated man would enjoy serving in the ranks.   When the sergeant found the young man adamant, he informed him that he would not enter

Cloud's educational achievements onto his record, or "otherwise [he would] be a marked man."[57] This friction between educated and uneducated rankers is most pronounced during the periods of war when large numbers of men are drafted into the military.

Court-martial statistics can also be used to show that the 1930s marks a major change in the personnel serving in the armed forces. In the entire navy, for example, between 1909-1937, there was a gradual decrease in cases, except for the war years. This is further illustrated by examining the years 1920 to 1937. The high ran from 3,217 in 1920, to 273 in 1936. Similar numbers can be shown for summary courts (Table 20). During the same time span, desertions dropped from a high of 10,261 in 1921, to a low of 318 in 1936. The 1936 figure was the lowest in forty years (Table 21). In July 1912, Company A of the marine corps' legation guard at Peking, had eleven offenses, all of which were of military types. In July 1925, the same company had three cases, again, all of military types. By July 1935, there were no offenses recorded.[58]

Two reasons account for this change. The first is that very few men would take a chance on losing a secure position during poor economic times. The second is that, in spite of the vast differences between officers and enlisted men, which are discussed below, conditions had been improving for the rank and file, especially in the navy. Which of these two reasons most affected the men? The lack of in-depth studies on enlisted men during this period precludes a definitive determination of the reason or reasons behind the improvement in court-martial rates. At present, it is sufficient to note that a combination of economic factors and improved treatment appears to have changed the type of enlisted man serving in the American military during the 1930s, as indicated by court-martial statistics.

Another aspect of military life in China deserves comment: officer-enlisted relationships. There is no doubt that a very large gap existed between the two groups. In general, many officers believed that the men were uneducated and lazy, drank to excess, and were only interested in three meals a day, a place to sleep, and enough time off to have a good time. In short, they were little better than useless. Enlisted men, on the other hand, felt officers acted superior, used their

Table 20

Navy Enlisted Men Tried by Courts-Martial, 1909–1937 (In percentages)

Fiscal Year	Enlisted Force[1]	General Courts-Martial		Summary Courts-Martial	
		No.		No.	
1909	57,769	1,781	3.08	7,630	13.21
1910	54,791	1,339	2.44	8,457	15.43
1911	61,832	1,226	1.98	8,246	13.33
1912	65,286	1,265	1.94	9,202	14.09
1913	65,126	1,295	1.99	9,946	15.27
1914	67,015	1,342	2.00	7,542	11.25
1915	71,511	1,384	1.93	9,084	12.70
1916	72,885	1,239	1.70	8,274	11.35
1917	81,097	1,423	1.75	7,979	9.83
1918	378,858	4,428	1.17	14,552	3.84
1919	393,802	4,900	1.24	21,101	5.36
1920	137,456	3,217	2.34	20,311	14.78
1921	------------------not available------------------				
1922	98,946	1,624	1.74	12,702	12.74
1923	83,185	1,154	1.39	9,795	11.77
1924	85,603	2,204	2.57	9,057	10.58
1925	85,945	1,880	2.18	9,384	10.91
1926	82,128	1,307	1.59	8,619	10.49
1927	82,932	1,485	1.79	8,224	9.91
1928	84,010	1,612	1.92	8,639	10.28
1929	84,443	1,269	1.50	7,719	9.14
1930	85,270	1,181	1.38	6,058	7.10
1931	82,564	866	1.05	6,252	7.55
1932	80,711	692	.86	5,387	6.70
1933	80,735	457	.57	5,048	6.25
1934	78,260	394	.50	4,352	5.56
1935	81,510	261	.32	3,100	3.80
1936	86,574	223	.26	3,090	3.53
1937	96,360	228	.24	3,127	3.25

Source: Annual Report of the Judge Advocate General for the years 1909–37.

[1] For 1909–1916, this column gives the total number of men in the navy during the fiscal year; for 1917–1937, it lists the average number of men under naval jurisdiction during each year.

Table 21
Desertion, U.S. Navy, 1901–1937

Fiscal Year	Enlisted Force	No.of Desertions	Desertions as Percentage Enlisted Force
1901	18,825	3,158	16.8
1902	21,435	3,037	14.1
1903	27,245	4,136	15.1
1904	29,321	4,488	15.3
1905	30,804	4,427	14.4
1906	32,163	4,867	15.1
1907	33,027	5,105	15.5
1908	39,048	6,054	15.5
1909	42,861	3,836	8.8
1910	45,076	3,549	7.9
1911	47,612	3,284	6.9
1912	47,515	3,055	6.4
1913	48,068	3,237	6.7
1914	52,667	2,728	5.2
1915	52,561	2,320	4.4
1916	54,234	2,064	3.8
1917	100,539	2,826	2.8
1918	435,406	3,133	0.7
1919	250,833	6,138	2.5
1920	108,950	10,036	9.5
1921	119,205	10,261	8.6
1922	85,580	Not available	--------
1923	82,355	5,820	7.1
1924	87,327	7,787	8.9
1925	84,289	4,657	4.9
1926	82,161	2,675	3.2
1927	83,566	3,123	3.8
1928	84,355	2,906	3.5
1929	85,321	2,055	2.4
1930	84,938	1,884	2.2
1932	80,910	1,123	1.4
1932	81,120	757	.9
1933	79,243	604	.8
1934	80,359	580	.7
1935	82,839	332	.4
1936	93,077	318	.3
1937	100,178	467	.5

Source: Annual Report of the Chief of the Bureau of Navigation for the years 1901-37.

power to   excess, and believed that they were
members of the upper class, as compared to the men
in the ranks whom they regarded as little better
than serfs. The misunderstandings and inability to
understand one another at times seem to have caused
the gap to widen to an unbridgeable chasm.

Traditionally,   both   officers   and   civilians
have had a low regard for enlisted men.   One
contributing factor to the civilian point of view
is that, until very recently, it was not uncommon
for a judge to give a young offender a choice
between going to jail and entering the armed forces
as a ranker.   This type of punishment was a well-
known fact to the general public and did little to
enhance the image of men in military uniforms.   It
is not too surprising, then, that enlisteds met
with signs barring them from the better establishments or recreation areas. The Sentinel, in 1924,
proclaimed that one park in Tientsin had stopped
soldiers from entering while in uniform.[59] It can
perhaps be understood why civilians might have mis-
givings about the men.   After all, they saw them
only infrequently, and some of the enlisted men
they observed were not the best.

It is, however, a little more difficult to
understand why the officer corps of the time could
not comprehend the men, for they were in the same
profession.   One is forced to see an element of
class differences in the relationship.   James
Jones, in an essay on the old regular army just
prior to and during World War II, touches upon this
friction.[60] There is very little doubt that most
officers saw themselves as at least middle-class
and more likely as upper-middle-class.   Further,
Col. Noel F. Parrish, writing in 1947, recognized
that the interwar years, with the lack of funds for
proper training, the small dreary posts, and a
public that cared little for the military, could
cause an "atmosphere of unreality" to develop in
the officer corps, which made some leaders turn to
the "affectation of imported uniforms and manner-
isms . . . [and] the imitation of the well-to-
do."[61]

The writings and utterances of some senior
military leaders furthered the image of superiority. MacArthur, while serving as Chief of Staff of
the Army and in the process of trying to stop
reductions in the officer corps, reported to
Congress that, "If you had to discharge every

soldier, if you had to do away with everything
else, I would still professionally advise you to
keep these 12,000 officers. They are the main-
spring of the whole mechanism."[62] The chief of
staff was correct in pointing out the need for
officers, but his words certainly imply that
enlisted men were not professional and that their
loss would be of no great moment to the army.
Further, C. Robert Kemble has pointed out that in
the United States, it is the officer "who has
symbolized the profession of arms," because the
enlisted man is "of little interest to Americans."[63] These attitudes were certainly known and
felt by those in the rank and file. Lastly, the
military academies taught future officers that they
were, indeed, special leaders. Men in the ranks
too felt this indoctrination. As former navy
enlisted man William R. Hardcastle aptly put it,
"Many Academy officers . . . were given a false
sense of their importance at the Academy; that they
were somehow different and smarter than the average
civilian and all enlisted men."[64]   In short, the
training and backgrounds of the men in command
almost forced those who wore the gold to feel
superior.

Enlisted men in China, and generally throughout the American military until the 1930s, were
not well-educated, and many were foreign-born.
Some came from backgrounds that can only be
described as squalid. Most entered the military
when very young and had no skills. Many who
entered the rank and file quickly learned, or
perceived, the vast gap between officers and enlisted men, which even carried over into their
private lives. Even at some of the best posts,
most married enlisted men lived in poor conditions.
At some locations, families were forced to live in
tents. Furthermore, the area where married army
rankers lived has traditionally been called
"soapsuds row," because of the need for wives to
take in washing in order to supplement the meager
earnings of their soldier-husbands. One student of
the army during the interwar years, after detailing
the low pay and poor living conditions, was forced
to describe these men and their families as "this
wretched class of people."[65] It is no wonder that
when rankers, aware of their past inferiority to
officers in pay and living conditions, saw them
attending large affairs at the officers' club or

naval gold stripers served by stewards, the men
grumbled rather vociferously.

A young man who wore the gold did in fact come
from a background that was the antithesis of that
of the men he commanded. It took a very special
person not to develop certain attitudes of
superiority because of this circumstance. Most
officers ignored rankers, except in the line of
duty, internalized stereotypes of the men, and
sometimes condescended to them. A few accepted the
rankers for who they were and tried to treat the
men fairly while working within the system.

It was a simple matter for an officer to slip
into the paternal role. In the early 1900s, for
example, a form-type letter circulated through the
navy that enumerated all the stereotypes of the
white hats (gobs), such as being "eminenity [sic]
fitted to sleep curled up around torpedo tubes,
under boilers," and in other unusual locations.
The description ends with the sailor standing "by
his skipper, his ship, his country, and his bunkie
with all he has to give, and a little more; and is
the best pal God ever gave a man."[66]   Even
accomplished writers, such as John W. Thomason,
Jr., probably the best of the very few marine
officers to be a highly successful fiction
writer, could portray enlisted leathernecks as
"simple Marines in a confusing Orient."[67]
Secretary of the Navy Josephus Daniels, one of the
early-twentieth-century advocates for enlisted
reforms, was paternalistic in his feelings toward
the rankers. Harrod has noted that in reading
the secretary's annual reports concerning the rank
and file, one is left with "the impression that
Daniels must have invented enlisted men."[68]

Adding to the problems of understanding was
the officially accepted manner of how an officer
should conduct himself. The leader was not
expected to take care of day-to-day operations or
the supervision of the men. This was left to the
non-commissioned officers. Officer-enlisted contact was usually reserved for only disciplinary
measures, or formal requests, or ceremonies, such
as inspections. Anthony Ingrisano recalled that
when he soldiered in the Fifteenth Infantry in the
1930s, "officers had little to do with us. We
sometimes saw them during duty hours. Sometimes."[69] Such a system, of course, perpetuated
the gap by making the officer seem remote, aloof,

and impersonal. This type of routine could also lead to abuses. James Jones, in his novel From Here to Eternity, captured this problem by showing Captain Holms effectively turning over control of the company to Sergeant Warden, while Holms pursues his own interests.[70]   The remoteness was further heightened by the accepted manner of address on formal occasions. The two groups were expected to speak to each other in the third person.   For example, if a private in the army wished to speak to a captain, the proper manner of address was: "Private Smith wishes to speak to the captain."

Some officers, who at first blush may have seemed to have had the welfare of their men at heart, could not rise above their training and backgrounds. The best example is supplied by naval officer Howell on the Yangtze River.   When in command of the gunboat Palos in 1921, the officer rented a bungalow at Changsha so that his men would have a wholesome place to pass their off-duty hours.   His diaries are replete with entries of taking some of the crew on hikes and other activities.   Of course, one may also say that this activity was undertaken to keep the men from the bars and brothels. In 1926, however, while serving on the staff of the commander of the Yangtze Patrol, Howell learned that an officer who had come up from the ranks had been ordered to the executive officer's billet aboard the gunboat Penguin. "This makes me furious," Howell confided to his journal. "[T]he River is the last place to which this ex-gob trash should come."   The lieutenant commander felt that only an Annapolis graduate had the necessary training to handle the complexities of duty on the Yangtze.   His objections were so strong that he was instrumental in having the officer's orders canceled.[71]

The reader, however, should not believe that all officers were unfeeling toward the men they commanded.   Some leaders did try to accept the men as they were and to treat them fairly.   Ingrisano, fifty years later, remembered Lt. Col.   Karl Truesdell.   While on maneuvers, the officer refused to ride a horse, as was the normal practice for a senior officer.   Instead, he would march in front of the column in "poncho & campaign hat," no matter what the weather. When asked why he did not ride, Truesdell would point to the troops and say, "if [those] sons of bitches can walk I can walk." The former infantryman also remembered the then-Capt. Don Pratt, because he "always had time to listen."[72] Indeed, of the people who responded to the questionnaires used in this study, a great many reported that the officers they thought were good leaders were those who took the time to listen to what the men had to say and who also had the ability to let the troops know what was happening without condescending to them. These simple attributes speak volumes about how the men per-ceived their leaders.

It should also be emphasized that not all enlisted men in China, and throughout the American military establishment, conformed to the down-trodden lower-class pattern described above. That many of the men drank to excess and were constantly in trouble does not mean that the majority behaved in this manner.

The officer-enlisted relationship is an important factor in understanding the men who served in China. Very few rankers have published their experiences or kept journals. Therefore, much of what has come down to us is from the officer viewpoint. Much of the myth of the enlisted China hand comes from sea stories and barracks tales. As Richard McKenna correctly pointed out, sea stories usually begin from acts that are generally outrageous. After all, very few people will remember, or even be interested in, stories of everyday events, such as staying aboard ship and studying for promotion examinations. What is recalled and improved upon over the years is the man who is "Asiatic" (a little crazy), who commits some indiscretion on his off-duty time.[73] Officers heard these stories and, because they fit neatly into their view of the rank and file, passed them on, until it has become difficult to separate truth from fiction. It is therefore important to realize that many of the stories about enlisted men in China come from officers' perceptions.

By using questionnaires, diaries, regimental newspapers, and other information, a hypothetical man in the ranks in China can be sketched. Since there is more data for army men than for the other services in the Middle Kingdom, the hypothetical ranker is a soldier serving in the Fifteenth Infantry; preliminary evidence, however, suggests that this description may well fit many of the other men serving in East Asia. From 1912 to at least 1925, a soldier at Tientsin would speak with a Midwestern accent and be on his first enlistment. He would have entered the service because of patriotism, interest in travel or adventure, or a dissatisfaction with his lot in civilian life. He was very likely, at one time or another, to run afoul of regulations and be convicted of a military offense. Generally, this would be related to drinking. The infantryman would have had an elementary-level education.

By the end of the 1920s, however, because of a shortage of troops throughout the military establishment and the growing perception among enlisted men that China was good duty, there was a change in the composition of the ranks. The soldier still continued to speak with a Midwestern accent, but his age would have increased to a least twenty-four and probably a little older. He would have served at least one enlistment in the army. His education level would still be at the elementary level, but more men held a high school diploma. The infantryman would have spent at least one tour of duty outside of the Zone of the Interior, probably in the Philippine Islands. He would have left the service at least once for a try at civilian life. The perceived nature of the duty in East Asia made the soldier willing to buy his discharge or to take a voluntary reduction in rank to be assigned to Tientsin.

The Great Depression, the best recruiter for the American armed forces, caused a major change in the type of soldier in the Fifteenth Infantry. Midwesterners probably continued to dominate the regiment. The education level increased so that a high school diploma was not uncommon. Men caused fewer disciplinary problems, probably because they were afraid to lose a secure position in difficult economic times or because of improving conditions of service. The ages of the men would fall into a wider range as recruiters had a larger variety of men to choose from, including college graduates. Men tended to remain in the army longer, again because of the depression or because of improved conditions.

Even with the improvement in the caliber of men in the enlisted ranks in the 1930s, there is no indication that either officers or civilians had shed the traditional stereotypes of the rank and file. When a new group of enlisted men arrived at

Tientsin, in 1937, one officer felt they looked like convicts.[74] However, enlisted men in the Middle Kingdom were a far more diverse group than portrayed in the simplistic accounts of the old China hand.

NOTES

1. Roy K. Flint, "The United States Army on the Pacific Frontier, 1899-1939," in The American Military and the Far East: Proceedings of the Ninth Military History Symposium, United States Air Force Academy, 1-3 October 1980, ed. Joe C. Dixon, (Washington: Government Printing Office, 1980), 149.

2. The Sentinel (Tientsin, China), 27 March 1925, p. 11.

3. Edward M. Coffman and Peter F. Herrly, "The American Regular Army Officer Corps Between the World Wars," Armed Forces and Society, 4, no. 1 (November 1977): 59.

4. Frederick S. Harrod, Manning the New Navy: The Development of a Modern Naval Enlisted Force, 1899-1940 (Westport, CT: Greenwood Press, 1978), x-xi.

5. "The Log of Glenn Howell," VIII, passim, Naval Operational Archives (NOA), U.S. Navy Historical Center (NHC), Washington, DC.

6. Don Rickey, Jr., Forty Miles A Day on Beans and Hay: The Enlisted Soldier Fighting the Indian Wars (Norman, OK: University of Oklahoma Press, 1963), viii.

7. The literature on the officer corps is becoming large, for, as C. Robert Kemble has noted, in the United States it is the officer "who has symbolized the profession of arms." Furthermore, because officers were more educated and left papers, they have been the easiest to study. C. Robert Kemble, The Image of the Army Officer in America: Background for Current Views (Westport, CT: Greenwood Press, 1973), 7.

8. Barbara W. Tuchman, Stilwell and the American Experience in China, 1911-45 (New York: Macmillan 1970), 12; RADM Charles J. Wheeler interview by CDR Etta-Belle Kitchen (1970), 1-2, Oral History Program, U.S. Naval Institute (OHNI), Annapolis, MD; RADM William D. Irvin interview by John T. Mason, Jr. (1980), 1-3, OHNI; GEN Matthew B. Ridgway interview by COL John M. Blair (1971-1972), 1-2, 4, Senior Officer Debriefing Program

(SODP), U.S. Army War College (AWC), Archives, U.S. Military History Institute (A, USMHI), Carlisle Barracks, PA; Hans Schmidt, Maverick Marine: General Smedley D. Butler and the Contradictions of American Military History (Lexington, KY: University Press of Kentucky, 1987), 6-7.

9. Coffman and Herrly, "American Regular Army Officer Corps," 59-62.

10. Quoted in ibid., 62.

11. Peter Karsten, The Naval Aristocracy: The Golden Age of Annapolis and the Emergence of Modern American Navalism (New York: Free Press, 1972), 23-46.

12. Ibid.

13. Quoted in Coffman and Herrly, "American Regular Army Officer Corps," 67.

14. Doe retired as a major general. Charles G. Finney, The Old China Hands (Garden City, NY: Doubleday, 1959; reprint, Westport, CT: Greenwood Press, 1977), 7, 13 (page references are to reprint edition).

15. GEN Charles Bolte interview by Arthur J. Zoebelein (1971-1972), 15, SODP, AWC, A, USMHI: Ridgway interview, 20; GEN Paul L. Freeman interview by COL James N. Ellis (1973), 18, SODP, AWC, A, USMHI; Larry I. Bland and Sharon R. Ritenour, eds., The Papers of George Catlett Marshall Vol. 1, "The Soldierly Spirit," December 1880-June 1939 (Baltimore: Johns Hopkins University Press, 1981), 277.

16. "Log of Howell," XIII, December 1922.

17. Schmidt, Maverick Marine, passim.; Finney, Old China Hands, 13; Allan R. Millett, Semper Fidelis: The History of the United States Marine Corps (New York: Macmillan, 1980), 627.

18. Joseph G. Felder, China Service Question-naire (CSQ) to Dennis L. Noble (DLN), 6 August 1984.

19. George Stevenson to Sonya Leyton, 29 May 1927; Stevenson to [Sister], 12 June 1927, Papers of George Stevenson, Special Collections, Nimitz Library, U.S. Naval Academy, Annapolis, MD.

20. Samuel B. Griffith II, The Battle for Guadalcanal (New York: Nautical and Aviation Publishing, 1963), 21-22.

21. CAPT Henri Smith-Hutton interview by CAPT Paul Ryan (1973), 26, OHNI.

22. Freeeman interview, 21-22.

23. All material for Company E comes from: L. L.

Williams, ed., 15th Infantry Annual: May 4, 1924-May 4, 1925 (Tientsin, China: Tientsin Press, 1925 ?), 33-39.

24. The Sentinel ran short articles on the quality of the men from 1921 until the end of its publication. See, for example, The Sentinel, 7 December 1929, p. 19.

25. Among the many who stressed this point were: Frank H. Farley, CSQ to DLN, 1 August 1984; Laney E. Rutledge, CSQ to DLN, 20 August 1984; Robert J. Plummer, CSQ to DLN, 22 July 1984; Arthur G. Gullickson, CSQ to DLN, 18 August 1984; and Edward J. Ormiston, CSQ to DLN, 10 August 1984.

26. Finney, Old China Hands, 16-17; "Smith, Robert F., Pvt. WWI-6639 15th Infantry, Company D," typewritten questionnaire, 7 October 1983, China Expedition, The World War I Survey, A, USMHI.

27. The Sentinel, 11 March, 10 June 1921, pp. 2, 13.

28. Ibid., 18 May 1923, p. 8.

29. Ibid., 18 January 1924, p. 9.

30. Memorandum for Adjutant General from W. D. Connor, 2 November 1922, American Forces in China, 123.61 to 333.2, box 1350, Record Group (RG) 407, Records of the Adjutant General's Office (AGO), National Archives, Washington, DC.; J.C. Castner to the Adjutant General, with enclosures, file 370.5, 17 January 1927, Countries Files, China, box 483, RG 407; The Sentinel, 28 October 1921, p. 14; ibid. 20 June 1924, p. 12; Infantry Journal, 33, no. 2 (August 1924): 203.

31. The Sentinel, 18 August 1929, p. 9.

32. Ibid., 5 October 1929, p. 10.

33. "Log of Howell," X, 15 March 1921, pp. 2774-79.

34. MGEN George H. Cloud interview by Benis M. Frank (1970), 2, Marine Corps Oral History Program (MCOH), Marine Corps Historical Center (MCHC), Washington, DC.; Julius Isaacson, CSQ to DLN, 20 August 1984.

35. Wheeler interview, 22-24.

36. Statistics are found in: Harrod, Manning the New Navy, 186-7; Fleet Review, 13, no. 1 (January 1922): 18.

37. Bureau of Navigation to Commanding Officer, Submarine Division, Asiatic Fleet, 5 April 1927, FF 6-2 to FF 6-5, Box 2194, RG 80, General Records of the Department of the Navy (RDN), National Archives.

38. "Annual Report," 24 August 1923, 123.61 to 333.3, American Forces in China, Box 1350, RG 407.

39. Commander, Fifteeth Infantry, to Adjutant General, 8 May 1924, China 014.5 to 251.2, Box 1349, RG 407.

40. Bland and Ritenour, Papers of Marshall, I, 279; "Annual Report, 1926," 000.71 AF (3-7-29) to 253 China AT (13 September 1925), Countries File, 1926-1929, Box 483, RG 407.

41. Adolph B. Miller, "Diary," 7 June 1927, Box 4, Papers of Adolph B. Miller, P.C. 196, Personal Papers Collection (PPC), MCHC.

42. GEN Vernon E. Megee interview by Benis M. Frank (1967), 55-57, MCOH.

43. Harrod, Manning the New Navy, 116-17, 120-23; Robinson O. Everett, Military Justice in the Armed Forces of the United States (Harrisburg, PA: Military Service Publishing, 1956), 1-16.

44. "Courts-Martials," Countries file, 1926-1929, Box 483, RG 407.

45. Logbook of the U.S.S. Helena, 8 November 1911, RG 24, Records of the Bureau of Navigation (RBN), National Archives.

46. Quoted in Harrod, Manning the New Navy, 118.

47. "Log of Howell," 5 November 1921, XI, 2843-2856; 22 December 1925, XL, 11,094-99.

48. Pfeiffer's oral history does not give the names of the officers involved. Comments by other officers also fail to give complete names. Robert C. Giffen, for example, noted that officers who became troublesome were removed from the station. Because these cases could not be documented without the full names, I felt it better not to include the comments in the narrative. MGEN Omar T. Pfeiffer interview by MAJ Lloyd E. Tatem (1968), 72-78 and passim, MCOH; VADM Robert C. Giffen Papers, China Repository (CR), NOA, NHC.

49. LGEN James P. Berkeley interview by Benis M. Frank (1969), 50-51, MCOH.

50. The highest number of men convicted was 574 in the Third Corps area. U.S., Department of War, Report of the Secretary of War to the President, 1929 (Washington: Government Printing Office, 1929), 246.

51. Robert K. Griffith, Jr., Men Wanted for the U.S. Army: America's Experience with an All-Volunteer Army Between the World Wars (Westport, CT: Greenwood Press, 1982), 149.

52. Edwin C. Schierhorst, CSQ to DLN, 15 July 1984; Albert Tidwell, CSQ to DLN, 14 July 1984; Glenn M. Hargrave, CSQ to DLN, 30 May 1983; Howard L. Povey, CSQ to DLN, 5 July 1984; and Malcolm P. Stimmers, CSQ to DLN, 10 January 1985.

53. American Embassy Guard News (Peking), 1 November 1936; The Sentinel, 7 March 1936, p. 5.

54. Berkeley interview, 76; Legation Guard News Annual 1931, 63; American Embassy Guard News, 1 July 1935, p. 1.

55. American Embassy Guard News, 1 March 1936, p. 18.

56. Robert Shenk, ed., The Left-Handed Monkey Wrench: Stories and Essays by Richard McKenna (Annapolis, MD: Naval Institute Press, 1986), 5.

57. Cloud interview, 3-5.

58. In 1912, the charges were: drunk (2); AWOL (3); smuggling liquor (1); others (5). The 1925 charges were: AWOL (1); absent from guard (1); and sitting down on post (1). Microfilm Muster Rolls, U.S. Marine Corps, 1912, 1925, 1935, Reference Section, MCHC.

59. "No Soldiers in Uniform Allowed," The Sentinel, 30 May 1924, p. 5.

60. James Jones, World War II (New York: Grosset & Dunlap, 1975), 70-71.

61. Noel F. Parrish, "New Responsibilities of Air Force Officers," Air University Review, 23, no. 3 (March-April 1972): 16 (originally printed in 1947).

62. Quoted in Griffith, Men Wanted, 129.

63. Kemble, Image of the Army Officer, 7.

64. William R. Hardcastle, CSQ to DLN, 5 September 1984.

65. Griffith, Men Wanted, 156.

66. A Shipboard (?) newsletter located within "Enlisted Personnel, 1906-1917," Box 56, Papers of William S. Sims, Manuscript Divison, Library of Congress, Washington, DC.

67. Millett, Semper Fidelis, 230.

68. Harrod, Manning the New Navy, 29.

69. Anthony Ingrisano, CSQ to DLN, 16 July 1984.

70. James Jones, From Here to Eternity (New York: Charles Scribner's, 1954), passim.

71. "Log of Howell," XL, 10 December 1925, 11,033-34.

72. Ingrisano, CSQ.

73. Richard McKenna, "Life Aboard the U.S.S.

Goldstar," in Shenk, ed., <u>Left-Handed Monkey Wrench</u>, 129-31; Hardcastle, when asked if there were any enlisted man who stood out in his memory, replied: "after thinking it over, none were admired for their professional ability, brilliance, or ability to shape their lives. The ones we admired most were the 'clowns,' the ones that were always coming close to getting in trouble and barely escaping, and were always lying about their amorous conquests. None were in a position to be admired for much else; not while in the service." Hardcastle CSQ.

    74. Paul W. Caraway to Forrest Caraway, 26 February 1937, Personal Letters, 1937-1940, Paul W. Caraway papers, A, USMHI.

3

TROOP AND STOMP:
THE DUTY DAY
AND ROUTINE

Military mythology sometimes endows the men who
served on the China Station with the reputation of
being among the most professional in the armed
forces. Marine officer James P. Berkeley recalled
that more training--"and real training"--was
accomplished in a shorter period of time than was
ever accomplished at the Quantico, Virginia, marine
base. Marine officer William F. Battell related
that the training was hard, while George H. Cloud
remembered that the Fourth Marines in Shanghai were
the "finest outfit" with whom he had ever served.
On the other hand, marine officer Graves B. Erskine
recalled that in 1935 the performance of the
Peking-based marines as professional military men
"had dropped to a pretty low level." Yet another
leatherneck officer, Joseph C. Burger, echoed this
comment, stating that many leaders "were not capable of carrying out their jobs." Similar dissent
can be found concerning the soldiers and sailors
serving in the Middle Kingdom. In short, the men
who served in China seem to have had mixed ideas
about the quality of their fellow soldiers,
sailors, and marines. This chapter will examine
the duty day and duties of the armed forces in East
Asia to see whether the above dichotomy can be
resolved.[1]

Men reporting to the Fifteenth Infantry at
Tientsin would debark from a troopship at
Chinwangtao and then board a train to their new
duty station. Robert F. Smith, recalled that in
1914, sitting on the wooden benches in the second-
class compartment made the four-hour train ride

seem very long.[2]

According to the custom of the Fifteenth, all the officers not on duty were expected to meet the train upon its arrival at the station, and the band was to play "appropriate airs."[3] The enlisted troops were formed up and marched to a barracks area. Smith recalled that an officer would walk down the ranks of men with the first sergeant of each company and, after counting off a certain number of men, would order the selected men to do a right face. The non-commissioned officer would then be informed that here were his replacements. This procedure continued until all the men were assigned to their respective companies, and then the order was given to march to barracks.[4] Until 1927, the Fifteenth Infantry was not quartered in a central area, but scattered throughout the various international concessions in Tientsin. The living conditions were far from pleasant. There were, for example, no bathrooms, no wash basins--no water system. According to the regimental newspaper, soldiers were required to purchase their own wash basins and obtained fresh water from large cans that were stored on each floor. Eventually, a central barracks was erected on Woodrow Wilson Road.[5]

Newly arrived officers were formally introduced to their fellow officers, given an informational packet about China and Tientsin, shown to temporary quarters, and, lastly, photographed for the Fifteenth Infantry's regimental photograph album.[6] Enlisted men, meanwhile, were confined to their barracks area until they completed their basic training. At this time, the army had no central recruit training bases. New soldiers were simply issued their uniforms and given the rudiments of military drill while being processed into the service. The novice soldiers were expected to learn their trade once they reported to their commands. Smith, for example, enlisted at Indianapolis, Indiana, and was sent to Columbus, Ohio, for about two weeks before being assigned to the Fifteenth Infantry.[7]

In the "Can Do" regiment, besides the normal training required of newly arrived enlisted men, there were a few extra touches. Troops were marched around the immediate neighborhood of the barracks to acquaint them with the city. Another reason for the confinement of the men to barracks was to fit the new soldiers with specially tailored uniforms. Charles G. Finney recalled that, when he arrived in Tientsin in 1927, he wore a World War I-vintage outfit that "could hardly be called proper dress for scarecrows."[8] The troops were fitted with tailored "Hong Kong khaki uniforms." Army officer Paul L. Freeman recalled that the winter uniform of the regiment included "rabbit fur caps as they used to wear on the great plains and turtle neck sweaters and sheep skin coats."[9] Even enlisted men carried swagger sticks while in uniform in Tientsin. The Fifteenth Infantry appears to have been one of the few regiments in the army in which all the troops wore tailored uniforms to improve their appearance.[10]

The length of the recruit training period depended upon how long it took to fit the men with their new uniforms and how unskilled the new group of men was in military drill. Once the first instruction period was at an end, a soldier would be issued a pass that allowed him to leave the barracks area, when not on duty, until midnight. After six months, the soldier would be issued an overnight pass.[11]

The training for the regiment was broken up into two broad periods: time in Tientsin and in the field. The former usually stretched from December to March, while the latter was conducted from summer into November. During training in Tientsin, the duty week was divided into company and regimental functions. Mondays through Fridays beginning at 8:00 am the troops were employed in calisthenics and underwent training in the many skills required of an infantryman, such as assembling a rifle and reading maps. Those who had technical duties were given special instructions beyond the normal military training. Officers attended their own special schools. Saturdays were for inspections or marches.[12] As a new recruit, Smith felt it took "about a year" to know what was expected of a private in a rifle company.[13] Except for retreat and those selected for guard mount, the duty day ended at 11:30.

The type and intensity of training depended largely on who was in command. In 1928, for example, officers and troops were required to learn the rudiments of the Chinese language.[14] One of the strongest training programs, both in Tientsin and in the field, was marching. Brig. Gen. Joseph

Castner was an inveterate hiker who, during his spare time, would walk around a track and time his speed. Regimental rumor had it that Castner had hiked from Alaska to Seattle and had outdistanced his Indian guide.[15] The general's reputation for marching was so legendary that even the regimental newspaper, The Sentinel, could play on it to amuse the troops. The periodical reported that Col. Isaac Newell led a delegation of officers to wish Castner a happy fifty-eighth birthday. Newell remarked that everyone wished to be able to walk as far and as fast as the general when they reached his age. To which Castner replied: "You shall have practice."[16]

It should come as no surprise, then, that company commanders received a great deal of pressure to make sure their men could hike. On 10 January 1927, for example, officers were given three months to whip their troops into sufficient shape to make a fifteen-mile march in heavy marching order.[17] As early as July 1924, however, The Sentinel reported that Company L had left Tongshan and marched eighty-five miles to Tientsin in four days. The newspaper noted that the performance was "remarkable," considering the "intense heat," the lack of roads, and that, in some locations, "the only water to be had . . . [was] in ditches.[18] The newspaper probably mirrored the average foot soldier's reaction to Castner's emphasis on marching by describing marches "over dusty road, wandering through . . . ditches and beside the ancient graves and . . . through the ungodly smells of dirty villages."[19]

Garrison duty also consisted of weekly and annual athletic contests, which also included marching. In 1928, for example, the Infantry Journal reported that Newell had held a marching competition between companies, without packs, over a five mile course, with half of the course over paved city streets and half on dirt roads. The winner in 1928 was Company L, with an elapsed time of 47 minutes, 19 seconds and a speed of 6.34 miles per hour, as compared to the regiment's time of 49 minutes, 29 seconds.[20]

The highlight of the physical training took place during "Can Do" week--the celebration of the regiment's organization--in July. The week featured speeches, picnics, and athletic contests, climaxed by a five-mile running march. Each

athletic event received a certain score, with the
running march event receiving the highest number
of points. The company with the most points at the
end of the day was entitled to carry the
Chickamauga guidon, a flag with a red acorn
emblazed upon it, symbolic of the regiment's
engagement during the American Civil War. Company
commanders coveted the pennant for the prestige,
while the troops irreverently called it the "red
raspberry." The men had to carry the Springfield
rifle, ammunition, full canteen, rations, and the
other items that made up a full pack, totaling
about sixty pounds. The "only ground rules were
that the head of the column could not go faster
than the authorized double time [180 steps per
minute]," and, if a man dropped out, points were
taken away. Further, once across the finish line,
the men then had to go to an inspection area to
insure that everyone had carried the proper
equipment. If a man fell out during this time, it
was also counted against the company's total
points.

Many years after his service with the Fifteenth,
Freeman recalled how Company I's captain wanted
first place. To prepare for the event, the men
were required to run "a couple of miles every day"
for most of the year. On the day of the event, the
company set off on their endurance test. After
running "over dikes, through Chinese burial
grounds," all during weather that was "hotter than
Hell," the men began to cross the finish line, and
it looked as if a new record would be set.
However, apparently some of the troops did not know
the rule about having to go to an inspection,
because a bugler named Foote "made a spectacular
nose dive [across the finish line] not knowing that
he . . . had to go another 100 yards." Foote's
flourish cost the company first place.[21]

The highlight of the training year took place
during the hot summer months, when training in
Tientsin was over and companies were rotated to the
firing range. There had been at least two firing
ranges for the regiment before a permanent location
was selected at Chingwangtao, some 150 miles from
Tientsin and 25 miles from where the Great Wall
begins.[22] The location was near a sandy beach and
the resort area of Pei-hao [Beidaihe]. A few permanent buildings were erected for storage,
administrative offices, and living quarters for

those who were detailed to remain during the winter, but most of the men lived in large pyramidal tents.[23]

Over thirty years after his service in China, Finney recalled that the Fifteenth had a tradition of being "quite a shooting regiment." During the "loafing, lissome days of the summers at Chingwangtao, just one thing counted: rifle shooting." The rifle range had firing lines at 200, 300, 500, 600, and 1,000 yards. There were also ranges for pistol, Stokes mortar, 37mm howitzer, and machine-gun fire. The officers and non-commissioned officers made the atmosphere as relaxed as possible, probably in the hopes of having the men concentrate on their shooting. Reveille was usually sounded at 4:30 in the morning, with the sergeants announcing a maskee uniform (wear what you please) of the day. The men were usually on the line shortly after sunrise. Firing generally stopped by noon and, if a soldier did not have guard, he was free the rest of the day. Indeed, the situation was as idyllic as could be made in the military. Finney remember- ed, "all we did was eat and swim and shoot . . ., and drink beer at Jawbone Charlie's peng back of the camp."[24]   Officers were not immune to the pleasant surroundings. George C. Marshall wrote that, "Bathing, riding and shooting occupies the time," while "riding in the picturesque country" was always a pleasure.[25]   The area was so pleasant that officers brought their wives and families to Pei-hao for the entire summer, where they lived in large resort-type houses.

At first glance, the strategy of easy living seems to have paid off on the firing range.   In 1924, for example, Company I, with eighty-one men firing, had thirty-one experts, twenty-six sharpshooters, seventeen marksmen, and seven who did not qualify.   The same year, the Service Company, with thirty-eight men firing, produced thirteen experts, eleven sharpshooters, ten marksmen, and four who did not qualify. In July of the same year, the Fifteenth Infantry shooters competed with the marines from Peking in an interservice shooting match and outscored the leathernecks by some 152 points. Another factor providing an incentive to score high was an additional five dollars in pay for qualification as an expert. While the recollections of Finney and

and others, plus the above record, seem to
indicate that the soldiers were more than adequate,
a perusal of the Infantry Journal reveals that the
Fifteenth was not the best in the army. In August
1929, for example, the regiment finished third out
of five organizations reporting their scores to the
Chief of Infantry. In June 1928, machine-gunners
from the Fifteenth finished fourteenth out of
nineteen regiments reporting to the Chief of
Infantry. In short, while the men of the "Can Do"
regiment were good, they were not the best in the
army.[26]

After the shooting season was completed, usually
in August, the regiment was scheduled to conduct
field exercises. The highly cultivated fields
around Tientsin, however, prevented any intensive
maneuvers. Generally, the troops would practice
manning defensive positions around Tientsin in
order to be prepared for their primary mission of
protecting American lives and interests.[27]

The protection of American lives and interests
was the main duty of the Fifteenth Infantry--as it
was for all the American armed forces in China. In
addition to protecting portions of the concessions
in Tientsin, the regiment had one company on
detached duty at Tongshan to protect the locomotive
and car shops. The soldiers also made up a part of
the international guard detachment that protected
the train from Peking to Tientsin--the main escape
and supply route between the capital city and the
sea. In 1912, for example, Company A's muster roll
shows that from September to October, the soldiers
guarded the railroad along with their usual guard
and garrison duties.[28]

Most of the soldier's time, however, was
consumed with normal garrison duties and providing
a showpiece for ceremonial purposes. In fact, the
search for perfection in drill and parades became
an obsession for some commanding officers. Col.
Reynolds J. Burt had some of the troops equipped
with wooden pistols, carved by local Chinese, so
that their belts would not sag when they were in
formation; the blanket rolls for the packs were
actually stovepipes wrapped in blanket material.
Further, in the last second before the troops were
inspected, some Chinese would come "out to dust off
the shoes . . . so that in inspections the ranks
would shine."[29] Burt, however, would not go out
into the field for training. Indeed, this points

up the reason some military men remembered China hands as being well-trained and others recalled a poor quality: the nature of the training and efficiency of the troops reflected the commander. This applies to all military units at any place or time, of course, but it was especially noticeable in China because of the small numbers of men involved.   Years later, Charles L. Bolte remembered that soldiering in the Fifteenth under the command of Burt "was artificial" and could have led to "serious" problems should the troops have been required to handle an incident involving combat. Or, as the former infantry officer put it: "It was one of those tendencies of getting away from the realities of military life, and going into a fairy tale."[30]

Leathernecks stationed at either Peking or Shanghai followed a garrison routine not unlike that of the soldiers in Tientsin.   Joseph E. Johnson, for example, recalled that while serving with the Fourth Marines in Shanghai during the 1930s, the normal routine, from Mondays through Wednesdays, had colors at 8:00, "troop and stomp" (marching), and then school in squad bays in the morning and for a short period in the afternoons during the winter.   Afternoons were generally devoted to athletics.   Thursdays the regiment would march to the Shanghai Race Track for parades. Fridays were devoted to field days (cleaning), and inspections were scheduled for Saturdays.[31]

Marines bound for duty at Peking arrived in China at Chinwangtao and embarked upon the train to Tientsin and then to their duty station. Leather-necks ordered to duty with the Fourth Marines usually took the navy transport directly to Shanghai. Leathernecks in Peking were quartered near the Chien Men Gate, within the walls of the old Tartar City and bounded on the north by Legation Street and on the south by Wall Street and the Tartar Wall.

During part of the period when the Third Marine Brigade served in China (1927-29), Gen. Butler moved a large portion of his command to Tientsin, and the men were forced to live in tents throughout the summer of 1927 in rather squalid conditions. Marine officer John N. Hart recalled that, in the summer the dust was at least two feet deep, and during the winter the mud was the same depth.   By the onset of winter, however, the marines were finally moved into leased quarters.[32] In Shanghai, there was no central barracks area for the leathernecks. Like soldiers in the early days at Tientsin, marines were scattered throughout the International Settlement. Unlike the Fifteenth Infantry, however, the Fourth Marines never obtained one central location.[33]

The enlisted leathernecks were limited to set hours when they could be away from their barracks on liberty. Johnson recalled that in Shanghai, staff non-commissioned officers had no restrictions, but other rankers were divided into three classes of liberty: first-class could remain in town until 1:00 in the morning, second-class until midnight, and third-class until 10:00 in the evening. Furthermore, second- and third-class liberty pass-holders could not wear civilian clothes in town.[34]

The marines also placed a great deal of emphasis on shooting. Robert Hugh Williams recalled that the corps made a "cult out of the rifle."[35] The leathernecks at Peking used a small-bore range and also fired at Chingwangtao. Those stationed in Shanghai fired at an international range. Many times contests developed between the armed forces of various countries and the U.S. Marines, with the losers buying beer.[36]

The marines at Shanghai and Peking had slightly different duties, but basically the leathernecks were to man either barricades or posts to protect designated areas of international settlements. A description of the duty day at Peking conveys the rhythms of marine routine in China.

The marines at the American legation were required to perform both ceremonial and military guard duties. The number of leathernecks at Peking fluctuated. In 1932, the complement was a Headquarters Detachment and the 38th, 39th, and 62nd Companies, plus a mounted detachment and signal platoon, a navy detachment, and a U.S. Navy Radio Station.[37] By "gentleman's agreement" among the international armed forces in Peking, the American commandant was in command of the defense of the international guard. In the diplomatic corps area, there was a cleared area for at least 100 meters "to give . . . fields of fire" in case it was needed.[38] The main weapons the leathernecks had for defense were Springfield rifles, Colt machine-guns, and a few light artillery pieces.

Fred D. Beans recalled that the guard was expected "to put up a token fight" if trouble arose, and then be captured so that the "United States would have some reason to protest."[39]   To keep the men prepared for any possible attacks--the specter of the Boxer Uprising was always before the legation residents--there were constant alerts during which the marines would man the walls.   According to one officer, "you never knew what might happen."[40]

Marine officer Beans recalled that the duty day included inspections at 7:30 in the morning, and "then we'd go out and run a few problems, out in the [Western] hills or hold schools" until 11:30 and that usually ended the working day.[41]   One of the duties of the Officer of the Day was to inspect the alertness of the guards at the various posts at night.   Berkeley recalled that during the winter it could be a long "cold, cold walk" to accomplish the rounds. The officer also recalled that the enlisted guards received help from an unexpected source. The marines had an English bulldog as a mascot that lived in the Officer of the Day's office.   The dog knew where all the posts were, and he "was in cahoots with the sentries" and warned of the officer's approach by barking.[42]

In addition to guard duties, the marines were required to undertake normal military training. Erskine noted that, when he arrived in Peking, the training was at a "pretty low level" and not "befitting to the Marine Corps."   Further, there had been a great deal of illness and some deaths, especially in the winter.   The newly arrived officer and others set up "a pretty stiff training schedule," which included hikes in cold weather.[43] Soon there was a marked drop in sick call.   Indeed, the winter hiking soon became a constant factor in the routine. The American Embassy Guard News reported that by New Year's Day of 1936, there had already been three marches.[44]   Some of these exercises could be rugged.   Berkeley recalled that when he reported to the 38th Company in 1932, the first assignment he received was to "take a hike the likes of which I've never seen." The marines went farther and farther away from the legation, and the leathernecks began to grumble about the length of the march.   Capt. John W. Thomason, Jr., the company commander, ordered the troops to sing and then, Berkeley remembered, the marines "walked, oh my God, we walked."   Thomason, according to the officer, was testing to see "whether the new lieutenant could take it."[45]

Before proceeding to some of the navy's duties and routine, it is necessary to discuss one of the unique features of duty on the old China Station: the employment of Chinese to undertake all of the mundane and unpleasant everyday features of military life, such as cleaning and kitchen police or mess cook duties.   In fact, the Legation Guard regulations of 1932, allowed "1 boy for every 16 men occupying squad rooms . . .; 1 boy for every 3 sergeants; [and] . . . 1 boy for every Non Commissioned Officer above the grade of sergeant."[46] Richard McKenna, in his novel The Sand Pebbles, has all of the routine duties aboard a gunboat being completed by Chinese, with only duties involving weapons being accomplished by sailors.   When a problem develops and the Chinese flee the ship, the men do not even have the material to shave themselves.   At present, there is no evidence to support this ultimate use of Chinese aboard a naval vessel.   There is no doubt, however, that McKenna drew on observations that were common aboard naval ships in China.   Indeed, even submarines that were deployed to China employed a few Chinese.[47]

Soldiers and marines at Tientsin, Shanghai, and Peking had Chinese do all the unpleasant duties, except to clean weapons.   Some marines from Peking, who were visiting the Fifteenth Infantry in 1936, felt that the servants employed by the army were "too sophisticated," and that the marines were lucky if the "room-boy" would make their bunks or shine their shoes.   The leathernecks found the Chinese practically ignoring them, and "it was quite a blow" to their pride, according to the correspondent, to have a "boy" do this.[48] The Chinese servants were paid a monthly wage, which was collected from the men at payday.   Erskine recalled that mess duties had been accomplished by the Chinese for so long "that the Marines sort of forgot how to run their own mess." Even the rule about Chinese not touching weapons was sometimes overlooked.   Erskine recalled that sometimes when a leatherneck would be caught with a dirty rifle, he would plead an excuse that his "boy" did not do it correctly.   "Boy, I'd let . . . [the marine] have a piece of my mind right there," the officer remembered.   In addition to a verbal lashing, the offender would be punished with extra duty and have no Chinese help for a specified period.[49]   In short, for inspections American military men had only to make certain their rifles were clean and stand in formation.   All of the drudgery of polishing brass, cleaning uniforms, and polishing shoes was accomplished by the Chinese.

Naval officer Glenn Howell wrote how some Chinese came to be employed aboard a navy gunboat that he commanded on the Yangtze River in 1920. During a baseball game, a small boy was hit in the ribs by a sharply hit ball.   The young waif, who had been selling peanuts, was taken to the Palos for medical treatment and, so Howell thought, released.   A few days later, the crewman who had hit the boy brought him to the skipper and requested that he be allowed to remain aboard until completely recovered.   "That started the whole business," the naval officer later recalled.   The boy was quickly dubbed "Peanuts," and Howell began to notice that never before had the crew's shoes shone so well at inspection.   "Then came Polly, Acey, Ducey, Apollo, and others." The ship began "smarten up" noticeably after each new arrival, with the admiral giving great compliments about how good the Palos looked. At this time, it was illegal to keep the Chinese aboard, so the children would be put into sampans when inspection parties reported aboard.   Howell wrote that he had "no compunctions" about breaking navy regulations on this subject.   Later, the navy allowed Chinese to be shipped aboard as mess attendants.[50]

Some Chinese served for many years with the American military forces and apparently developed an attachment for a particular unit.   In 1921, for example, the reporter for Company A's gossip column wrote to The Sentinel that, while the men were confined to barracks due to a medical quarantine, several boxes of candy were sent by "Mao." The reporter noted that he was "not surprised" by this act of kindness, as Mao had shown other acts of a similar nature in the past.[51]   The Walla Walla, the newspaper of Shanghai's Fourth Marine Regiment, reported the death of "Jimmy," who had served as a "room-boy" for twenty years.   "Jimmy," it stated, could perform the manual of arms for the armed forces of England, Italy, France, Germany, Russia, China, and the United States.[52]

With a few major exceptions, the officers and men of the Asiatic Fleet units carried out a duty

day not unlike that performed on any ship in the
navy.   That is, a great deal of the time while at
sea was spent in preventive maintenance--chipping
and painting--of the ship, drilling, and standing
watches.   One of the major differences in the
Asiatic units was that, until the late 1930s,
isolation and poor communications left the
commander in chief with more freedom of operation
than on any other command.   As one former officer
put it, the admiral "was the whole Navy Department
himself."[53]

By the middle of the 1920s, the Asiatic Fleet's
main support base, except for the gunboats assigned
to the South China Patrol and the Yangtze River
Patrol, was at Cavite on the Philippine Island of
Luzon.   The fleet spent from October through March
in maneuvers in Philippine waters or in routine
maintenance.   The remainder of the year the fleet
spent in cruising, with Tsingtao being the port for
submarines and Chefoo for destroyers.   This routine
was disrupted from time to time by periods of
unrest in China.

The Asiatic Fleet traditionally employed older
equipment and ships.   The flagship during the
1920s, the Marblehead, was known as the "Swayback
Maru" throughout the China Station.[54]   Even when
the navy began to assign aircraft to the fleet,
there were problems.   Early naval aviator George
Van Deurs recalled that there were never enough
planes to do any good, and the ones that were
available left much to be desired.   The officer
remembered that the T3M-2 torpedo planes aboard the
Jason would, for some unexplained reason, run for
"fifteen minutes by the clock" and then quit.
Pilots would then land, wait another fifteen
minutes for the engine to start, and off they would
go for another quarter of an hour.   The exception
to the rule of older equipment was when the Third
Brigade, under Butler, arrived in China in 1927.
The marine general brought state-of-the-art
equipment and had argued successfully for marine
aviation to be attached to the brigade.[55]

The major change in normal navy routine was
aboard the gunboats assigned to either the Yangtze
River or South China Patrol.   The ships were prizes
from Spain, taken during the Spanish-American War.
The officers who commanded these units, usually
lieutenant commanders, had even more freedom of
action that the admiral of the Asiatic Fleet.

Radio technology, in its infancy, could not be relied upon to deliver messages, especially to ships operating above Wuhan. Most young officers relished getting underway and operating independently. As Howell put it, "we are forgotten by the world."[56]

Probably no other duty in the Middle Kingdom gave its men more of a "slice" of rural China than on the gunboats. Further, the white-hulled ships, trimmed in teak, with steel decks and white canvas awnings, have become the most symbolic emblem of the American military in the Middle Kingdom. There seems to have been a concerted effort on the part of some sailors first to be assigned to one of the larger units of the Asiatic Fleet, then to request duty in a gunboat and attempt to remain there for as long as possible. The idea of getting away from crowded Shanghai into rural China and the chance of excitement led many marines to volunteer to serve on the ships as extra landing-party personnel in times of unrest.[57]

The freedom that most skippers enjoyed came at a price. Most of the gunboats were old and very undependable coal-burners. It was not unusual for a logbook to show numerous breakdowns. Most serious work could not be accomplished by the ship's force, and captains were forced to find yards, usually in Shanghai, to undertake major repairs. The ships were also underpowered and could not compete with the strong currents sweeping out of the Yangtze River gorges. Howell at one point could not get the _Palos_ upstream against the current and was forced to tie up alongside a farmer's field. In exasperation, the naval officer confided to his diary: "What a situation! An American war vessel . . . tied up to trees on the edge of a cornfield." Because the ships had no refrigeration, the gunboat commanders had to buy all their food from local villages and cities. Further, the coal-fired ships also obtain their fuel from local sources. Even though the craft employed Chinese pilots on the Yangtze River, there was always the chance of running afoul of the "river dragon" (the superstition Chinese boatmen used to explain the cause of shipwrecks) in the poorly charted and ever-changing river. Howell, according to his diary, professed pleasure at commanding the _Palos_. After a few misfortunes, however, such as losing all power and drifting

helplessly in the swift current of the river, the
naval officer recorded that he was getting tired of
"hair raising experiences." Eventually the officer
would spell out his formula for surviving a tour
aboard the gunboats: "trust in the lead, the pilot,
and your luck, and [then] not . . . trust any of
them too far."[58]

The duty day aboard a gunboat was, again,
standard naval routine.   Repelling boarders, however, was practiced with more frequency on the
rivers of China.   There was also more emphasis
placed on landing-party operations, as the gunboats
were likely to be the first ones called upon to go
to the aid of missionaries in trouble.   The
isolation of the ships also allowed the sailors to
enjoy a more relaxed standard in their uniforms.
In the areas where there were fewer foreign
sailors, undress blues or whites, depending on the
season, were worn ashore.   During the hot summer
months, short white pants, white sport shirts with
open collars, pith helmets, and black shoes and
white socks were de rigueur for enlisted men.
Officer's dress differed only in that they wore
white shoes.[59]

Living conditions aboard the gunboats have,
under the influence of McKenna's novel, been
pictured as ideal. The protagonist of The Sand
Pebbles called his gunboat a "home," the best
accolade a sailor could give a ship.   In reality,
however, many of the craft were far from ideal.
The engine rooms were designed to be shut tight
with blowers providing ventilation.   With the
hatches dogged down tight, however, the spaces
became so hot that the "black gang" could take
only half-hour watches in the heat.[60]   Most of the
older gunboats had very small berthing areas, with
poor ventilation. In the heat of the summer months,
most sailors were forced to sleep on deck in order
to endure the night.   In a nonfiction account of
his time in China, McKenna recalled that one of his
first priorities when he reported aboard a gunboat
was to buy a cot in order to sleep on deck.[61]
Sleeping topside sometimes led to disastrous
results.   Henry J. Poy recalled a shipmate who,
while inebriated and trying to get off his uniform
jumper, fell overboard and was drowned.   An
investigation by the navy revealed that there had
been twelve deaths due to drowning aboard gunboats
on the Yangtze Patrol.   While the report did

concede that some modifications to life lines should be made on the ships, most of the cases dealt with intoxicated enlisted men. Therefore, the men themselves were adjudged to have been at fault.[62] Once new ships began to appear on the rivers, in 1927, some of these conditions were alleviated. Most men, however, were willing to put up with the poor environment for the freedom of serving on the river.

In general, most of the duties of the American armed forces in China came under the rubric of protection of lives and property. That sometimes entailed unusual duties. In 1931, for example, the Legation Guard News reported that three men from each company were to be picked for a detail to escort a camel caravan carrying U.S. mail to Harbin. The leathernecks selected were informed that they must be able to use the automatic rifle and capable of handling a pistol in case of an attack. Further, the men had to be in good health and "unafraid of combat with the alien tribes who make it a point to molest our mail trains." The chosen men were expected to be in the desert for one month. There is, however, no report on the results of this mission.[63]

One type of escort duty that is well-documented is the placing of armed guards aboard merchant ships plying the Yangtze River during periods of unrest. A detachment of either marines or sailors was assigned to provide firepower to unarmed ships that were receiving gunfire from the shore. This became a fairly common assignment during the 1920s and into the 1930s.

When marines made up the detachment, it usually consisted of two non-commissioned officers, two privates, and at least one officer. The men were armed with Browning automatic rifles, Thompson submachine guns, shotguns, rifles, and pistols. In 1934, Lt. James F. Moriarty kept a log, written in pencil, about his experiences aboard one merchant vessel. While the account does detail some firing upon the ship, the journal is a delightful exposition of how a military man viewed service aboard a civilian ship on the Yangtze River. On 24 April, the leatherneck recorded that they were tied up at Hankow and in a fog, but "so is the captain." The next day, the ship, after a long delay, got underway with the "Captain's sweetie" waving farewell. For dinner the next day, Moriarty feasted upon a repast of "rubber chicken," but at least the skipper had come "out of his fog." Five days later, the ship was moored and everyone was "twiddling thumbs." By the end of the escort duty, the marine recommended that there be no more than two men of the armed guard to a room, especially on hot days, and that there should be "ointment for bug infection or spider bites, [and] sunburn," plus medicine to combat dysentry.[64]

The nature of the terrain around Peking and Tientsin, as noted, was not conducive to large-scale manuevers or the use of motor vehicles. At Peking, a mounted unit was formed to perform scout duties, and horse marines became a part of the Corps' China legend. The Fifteenth Infantry also had a mounted platoon. Edward J. Ormiston, a former member of the army unit, recalled that the horses were Mongolian ponies, since they were immune to most of the diseases in the area, rugged, and noted for their ability to withstand harsh conditions. The ponies had to be at least thirteen-and-a-half hands high and weigh no less than seven-hundred-fifty pounds.[65]

At Peking, the horse marines were armed with rifles, pistols, Thompson submachine guns, one heavy machine-gun, and sabers. In addition to scouting duties, the mounted unit was also to perform a census of American citizens residing in the area and to come to the aid of these people if they were in distress. The men wore the marine corps blue blouse with blue jodhpurs, and, unique to Peking in winter, a fur cap with a red diamond in the center with the Corps' distinguishing device. (The headgear was, however, worn by all the men in the legation guard.)[66]

Ormiston recalled that the army's mounted platoon consisted of one officer, twenty-seven enlisted men, and fifty-two horses. He was armed with a Springfield rifle and a .45-caliber pistol. The unit was to scout and patrol, provide a communications link between the various army outposts around Tientsin in case the regiment should have to defend the International Settlement, and help in "rescue missions when necessary." The unrest around the city during 1927 and 1928 kept the platoon "on the jump." At one time, Ormiston was fired upon while making a reconnaissance. By 1929 and early 1930, the former infantryman noted, conditions had become more stable, and the men were able to enjoy a more relaxed routine.[67]

One duty common to all of the American forces in China was the gathering of intelligence data. Officers on the Yangtze River Patrol, for example, would routinely report on the various villages, towns, and cities that they visited during their patrols. The emphasis on what type of data depended on the era in which a military man was stationed in the Middle Kingdom. That is, if reports were during the 1920s, they stressed Chiang Kai-shek, the Communists, and the Japanese. As the 1930s progressed, more emphasis was placed on Japan. A marine corps radio station, for example, was established at Shanghai to intercept Japanese radio signals. The station was closed by Secretary of War Henry Stimpson, because the State Department would have no part in "reading the mail of friends of our country."[68] The voluminous information in the intelligence reports from China has been only lightly plowed, if at all, by scholars. One unusual mission, was performed by marine officer William A. Worton in 1935. The marine officer, who spoke excellent Chinese, undertook a covert operation in Shanghai. Posing as a businessman in the International Settlement, Worton recruited and sent agents into Japan in order to gain information on the Japanese fleet.[69]

All of the U.S. military forces in China also participated in activities that did not fall under the heading of protecting American lives and property. One of these duties was humanitarian. Apparently as a part of the Fifteenth Infantry's efforts to help the Chinese, The Sentinel in 1921 reported that Pfc. Orpheus A. Staples had spent two months completing "first class work" among Chinese famine sufferers "down Shantung way."[70] Another activity was ceremonial. The Fifteenth Infantry, on Memorial Day and other special occasions, decorated the graves of Americans and important foreign nationals who had died in China. Similar duties were carried on by marines and sailors. Lastly, all military units in the Middle Kingdom were expected to provide honor guards for visiting dignitaries, both civilian and military.[71]

Military mythology has portrayed the men who served in China as the best in the American armed forces. There were times when the myth was indeed correct. During the unrest in the late 1920s, when the Third Marine Brigade was deployed to China,

General Butler insisted that his men be able to react quickly in case they were needed to go to the aid of the Legation in Peking. Marine officer Adolf B. Miller recorded that when a practice call to arms sounded, the leathernecks were able in "37 minutes . . . [to have the] Battalion entrucked with 5 days rations & ammunition for rescue party to Peking."[72]

As the various alarms and unsettled conditions receded, however, the men succumbed to the indolent routines of East Asia duty. With Chinese to perform all of the normal drudgery of garrison life, U.S. service men were free to sample some of the nearby exotic delights and quickly became lethargic. In one case, the commander of the marine guard in Peking decided to have a mobilization drill; after sounding the general alarm, "he counted noses and there were more Chinese than there were Marines" at muster.[73] On the other hand, if a commander was especially enthusiastic in stressing military drill, then the unit could still remain sharp. In this case, because the Chinese freed the men from mundane duties, they could devote more time to their military ones. The evidence suggests, however, that the demanding senior leaders were in the minority in the Middle Kingdom. All too often, officers tended to be on the order of Burt, whose "artificial" training caused troops to move away "from the realities of military life" and enter into a "fairy tale" routine. In some cases, this "artificial" training--the stress on spit and polish--would be mistaken for high efficiency. This common mistake is often made by military leaders. According to Freeman, the routine in China was no different from that at any other army base of the period. Thus, we are left with the impression that even though the military in China gathered intelligence data, provided guards for ships, and assisted with humanitarian aid in cases of flood or famine, the question of their professional competence was entirely up to their commissioned and non-commissioned officers and to the events occurring in China. In sum, the evidence suggests that the military in the Middle Kingdom was no better, or no worse, than in any other location in the American armed forces.

NOTES

1. LGEN James P. Berkeley interview by Benis M. Frank (1972), 75, Marine Corps Oral History Program (MCOH), Marine Corps Historical Center (MCHC), Washington, DC.; MGEN William F. Battell interview by Frank (1971), 40, MCOH; MGEN George H. Cloud interview by Frank, (1970), 38, MCOH; GEN Graves B. Erskine interview by Frank, (1969), 129, MCOH; LGEN Joseph C. Burger interview by Frank (1973), 86, MCOH.

2. "Smith, Robert F., Pvt. WWI-6639 15th Infantry, Company D," typed questionnaire, 7 October 1983, China Expedition, The World War I Survey, Archives, U.S. Military History Institute (A,USMHI), Carlisle Barracks, PA.

3. Customs of the Fifteenth Infantry: American Barracks, Tientsin, China (Tientsin-Peping: Pelyan Press, 192[?]; reprint, Cornwallville, NY: Hope Farm Press, 1959), 17 (page references are to reprint edition).

4. Smith questionnaire.

5. One location was in the French Concession, another at the corner of Bruce and Taku Roads, and the stables were located on Taku Road. The new barracks area occupied "1/6 of an English acre" and was divided into the following: barracks and Headquarters, hospital, and Quartermaster buildings. The buildings were remodeled in 1936. The Sentinel (Tientsin, China), 12 February 1938, p. 2.

6. Customs of the Fifteenth Infantry, 3-4.

7. Smith questionnaire.

8. Charles G. Finney, The Old China Hands (Garden City, NY: Doubleday, 1961; reprint, Westport, CT: Greenwood Press, 1977), 36-37 (page references are to reprint edition).

9. GEN Paul L. Freeman interview by COL James N. Ellis, (1972-1974), 20, Senior Officer Debriefing Program (SODP), U.S. Army War College (AWC), A, USMHI; Letter to the Adjutant General, 19 June 1926, file 000.71 to 253, Box 483, Record Group (RG) 407, Records of the Adjutant General's Office (AGO), National Archives; Finney, Old China Hands, 37.

10. Customs of the Fifteenth Infantry, 5.

11. Finney, Old China Hands, 36-37; The Sentinel, 10 June 1921, p. 4.

12. Edward J. Ormiston, China Service Questionnaire (CSQ) to Dennis L. Noble (DLN), 10 August 1984; The Sentinel, 30 March 1928, p. 8; Charles W.

Thomas, "The United States Army Troops in China, 1912-1937" (History paper, Stanford University, June 1937), 29-30; The Sentinel, from time to time, published the regiment's training schedule, see: 2 December 1927, pp. 16, 24, 26.

13. Smith questionnaire.

14. Thomas, "Army Troops in China," 30.

15. Finney, Old China Hands, 75.   More details on Castner are found in: Forrest C. Pogue, with the editorial assistance of Gordon Harrison, George C. Marshall: Education of a General (New York: Viking Press, 1963), 241-42.

16. The Sentinel, 26 November 1927, p.8.

17. Ibid., 14 January 1927, p. 5.

18. Ibid., 11 July 1924, p. 7.

19. Ibid., 19 October 1923, p. 5.

20. Infantry Journal, 33, no. 1 (July 1928): 90-91.

21. Freeman interview, 24-25.

22. The previous ranges had been located at Leichuang [Luan Xian] and Tongshan. The Sentinel, 8 April 1921, p. 1; 25 May 1923, p. 4.

23. Finney, Old China Hands, 169-71.

24. Ibid., 170, 172-73.

25. Larry I. Bland and Sharon R. Ritenour, eds., The Papers of George Cattlett Marshall, Vol.1, "The Soldierly Spirit," December 1880-June 1939 (Baltimore: Johns Hopkins University Press, 1981), 281, 293.

26. The Sentinel, 20 June 15 August 1924, pp. 7, 13; Freeman interview, 37; L. L. Williams, ed., 15th Infantry Annual: May 4, 1924-May 4, 1925 (Tientsin, China: Tientsin Press, 1925 ?), 146; Infantry Journal, 32, no. 1 (June 1928): 72-73; Infantry Journal, 35, no. 2 (August 1929): 196.

27. Ormiston CSQ.

28. Muster Roll, Company A, 15th Infantry, October 1912, RG 407; Bland and Ritenour, Papers of Marshall, 267. The industrial city of Tongshan was not popular with the troops, because of the poor recreation available, and it was given the name "smoky city." The Sentinel, 9 September 1921, p. 1; 8 January 1926, p. 17.

29. GEN Charles L. Bolte interview by Arthur J. Zoebelein, (1971), 42, SODP, AC, A, USMHI.

30. Ibid., 42-43.

31. 1LT Joseph E. Johnson interview by COL. Joseph B. Ruth (1977), 15, MCOH.

32. MGEN John N. Hart interview by Frank (1977),

31, MCOH; GEN Vernon E. Megee interview by Frank (1970), 47, MCOH; Adolf B. Miller, Diary, May 1927, Box 4, Papers of Adolf B. Miller, Collection Numbers: P.C. 196, Personal Papers Collection (PPC), MCHC.

33. J. Robert Moskin made a survey of Shanghai in search of former marine quarters. J. Robert Moskin, "Tracing the Footsteps of the 4th Marines in Shanghai," Fortitudine: Newsletter of the Marine Corps Historical Program, 16, no. 3 (Winter 1986-1987): 13-16; Johnson interview, 13-14. All marine regiments after 1930 were called "Marines," without the word "Regiment." Allan Millett, Semper Fidelis: The History of the United States Marine Corps (New York: Macmillan, 1980), 230.

34. Johnson interview, 16-17.

35. Robert Hugh Williams, The Old Corps: A Portrait of the U.S. Marine Corps Between the Wars (Annapolis, MD: Naval Institute Press, 1982), 13.

36. Fred Osborn CSQ to DLN, 2 August 1984.

37. "Post Regulations, Marine Detachment, American Legation, Peiping, China, January 1, 1932," 1, photocopy located in "China, 1930-1936," file, Reference Section, Marine Corps Historical Center (MCHC).

38. Erskine interview, 126-27

39. BGEN Fred Dale Beans interview by MAJ Thomas E. Donnelly (1971), MCOH, MCHC.

40. Ibid.

41. Ibid., 42.

42. Berkeley interview, 93-94.

43. Erskine interview,127-28.

44. American Embassy Guard News (Peking, China), 1 January 1936, pp. 18-19.

45. Berkeley interview, 65. In 1931, the marine corps changed from numerical companies to letters, i.e., 32 Company became Company D. Burger interview, 59.

46. "Post Regulations, 1932," 8-9.

47. Julius Isaacson, CSQ to DLN, 20 August 1984; Horace Edward Tuckett, CSQ to DLN, 16 June 1984.

48. American Embassy Guard News, 15 November 1936, p. 17.

49. Erskine interview, 91, 132-33.

50 Unless otherwise noted, all information on the Chinese aboard the Palos is found in: Glenn Howell, "Cheeseye," typescript, Glenn Howell Papers, China Repository (CR), Naval Operational

Archives (NOA), U.S. Naval Historical Center (NHC), Washington, DC. "Cheeseye" is the Americanization of the Chinese dialect for children in the province where the Palos was operating.

51. The Sentinel, 14 January 1921, p. 15.
52. The Walla Walla, 2 May 1931, p. 4.
53. RADM George Van Deurs interview by CDR Etta-Belle Kitchen, (1974), 217, Oral History Program, Naval Institute (OHNI), Annapolis, MD. For an excellent overview of the daily naval routine, see: Frederick S. Harrod, Manning the New Navy: The Development of a Modern Naval Enlisted Force, 1899-1940 (Westport, CT: Greenwood Press, 1978), 140-65, 200-01.
54. Finney, Old China Hands, 178.
55. Van Deurs' interview failed to record the type of aircraft that was used in China. Using the information provided, that is, that the aircraft was powered by a Packard engine, I have determined that the craft was a T3M-2. Gordon Swanborough and Peter M. Bowers, United States Navy Aircraft Since 1911, 2nd ed. (Annapolis, MD: Naval Institute Press, 1976), 310-13; Van Deurs interview, 220-21. For the Third Brigade's equipment, see Finney, Old China Hands, 150-66; Gabrielle Neufeld and James S. Santelli, "Smedley Butler's Air Corps: The First Marine Aviators in China," U.S. Naval Institute Proceedings, 103 (April 1977): 48-59.
56. "The Log of Glenn Howell" VIII, 22 June 1920, p. 1879, NOA.
57. Johnson interview, 22, 29-30.
58. "Log of Howell," XI, 10 July 1920, p. 3268; ibid. VIII, 7, 12 October 1920, pp. 2064, 2082. The best account of navigational and ship-handling problems aboard the Yangtze River gunboats is found in: Kemp Tolley, Yangtze Patrol: The U.S. Navy in China (Annapolis, MD: Naval Institute Press, 1972; reprint 1984).
59. Tolley, Yangtze Patrol, 206 (page references are to reprint edition).
60. RADM Charles J. Wheeler interview by CDR Etta-Belle Kitchen, (1970), 44, OHNI. A 1925 navy report stated the Pamanga should be "placed out of commission as soon as a relief can be provided." Letter, Commander-in-Chief, Asiatic Fleet to Chief of Naval Operations, Material Reports Quarter Ending 30 June 1925, FF 6/8, Box 2193, RG 80, General Records of the Department of the Navy.
61. As Richard McKenna noted, " on my new ship

there were no bunks, and I got special liberty for a few hours to go ashore and buy a canvas cot." Richard McKenna, "Adventures with Libraries," in New Eyes for Old: Nonfiction Writings by Richard McKenna, eds. Eva Grice McKenna and Shirley Graves (Winston-Salem, NC: John F. Blair, 1972), 33.

62. Papers of Henry J. Poy, CR, NOA, "Record of Proceedings of a Board of Investigation on Board the U.S.S. Elcano," 10 Decemer 1927, file FF6-1 to L4-2, Box 2193, RG 80.

63. Legation Guard News (Peking, China), 15 February 1931, p. 15.

64. All details on Moriarty's guard duty are found in: Papers of Brig. Gen. James F. Moriarty (USMC), CR, NOA; Johnson interview, 28.

65. Ormiston, CSQ.

66. Legation Guard Annual (Peking, China: 1934), 170; Johnson interview, 43-44. The horse marines were disbanded in 1938. Time, 7 March 1938, p. 17.

67. Ormiston, CSQ.

68. The station was reestablished in 1932. CAPT Henri Smith-Hutton interview by CAPT Paul Ryan (1976), 202, OHNI. Peking also had a radio station. "A Brief History of the Radio Security Station, Marine Detachment, Peiping, China" (Washington [?]: U.S. Navy, 15 April 1981). Photocopy in possession of Dennis L. Noble.

69. An example of intelligence-gathering on the Yangtze Patrol is found in: Papers of VADM Robert C. Giffen, CR, NOA. The work of marine officer Evans F. Carlson in Shanghai in 1927 is detailed in: Michael Blankfort, The Big Yankee: The Life of Carlson of the Raiders (Boston: Little, Brown, 1947), 145-56. Jeffrey M. Dorwart, Conflict of Duty: The U.S. Navy's Intelligence Dilemma, 1919-1945 (Annapolis, MD: Naval Institute Press, 1983), 59-60; Worton's mission is described in the formerly classified attachment to MGEN William A. Worton interview by Frank, (1967), MCOH.

70. The Sentinel, 25 February 1921, p. 15. Other information on famine relief is found in 4 March 1924, pp. 14-15.

71. "Customs of the Fifteenth Infantry," 6; "Once each year, we welcome the Commander-in-Chief, U.S. Asiatic Fleet to Peiping, for his annual tour of inspection;" American Embassy Guard News, 1 September 1936, p. 1.

72. Miller, "Diary," Box 2, 9 January 1928.

73. Berkeley interview, 90.

4

"A MARVELOUS EXISTENCE": OFF-DUTY HOURS

The Army of the interwar years, according to William L. Hauser, was "quaint. . . by today's standards, or even by the standards of its own time."[1] Hauser's observation, of course, applies equally to the other armed forces of the United States. This "quaintness" is especially noticeable in the off duty social activities of the American military in the Middle Kingdom. Marine corps officer Graves B. Erskine correctly observed that the reason China "was considered to be choice duty was the social activities that were involved."[2] Indeed, the leisure amusements have been the basis of the stereotype of the military man in China, and this stereotype has been honed to a fine edge by countless barracks tales and sea stories that relate a life of indolence. Short duty hours, with large amounts of time to indulge in all the vices imaginable, provided ample opportunity for what Americans of an earlier day would surely have called dissipation. American military officers are pictured as "gentlemen," who employed large household staffs of Chinese servants, attended a constant round of parties, and enjoyed a truly international social life that would have been the envy of their peers stationed in the United States. Enlisted men are seen as a boorish breed, whose activities revolved around liquor and prostitutes, yet they perhaps possessed just enough intelligence to recognize that China was the only country where they could retire to maintain this type of life-style. By examining the off-duty activities of the American military in the Middle Kingdom, we will be able to see if, in fact, these stereotypes are correct. Furthermore, the examination will help to bring the men into sharper focus.

A look at the athletic activities of American personnel provides an illuminating introduction to the social phase of the American military experience in China. Military authorities stressed sports almost to the point of being an obsession. In one case, a marine officer was given written orders to play football when he mentioned that he was not interested in the game.[3] The reason given for this large interest in sports was that it helped build team spirit and fostered leadership abilities. Left unsaid was that it also kept some of the men from sampling the delights of the surrounding cities. The army and marine corps were involved in sports on a regular basis much more than the navy was, simply due to the nature of naval duty. Soldiers and marines usually began their sporting activities after the end of the duty day, at noon, while sailors could not always be sure their ships would be in port. Whenever possible, however, the navy placed the same strong emphasis on athletics. William D. Irvin, for example, relates that Adm. Mark Bristol, Commander-in-Chief of the Asiatic Fleet, was goaded by the British Commander-in-Chief about Americans being champions only in sports that no one else played--baseball, for instance. Bristol returned to his flagship and sent forth an order that required every ship under his command to have a soccer team. By fiat, everyone would play the game. This worked to Irvin's advantage when it was discovered he could coach soccer. He was transferred from a ship that he did not care to serve in to the flagship, and his only duty, for a period of time, was to whip some divisional teams into shape.[4]

Every sport in its season was played. Where possible, a company fielded a team and played other companies. Sometimes teams were collected representing the entire command to compete with teams from foreign military commands, civilians from the surrounding cities, or other U.S. military units. Peking marine officer James P. Berkeley recalled that "the [Manchurians] used to lick our pants off in basketball."[5] Anthony Ingrisano recalled that during baseball season the Fifteenth Infantry played "a college team from Japan. . . .

They were quite good, small and fast." He also noted that one year the Hawaii military boxing team journeyed to Tientsin to challenge the international community.[6] Glenn Howell, commander of the gunboat _Palos_ on the Yangtze River, found some football equipment in a storehouse and managed to put together two teams from his small crew of three officers and fifty enlisted men.[7] Robert B. Luckey detailed the strong competition between the marines of the Legation Guard in Peking and the Italian naval guards over tug of war. For practice, the leathernecks would take an old . . . truck, put it into gear, and then, tying a heavy line on the bumper, tow the truck around the parade ground. Luckey, however, related that for the two years he was there, the marines were never able to defeat the Italians.[8] The interest in sports was so great that even during the unrest around Tientsin in 1927, _The Sentinel_, devoted more space to athletics than to what was occurring around the city. Indeed, one would be hard pressed when reading the soldiers' newspaper for this year to know that there was any trouble at all in China. George C. Marshall wrote that he had an ice rink built at Tientsin, with lighting for night skating, warm dressing rooms, and even a band room, for those not wishing to participate in the more violent activities.[9]

In sports, as in every phase of life in the military, there was a distinct difference between the activities of officers and enlisted men. Hauser has written that in the interwar years, "the focus of military life was the horse: an officer's equestrianship was a major measure of his professional competence, and the social schedule of a post was filled with hunts, shows, polo matches, mounted parades, and gymkhanas."[10] Polo was considered an officer's sport. Peking marine officer William F. Battell's comments are typical of the period: "Several days a week we played polo. The rickshaw boy would take you down to the polo field on the French Glace and there you would play . . . for an hour or so."[11] Even officers on the Yangtze patrol tried to participate in polo. Robert Hugh Williams, for example, relates the story of a game in which he participated against British gunboat officers. There were only three players instead of the normal four, the mallets were made by a carpenter's mate who knew nothing about the game, and the ball was a recreational softball.[12]

While some officers did not enjoy riding or horses, enough did so that some officers of every branch of the American military owned the animal. Marine Fred D.   Beans noted that, even on a captain's pay, he had five polo ponies.[13]   While not playing polo, many officers in the Shanghai area raced their horses.   The Shanghai Race Course was a gentleman's track--that is, the owner of the horse rode the animal instead of hiring a jockey.

If neither polo nor racing interested officers, there was always riding through the countryside. Marshall, an inveterate rider, wrote to General of the Army John J. Pershing that "we are now doing a lot of riding in the regiment. . . . [W]e have several trips on the cards, to be taken poney [sic] back with our mounted detachment."[14] One Yangtze Patrol officer recalled that "at Chungking we had a riding club the 'Suicide Club' (so called because of the way we rode the Kwachow ponies up and down steps, along very narrow [and] steep mountain paths, on . . . narrow paths through rice patties, etc.) and rode several times a week."[15]   All of this, however, does not mean that officers did not participate in other sports, for many were active in a variety of activities.   It does indicate that horsemanship was an important part of an officer's life in China.

Travel   and   hunting   were   other   off-duty activities approved by the military.   Travel in China greatly depended upon when and where a man was stationed.   During years of unrest, most men were restricted to the particular area where they were stationed: Shanghai, Tientsin, or Peking. Naval personnel were usually confined to the city they were visiting.   Once conditions became more stable, the men were allowed to move more freely.

Hunting was a popular activity, even during periods of unrest.   Men sailing the Yangtze River had hunting parties to shoot duck and other waterfowl.   The Sentinel, as early as 1921, recorded a sheep-hunting expedition on the Mongolian Plateau by Lt. Col. Benjamin H. Pope.[16] Hunting passes were soon common for both officers and enlisted men.[17]   One of the dangers in hunting was detailed by the Legation Guard News in 1930, when a party of marines were thought to be spies for the Nanking government because a city was bombed shortly after the nimrods had passed through.[18] Peking Marine Ivan Buster recalled that he and three other enlisted men put in for a thirty-day hunting leave into Outer Mongolia in the spring of 1933 and returned with a "couple of hundred pieces of game." In all, Buster made "four trips through the wall."[19] Battell related that whenever he had a chance, he went tiger hunting in Manchuria for a few weeks at a time.[20]

For most of the first twenty years of the twentieth century, there were few, if any, efforts to organize tours for enlisted men or officers. George H. Cloud recalled that during his service in China, from 1927 to 1929, there were no organized tours or USO for marines.[21] Even during periods of peace, it was difficult for many enlisted men to do any type of traveling. A 1924 editorial in The Sentinel stated that travel entailed such a "considerable expense" that most soldiers were prohibited from engaging in tourist activities.[22] In the same year, however, the paper did make mention of a corporal returning from thirty-days furlough who had traveled to Peking, Tongshan, and Shanhaikwan [Shanhaiguan], and visited the Great Wall.[23]

Near the end of the 1920s, there was a greater effort on the part of some commands to provide organized tours. In 1926, for example, The Sentinel advertised a group tour especially for enlisted men to Peking at a very low rate.[24] In 1930, the U.S. Marine Corps news magazine, The Walla Walla, reported a chance for two-hundred enlisted Marines to travel aboard the Chaumont, the navy troop transport, for sight-seeing at Tsingtao, Chefoo, Tientsin, and Peking. "After years of duty and no chance to get outside of the [international] settlement limits of Shanghai," reported The Walla Walla, "a proposal of this kind is certain to be very popular with the enlisted men of this port."[25] By the middle of the 1930s, the YMCA was advertising in The Walla Walla for guided tours of Peking and excursions to Soochow [Suzhou].[26]

Officers, given their larger paychecks, were able to do more traveling, if they desired. Marshall, when writing to Pershing, noted a planned trip "north to the Eastern Tombs, on through the Royal Hunting Park to [Jehol?], and thence down to the Lan River on barges to Lanchow a station on the railroad 100 miles from here."[27] Marine officer

Samuel B. Griffith II related that he had made a two-week walking tour from Peking "out almost to Shansi [Shanxi] Province" with three companions, spending their nights in temples and little inns.[28]

The American sailors and marines on the Yangtze Patrol had the best view of rural China. Old China hands who were invited as guests aboard one of the gunboats or had irregular duties aboard the craft have all commented on the uniqueness of this duty and the chance it offered to observe the passing scene. If officers or crewmen were interested enough, they could see things that very few Westerners had ever viewed. In 1923, for example, Lt. Scott Umsted, skipper of the Palos, recorded an outing with the ship's doctor in the vicinity of Wanhsien [Wanxian]. "I never in all my life saw anything like it," Umsted wrote. Climbing a mountainside, the two officers came upon a walled city, but found the gate closed to them and "we were told in good Chinese that foreign devils were not wanted." After much pleading and cajoling, the two men managed to slip inside the walls and found themselves in an "apparently feudal state." The land was one "immense garden." The lakes, temples, winding pathways, stone bridges, streams, closely trimmed trees, "were a sight to delight the eye."[29]

Travel in China, then, to a large degree depended upon when and where a man was stationed in the Middle Kingdom and, to some extent, whether he was an officer or an enlisted man. The comments of many China hands about not having enough money to travel, however, are only partially valid. During periods of peace, the decision to travel depended on one's interests and priorities. If a soldier, sailor, or marine wished to sample the bars and other sensual delights of a city, then of course there would be little money left to travel. The people most apt to travel were those interested in China and the Chinese. Robert J. Plummer, an enlisted man in the Fifteenth Infantry from 1933 to 1937 who spoke Chinese, wrote, "I went all over China, inner-Mongolia [sic] to Harbin, and up north as far as the Russian border by train."[30] Men who saw the Chinese as a backward, dirty people--and there were a great many of these--were unlikely to move about the countryside or to take an interest in Chinese culture. These men would use lack of money as an excuse for not traveling. In short, while travel was sometimes difficult or even impossible, during periods of peace, those who had a desire and interest to travel could and did travel to the extent that their pay would allow.

There was an effort on the part of the U.S. military to provide off-duty recreational activities for the men on post.   In January 1924, for example, The Sentinel listed the weekly recreational activities for the Fifteenth Infantry. Besides the normal athletic events, there were movies on Sunday and Thursday. On Monday, Tuesday, Thursday, and Friday, there was an amateur stage production by members of the regiment.   In addition, there were regularly scheduled dances or "hops" for enlisted men, along with band concerts.[31]

A variety of facilities was available at or near the barracks area.   For example, the Fifteenth Infantry soldiers had a club nearby erected by "a group of businessmen."[32]   In addition, the Knights of Columbus and the YMCA ran a cafeteria and meeting place.   There were also three separate libraries available to the soldiers.   One was run by the army and the other two by the YMCA and the Knights of Columbus.   In 1921, the latter reported a circulation of 10,000.[33]   The post library, in the same year, contained 3,000 volumes, including books to help "understand China and the Chinese."[34] The Sentinel reported that among the periodicals were such titles as: North American Review, National Geographic, Asia Magazine, Literary Digest, Scribner's Magazine, Everybody's, and others.[35] The marine corps in Peking also provided recreational activities on post.   Like the army, the marines offered a post library and "sound movies," plus dances.[36]

Naval personnel aboard units of the Asiatic Fleet had movies, band concerts, and libraries aboard ship.   These activities, however, depended on the size of the ship on which a sailor served. A cruiser, for example, would be likely to provide these amenities, while a destroyer, and certainly a gunboat, would not.   Richard McKenna has noted the lack of libraries on the ships he served in prior to World War II.[37]   The men who had very little in the way of wholesome activities were those sailors aboard gunboats.   Howell, for example, when commanding the Palos, commented that "there is so little available for the men, so little occupation of their time."[38]   In an effort to provide some-

thing for the sailors other than bars, Howell
rented a bungalow while in his home port of
Chingling [Jingling].[39] It was, however, the off-
base social activities that most soldiers, sailors,
and marines looked forward to after a duty day.

Before proceeding to the off-base activities of
the men in China, we should pause briefly to
consider money--for it was one of the main reasons
the China Station was so popular. Chinese money
proved complex to Westerners. When most of the
silver was drained out of China at the end of the
nineteenth century, replenishment came from silver
dollars minted in Mexico. These silver dollars
were not reminted, but circulated "as was" and
prices were quoted in "dollars mex."[40] Some
inventive Chinese found ways to split the dollars
lengthwise, scoop out most of the silver, and then
refill and seal the coin with lead--producing what
was known as a "three-piece mex." Most shop owners
would bounce a silver coin (known as "dinging")
against a hard object to hear the proper ring
before accepting a silver "mex." The gunboats
plying the Yangtze River for many years paid their
crews in silver dollars and the disbursing officer
was faced with large amounts of silver and few
places to store it safely, plus the risk of
accepting counterfeit money. Joe W. Stryker,
when disbursing officer aboard the Penguin, was
told that between 5 to 7 percent of the silver he
would receive would be counterfeit, even though he
had received it "directly from the mint via the
bank."[41] Tolley noted that gunboat magazines
"offered the only secure storage for such a bulky
treasure, until one enterprising fellow cut his way
up from the bilges."

By the 1930s, the silver Mexican dollar had
largely disappeared. However, the official basic
unit of Chinese currency, the Yuan, inherited the
name "mex." In other words, when a price of twenty
dollars mex is mentioned in the 1930s, what is
usually meant is twenty Yuan.

Other coins were called "small money" and
consisted of copper and silver. The value of the
copper coins would fluctuate from day to day,
depending on the price of scrap copper. Silver
coins were somewhat more complicated to compute:
"Ten smaller dimes or five twenty cent pieces did
not equal a paper or silver dollar. . . . [T]he
smaller coins in total equaled the value of the

silver content of a dollar."

Paper money, called "big money," was made up of a galaxy of currency from various sources and never seemed to be withdrawn from circulation due to wear. Big money was usually in denominations of less than one dollar. "One bought them new in packs at the bank and carried them in a breast pocket like...visiting cards, for easy dispensation as tips and ricksa fare."

The pay of the American military man, as any veteran will loudly proclaim, has always been low. For example, the pay of a private in 1901 was $156 per year; by 1937, it had increased to $252 per year. A first lieutenant's annual pay for 1901 was $1,500 and, interestingly enough, was the same thirty years later.[42] During the depression, military pay was reduced by 15 percent, which amounted to approximately $17.85 for a private. Shooting pay and reenlistment bonuses were abolished.[43] Battell recalled that in 1932, a second lieutenant's pay, after the 15 percent reduction, was approximately $164.25 a month, including all allowances.[44] August Larson recalled that an officer could elect to take a month's leave without pay instead of taking the pay reduction.[45] Despite all of this, the American military received more pay than any other Western armed force in China. Ingrisano recalled that in Tientsin, American military men "were considered wealthy. There were places with signs that said: 'Men in uniform not allowed except Americans.' It was enough to turn your head."[46]

In addition to their larger paychecks, the exchange rate made Americans seem wealthy indeed. Ingrisano noted that Tientsin "was the only station I ever knew where the ordinary soldier read the financial pages to see what the rate of exchange was for that day." The soldier also recalled that when the United States went off the gold standard, even the rickshaw pullers seemed to know about the sudden drop in the value of soldier's money. Eventually, according to Ingrisano, "the dollar was established at 3.50 mex." The result was that American troops were still making more money. "I never understood [why,]" reported the former Fifteenth Infantry soldier, "but no one complained."[47] The Sentinel, in 1921, noted that the increase in the exchange rate caused a large rush for extensions of duty.[48]

The already complicated fiscal situation was made more difficult by the "chit" system. Most officers and men who have written about their tours of duty in China have expressed amazement at the "chits" employed by the Chinese. One needed only some big money when going out on the town for rickshaws and tips. For any other expense, all that was needed was to sign your name and duty station. Somehow, it was never understood how, the Chinese establishments would send someone around to present the bill. Stryker recalled that as a newly arrived ensign in China, he tried to beat the system by signing a false name and duty station, but was still located. Officers and enlisted men alike participated in the use of chits.[49]

The lending of money until payday is probably as old as the American military itself. In China, this was known as "jawboning." Buster recalled a marine by the name of Gegan who was always the big winner in poker games. Gegan would keep a "G.I. bucket (about 3 gal.) full of silver dollars for anyone to use, just pay back on pay day."[50]

Payday was also payback time for the services of the Chinese who took all the drudgery out of military life for those stationed in the Middle Kingdom. On some gunboats, in fact, the head Chinese aboard would sit at a separate table collecting the fees. In short, the credit system in use in China could cause some men who were not careful to be constantly in debt and never see their money.

The nature of off-duty life also had a family dimension. Normally, married officers who were stationed in China would arrive on station with their wives. Some families immediately found that things were somewhat different in East Asia. Marine Robert O. Bare noted that when he and his wife arrived at Tientsin, he found that there was fighting taking place along the route to his new duty station at Peking. The local Ford dealer, who was sending a convoy of vehicles to the capital city, offered free transportation to the marine and his wife, in the hope that the officer's presence would be protection from any possible attack. "We were young in those days," Bare recalled, "and didn't know better. [W]e immediately got into the midst of the troops which were moving towards Peking, include one group of White Russians. . . . There was some machine gun fire on one side of us and our driver got shot, but we landed in Peking." Bare also remembered that his senior officers "nearly tore my head off for being so foolish as coming up there that way and bringing my wife with me."[51]   Most   families   arrived   without   the adventures of the Bares.

The Fifteenth Infantry published a marvelous little booklet, The Customs of the Fifteenth Infantry, which spelled out the obligations of officers and their families while on the China Station.   A new bride joining the regiment, for example, was treated somewhat royally.   "Customs" decreed that the regimental band would serenade the bride at a suitable time after her arrival.   In addition,   a wedding present with the Fifteenth Infantry's coat of arms engraved upon it would be presented to the new wife.   Lastly, there was to be a yearly reception to honor the brides of the regiment.[52]

The Sentinel, in 1926, published a special issue detailing the facilities in Tientsin for the newly arrived officers and their families.   In describing the foreign concession, the newspaper noted that, but for the "absence of a red front five and ten cent store, the new arrival might easily forget, that for the moment, that the United States is some 7,000 miles away."[53]   In fact, the foreign concession did resemble a European town, but American military families nevertheless soon found that living conditions were far different on the China Station.

Battell   accurately   described   North   China in 1932 as a kind of "fairyland" to live in.   A married officer in Peking, he explained, could rent a house with at least three servants, including a cook and helper.   In addition, the officer's retinue could include "a personal amah for his wife, clothes amah, a baby amah, two rickshaw coolies, 2 coolies for the children, a horse amah--a 'mafoo.'"   All of this was on a second lieutenant's pay.   "And they were able to entertain--a little bit."[54]   The Sentinel noted that the average Army officer's family in China "has five servants . . . at a monthly expenditure of about 85 dollars, local currency."   The newspaper, however, warned the newcomer that "the prevailing idea that in China one can live like a Prince-of-the-Blood on the pay of a Second Lieutenant has as much foundation of fact as the

theory that two can live as cheaply as one." The
paper pointed out that an officer in the Middle
Kingdom spent as much as he got, "the difference
being [that in China] he lives on a higher scale."
Also, according to The Sentinel, if the officer was
married, his wife "invariably" bought a large
collection of "rugs, silver, linen, lingerie,
embroideries,and other impedimenta that would be
utterly beyond his means if priced on Fifth
Avenue."[55]

Single officers either rented rooms in hotels or
shared an apartment with other officers. Battell
recalled that while single and stationed in Peking
he lived in the Wagon Lits Hotel. The hotel
provided three meals and tea, plus a "boy" who
took care of the room and his clothing, all of
which cost $135 a month.[56]

The children of officers in Tientsin could
attend a school, from kindergarten to seventh
grade, at Number 53, Race Course Road, close to the
barracks. The Sentinel noted that the school was
ideal, as it gave American children the chance to
meet others from foreign nations, "[a]lthough the
number of these is kept down so as not to interfere
with the American atmosphere of the school." In
addition, there was also the English Tientsin
Grammar School. High school age children were sent
to a boarding school, the North China American
School, located about sixty-five from Tientsin.[57]
In Shanghai, there were also private schools, for
which the students would be picked up by a marine
corps truck.[58]

The wives of naval officers serving on ships
that were homeported in Manila lived a rather
unusual life. When the fleet sailed on its annual
deployment to China (Chapter 3), the women were
forced to follow their husbands the best way they
could. Caroline Bernard's husband explained that
she would have to "catch whatever commercial
transportation" was available and that she should
plan on being away from Manila for at least three
months. She would, however, have the "chance to
see interesting places."[59] The young wife usually
journeyed via commercial steamer to Shanghai and
Tsingtao.

Once settled, according to Battell, they found
that the "social life was something that no one
would ever believe. . ., it was strictly old Europe
formal."[60] This was especially true in the capital

city of Peking.   Marine officers were required to
call upon "every foreigner" in the capital.   (Old
China hands called all Westerners and Japanese
living in China "foreigners.") A list was provided to the new marine officer, and the "first duty"
of the new arrival was to follow the instructions
it contained.   "[T]here were little marks . . .
indicating those whom we should call on in person
and if they weren't home to come back again, and
others where it was perfectly all right to leave a
card.   The third mark meant you could send your
rickshaw boy with your card--you didn't have to go
yourself.   There were 200 or 300 of these people,
so it took a lot of time."[61]

When not visiting "foreigners," officers were
required to perform certain formal obligations
within their regiment.   One of the many social
duties of the newly arrived officer, or "griffin,"
was to take his place in the receiving line at the
first regimental formal party after his arrival.
All officers, and their families, of the post were
required to call upon the newly arrived officer and
his family as soon as they were settled into their
new quarters.[62]

Naval officers were constantly paying calls to
ships anchored or moored nearby, plus visiting
local officials at various ports.   Tolley has described official calls in the 1923-1931 navy on
the Yangtze River and noted that to "the average
citizen, the formality and inevitability of
official calls might seem straight out of Gilbert
and Sullivan."   The visiting officer wore a
knee-length   frock   coat,   "embellished   with
grapefruit-sized gold-fringed 'swabs' (epaulettes)
which extended the wearer's beam several inches,"
and the pants had "'railroad tracks,' wide gold
stripes." A "gold-encrusted belt" held a four-
foot sword.   "Topping off this magnificent display
was a cocked hat, projected fore and aft some eight
inches, decorated with cockade and gilt trim"   It
was traditional that a commodore rated having one
button of his fly undone and that anyone who had
rounded Cape Horn did not have to do up the top
bottom of his jacket.   Tolley has related that
"[c]lawing up the vertical ladder and through the
scuttle hatch of a British destroyer wardroom while
so attired called for finesse of a high order,
especially   after   three   or   four   glasses   of
hospitality."[63]

Once the formal activities were over, the social
whirl increased. Some officers went to established
clubs. Marshall wrote that the Country Club in
Tientsin was the focus of almost all social
activities. The lieutenant colonel went on to
describe a pool, twelve tennis courts, a large
ballroom, tea rooms, terraces, large dining room,
and a bar as "busy as a bee hive." The charges to
obtain membership were "ridiculously small." He
noted too the "swarms of servants" who stood
waiting for an officer's order.[64] Marine Adolf B.
Miller, while stationed at Tientsin, recorded in
his diary an almost dizzying round of daily social
activities: "Went to Tientsin Club, thence to Race
Club, thence to Country Club, then to Tientsin Club
for dinner. Ready for bed."[65] Battell recalled
that on some days in Peking, after polo was finished, the single marine officers would climb into
their rickshaws and go to a cocktail party. Then,
about seven or eight o'clock, the officers would
return to their hotels, change their clothes, and
go to dinner. This would be followed by even more
parties. At other times, the marine officer would
simply go to the Wagon Lits Hotel, take a nap, get
up around four in the afternoon, and then go to the
lobby, where he just had tea, "tea consisting of
mountains of sandwiches and scotch."[66]
The best description of the hectic whirl
experienced by some marine officers in Peking has
been recorded by Erskine:[67]

> [M]any times . . . there'd be some sort of
> reception at 10 o'clock. You might go to
> the Italian Embassy . . . and over there
> you would drink and end up with champagne.
> You had about all you needed for a whole
> day there, but then this was followed by
> something over at the British Embassy--you
> were invited there. And it seemed that if
> you declined these invitations, the person
> who invited you would have his feelings
> hurt. It was not an excuse. So we'd go to
> the British Embassy and drink gin until you
> were so tight you could hardly eat your
> lunch. Then from there we had a cocktail
> hour, maybe and that was followed by a
> dinner which kept you up at least till
> midnight.

Erskine quite rightly observed "there was no time, really, for an officer to get down to business."[68] Brooke Astor, as the daughter of the marine commander of the guard in Peking in 1919, related that her parents once went out thirty-six consecutive nights.[69]

One should not, however, think that all officers undertook the social whirl that Erskine and others have described. Officers did have to entertain socially, but this does not mean that everyone attended every party or that all officers drank at the functions. Donald R. Fox, Jr., wrote that his father, while serving as a marine officer in China, did not drink or smoke.[70] Families, as Griffith has pointed out, were not bothered with normal household drudgery and were thus able to make use of the available free time to sightsee or shop together. Griffith and his family shared leisure moments and discovered Chinese culture together. Together the family "spent many, many hours" walking in parks, visiting the museums and the Forbidden City. "Everytime it was an adventure . . . there was so much to do."[71] Fox recalled that at the "impressionable ages [of] 14-16 these were halcyon day--the greatest of times."[72]

In the heat of summer, most wives escaped the teeming city of Tientsin and moved to Pei-hao, near the firing range at Chinwangtao. In the early years, the families lived in tents near the range. As the years passed, however, a colony of officers' wives and children began living in permanent housing near the beach. A 1927 photograph reveals a summer colony, with cheerful-looking resort-style housing.[73]

For those women whose husbands were aboard fleet ships and had to move from Manila to the various Chinese port cities, life was not quite as secure as at Pei-hao. Alberta J. Matthews, for example, recalled that life could be hectic, pleasant, but sometimes frightening. She remembered staying in a hotel in Amoy, where the owner would be passed out on the steps. While she spent many evenings dancing, she spent more hours alone in her room, sewing or playing solitaire. One evening, while leaving the movie in Chefoo, Matthews found herself being jostled in the middle of a crowd of rickshaw pullers trying to get the departing theatergoers to take their carts. The shafts of the rickshaws were being pushed close to her. Suddenly, a tall sailor

lifted her up, carried her to the edge of the
crowd, and then gave her a long lecture on being
alone.   "I can see him now [over fifty years
later]" recalled Matthews, "wagging his finger and
telling me to stay home until my husband could take
me [out]."[74]

Duty in China also allowed American military
officers to meet a truly international group of
people.   In Tientsin, Shanghai, Peking, and the
port cities visited by ships, there were representatives of almost every Western nation and
Japan.   The large cities swarmed with people who
claimed to be everything from nobility to gun-
runners.   Miller, for example, recorded in his
diary: "Went to races. Met a Manchu Princess."[75]
Many officers took advantage of this opportunity
and cultivated friendships with nationals from a
variety of countries. Russell N. Jordahl felt that
any marine officer "missed a great deal in his
life" if he did not take advantage of this
chance.[76]   There could, however, be difficulties.
Berkeley remembered that at the monthly marine
corps dance, he invited many civilians to attend.
This brought censure from a number of captains who
wanted to know why "we play around with civilians
instead of our own people?"   Berekely let it be
known that if he "wanted to play around with
Marines I would have gone to Quantico."[77]

In general, however, Americans tended to be wary
of foreigners.   Howell wrote in his diary that he
disliked the English "on general principles."   He
claimed that those in Changsha were covertly anti-
American, for the United States' "position in the
world is now predominant, and is growing in the
Orient by leaps and bounds."   Least liked were the
Japanese.   The most strident of all descriptions
again comes from Howell, who noted that while he
could tolerate the Japanese, "I certainly hate
them."[78]   In short, American military officers
tended to be much like their country: national-
istic, and if forced to side with another
"foreigner," preferring those who spoke their
language and were white.

From the preceding, the reader can readily see
that in China, officers were considered--to use the
old phrase--"officers and gentlemen" and were
allowed to mingle with the Western social elite in
the Middle Kingdom. The same did not apply to the
enlisted men. Chapter 2 discussed the ostracizing

of these men and the difficulties of obtaining
accurate information on them. This applies even
more to their off-duty activities. The stereo-
typical picture of the enlisted China hand probably
emerges best from an entry in Howell's diary and
from McKenna, himself a former enlisted China hand.
Howell recorded an incident in which two sailors,
in a drunken argument, caused the death of a
Chinese by throwing him into the Yangtze River.[79]
McKenna wrote about Coxswain Duke Lee, "who wore
chin whiskers, went barefoot, scarcely even talked,
kept an ancient and equally silent parrot in number
four hold and smoked opium in the cordage locker."
Lee, while in Shanghai, would heat Chinese pennies
red hot and then throw them out the window to
beggars. In a bar in Shanghai's Blood Alley, he
"vomited the contents of his stomach over a table,
then used a pair of chopsticks to pick up the solid
pieces and swallow them again."[80]

In short, the picture of the enlisted man that
emerges from legend and from the very sparse information that we posses, is of a drunken boor, who
cared little for anything except liquor, fighting,
and prostitutes. This picture is easy to accept,
for in fact many men were exactly this way. Even
with the paucity of materials available, however,
it is possible to refine the stereotype.

Marshall, in a letter to Pershing, aptly summed
up the two greatest problems of the American
military in China: "Today is 'pay day' and we are
up against the problem of cheap liquor and cheaper
women."[81] The impressionistic evidence of heavy
drinking within the enlisted ranks is overwhelming. Berkeley said that during Prohibition, officers would tell the men that while China seemed to
contain all the liquor in the world, they could not
drink it all. "Of course they were always willing
to try, naturally."[82] Forty years after his service
in China, Charles Finney recalled that immediately
outside of the American barracks in Tientsin, the
"signs saying 'Bar' seemed to stretch into
infinity."[83] The Walla Walla, in an editorial
directed at newly arrived leathernecks, stated that
Shanghai had all the sins imaginable, and unless
"you want to fall . . ., you'd better take your
wine and beer with men who know the dope."[84] Carl
M. Tuttle remembered seeing the liberty parties
returning with the drunks "carried up the gangway
and laid out on deck, and if they were still there

in the morning, they were wet down with salt water."[85] The Sentinel's tongue-in-cheek comment probably came close to the mark for many men. The paper observed that soldiers in the Fifteenth Infantry had many reasons for serving in China, some for the sake of experience, others because it was an easy place to soldier, "but between friends I am going to tell the truth, I came to get a few drinks the same as the rest of them did."[86]

If the men didn't have the money for liquor, there was always a still. Oliver G. Webb described a concoction called "Pink Lady." A foam-type fire extinguisher was emptied and "pink lady" (torpedo alcohol) or shellac was placed in it and heated, with the resulting liquid dripped out through the hole and strained through a loaf of bread. This brew could be "improved upon" by adding lye to a glass of it. The lye would force the pink liquid to the lower third of the fluid. The clear portion would be poured off and then strained through bread. Webb recalled that it killed one person because he became too impatient and drank the concoction without straining it.[87]

Yet, despite all the evidence, most old China hands, when asked if drinking was a problem in China, replied in the negative. This requires some explanation. The military of this era did not consider drinking a problem unless it interfered with a man's duties. In other words, one could become drunk every night, but if he was able to get up in the morning and carry on with work, there was no difficulty. Further, there was no thought of excessive alcohol consumption being a disease. Indeed, this has been a continuing attitude of the military until at least the last decade. Part of the reasoning behind this thinking may be the officers' view that this was the only way uneducated enlisted men knew how to enjoy themselves.

It should be pointed out that drinking to excess was not confined to the lower ranks. The earlier descriptions of the social activities of officers clearly demonstrates that the constant round of parties could lead some to problems with alcohol. Further, some officers, like some rankers, could not handle the sudden freedom to drink as much as they wanted. Stryker mentioned a young officer who "went out of control" and had to be returned to the United States. Both enlisted men and officers faced intense peer pressure to drink, and it took a strong person to resist this pressure.[88]

Most of the enlisted men serving in China were single.   In fact, the military frowned upon marriage for anyone lower than the top three non-commissioned grades. Robert K. Griffith, Jr., has pointed out that married "enlisted men below non-commissioned officer rank constituted a class of soldier that always lived on the edge of poverty."[89]   In spite of this attitude, there were, of course, marriages by enlisted men in the lower grades. In 1927, the Sentinel reported the birth of a son to the wife of a private first class.[90]   Any enlisted man in China below the top three grades of non-commissioned officer, was required to pay for his wife's transportation to East Asia.

There is very little information on the legally married enlisted men in the Middle Kingdom, except for a few mentions of visits to each other's residences in the regimental newspaper.   In an era when some enlisted men's families were forced to live in tents at posts in the United States, it can be surmised that the families of the lower ranks enjoyed the relative luxury of China duty as much as their officer counterparts.   The pervasive lack of a family while on station contributed to the other major problem facing the American military in China.[91]

All of the armed forces spent an inordinate amount of time fighting venereal disease.   In the days before penicillin, men with VD were incapacitated and a unit's efficiency was thus lowered. Forrest Pogue has noted that some army company commanders provided free rickshaws to bring the men from bars at closing time.[92]   Erskine recalled that another attempted solution to the problem was to set aside a certain section of the city for prostitutes.   A doctor was employed to inspect the women at least twice a week.[93] Remarking upon a draft of thirty men returning to the United States, navy Cmdr. Robert C. Giffen wrote that twenty-six had VD. Of the twenty-six, fifteen had, or at least at one time had contracted, syphilis.   He then outlined his program for combating the problem aboard navy units: men were to be warned that contracting VD would mean restriction to the ship. In addition, a strong lecture program would be established.   Newly arrived men were to be subjected to examinations and lectures.   Giffen believed that the venereal disease rate could be reduced if commanding officers gave the matter at "least as much thought as we are . . . required to give to salinity in the boiler, rust in a double bottom and the thousand and one orders covering machinery and ships." The commander also stated that he did not feel he was "prudish" nor did he consider that men "are geldings," but he was concerned that pacifists would soon be able to coin the slogan: "Join the Asiatic and acquire venereal disease."[94]

Giffen would probably have applauded the efforts of the Fifteenth Infantry in its long war against VD. The army had good reason to wage this battle, for as Paul L. Freeman recalled, at one time every other man in the regiment was infected.[95] Brig. Gen. William D. Connor, in 1923, requested a ruling from the Adjutant General on the legality of his making the contracting of VD a military offense, punishable under the 96th Article of War. Connor noted that "diseased conditions" were so general in the Tientsin area that, after repeated warnings and instructions, any soldier contracting the disease was practically "causing self-inflicted incapacitation for duty." The Surgeon General of the Army, in his comments on Connor's request, noted that in the previous year, the American Social Hygiene Association, under the authority of the War Department, had sent a social worker trained in anti-venereal disease work to China in an attempt to improve conditions. Despite this effort, the VD rate had not decreased and the Surgeon General recommended that men be tried for the offense of contracting venereal disease. In a remarkable burst of speed for the War Department, the Adjutant General's approval was sent to Tientsin just twelve days after Connor's original message was transmitted.[96]

The man who waged total war on VD was Col. Reynolds J. Burt. Company officers were informed by the colonel that if more than two cases of venereal disease were reported in their company, "you've had it!"[97] Under his intense pressure, men with liquor on their breaths or simply returning to the barracks after five in the evening were required to undergo a prophylactic. If a man was reported infected, the company officer, the non-commissioned officers in the chain of command, and the offender were all hauled before Burt. Freeman recalled that there were very few company-grade officers in the regiment who did not have a comment on their fitness reports that stated the men "couldn't command" because they did not know how to eliminate VD and therefore "shouldn't ever get ahead in the Army."[98]

Inspections were a daily occurrence. Ingrisano recalled that the soldiers were inspected by the squad leaders, who in turn were inspected by the platoon leader, and this was followed by the first sergeant. William H. Arnold remembered that he even had to inspect the officers. In addition, according to Ingrisano, there were two in-depth medical inspections each month. To prepare for these, the men were required to run through the streets in company formation. This caused a diversion for the Tientsin civilian residents. Ingrisano recalled, "the women in the houses leaning out the windows laughing and crying out loudly, 'if you got something you no get it from me. I am a clean woman.' Everyone knew why we were running through the streets."[99]

One of the ways some men kept from contracting venereal disease was to find a woman and set up living arrangements with her. Joseph E. Johnson felt that the "powers that be" sanctioned living with a woman to prevent VD.[100] While there is, of course, no documentation to prove this assumption, there is some merit to this "feeling": witness marine officer Beans' comments that the best thing that could happen to a marine was for him to live with a woman, and then the leatherneck was just like a married person and would probably behave himself.[101]

U.S. consular records indicate that between 1879 and 1909, there were only 221 recorded American marriages in China to Asian women. From 1910 to 1918, there were 202 marriages, with 8.9 percent to Asians. Then, from 1920 to 1932, the percentage dropped to 2.2 percent. The radical drop in marriages was due to something "glamorous and exciting" in China: the White Russians had appeared on the scene.[102] Prior to this arrival, soldiers, sailors, and marines had lived with Chinese women, who were called "pigs" by many of the men. In fact, even with the great Russian influx, there remained those who preferred Asian women. Finney recalled that the men who lived with Chinese women often gave them a small allowance, which amounted to a fortune to the Chinese. In the early days,

most of the women came from brothels.   Later, as
Finney pointed out, the selection of women became
almost like economic freedom, for the Chinese, and
the taking of a woman "was merely a matter of
exercising one's choice among the multitude of
candidates frankly offered by the relatives of the
current kept woman."[103]   Officers usually did not
marry Asian women, for to do so would spell the end
of their careers.

Tolley has noted that Shanghai in the 1930s,
especially along Avenue Joffre, was almost like old
Russia.   This was the center of the Russian colony,
with signs in Cryillic, Russians strolling along
the crowded streets, and accordian music in the
background.[104]   Battell said that he felt sorry for
the White Russians.   They lived lower "than pigs.
You could go out and see [them] groveling in the
Chinese garbage dumps. . . .   The girls would dance
in cabarets."[105]   Cloud remembered that many of the
marines lived with White Russian women and
supported their families.   Many of the troops tried
to marry the women, but the "Corps frowned upon
it."   He then related that when the "dummy in the
company" tried to marry a cabaret woman, the
colonel confined the marine to the brig for three
weeks, until the man was rotated back to the United
States.[106]   What usually happened, according to
Berkeley, was that an enlisted man would stay with
"one gal, and when [he] left [he] turned her over
to someone else."[107]   Even though it was frowned
upon by most of the military, both officer and
enlisted men did marry Russian women.   In 1932, for
example, 62.1 percent of the men marrying Russians
in China were American.[108]

Enlisted men, like officers, usually had set
locations where they congregated.   As already
mentioned, some of these locations were red light
districts.   These   districts   were   considered
suitable for the common soldier, sailor, or marine
from any country.   Within the districts, a certain
bar would become the province of one country or
military force, say, the army.   Any military man
from another country or another branch of the
American armed forces would enter at his own risk.
Some very large brawls ensued.   The uniform
accoutrements of the men could make formidable
weapons.   Ingrisano, for instance, related how a
soldier's garrison belt could be wrapped around
one's fist until just the buckle remained as a

vicious weapon. Tuttle recalled making a blackjack out of his uniform tie by placing lead in it.[109]

It would be easy from the preceding to conclude that the stereotype of enlisted men in China does seem to be true. A great deal of the men's time appears to have been taken up in drinking, womanizing, and brawling. There is, however, some evidence to modify this stereotype.

Laurence C. Hanson, who served in China from 1925 to 1933, and a shipmate are example's of men who did not match the stereotype. Hanson recalled that he and his friend were "interested in photography and people" and, whenever possible, tried to wander about the countryside.[110] Buster wrote that when he first arrived in Peking, he did as the other marines were doing, that is, going to bars. After a period of time, however, he began to learn the Chinese language, "enough to be useful at least." A few fellow marines then became interested in exploring the arts and crafts of China, and about "once or twice a week . . . [we] would go into [the] Chinese city, pick a street, coppersmith's, goldsmith's, ... or whatever, and start with the first shop."[111] Howell, in trying to provide some recreational activities for his Palos crew, organized hikes in some of the ports along the Yangtze River.[112] In Chefoo in 1924, the local Western population organized a large party for the fleet sailors; contemporary photographs show a large gathering.[113] (Whether attendance by the sailors was mandatory is not known.) While many "old salts" attempted to lead newly arrived sailors astray, Tuttle, who was seventeen when he arrived in China, remembered that he was the youngest sailor aboard and that the "old timers took me under their wing," explaining how a young man from the midwestern United States should make his way in the Middle Kingdom.[114] The sailor who perhaps best defied the stereotype was Henry J. Poy, a first-generation Chinese-American from Portland, Oregon, who spent a great deal of his off-duty time learning about the country of his father.[115]

A Sentinel editorial noted that, for most enlisted men, it was not easy to find a wholesome social life as at home, but there were many opportunities to obtain good companionship by visiting with the citizens of Tientsin, for the soldier would find them "most hospitable."[116] Of course, the citizens referred to in the editorial

were other Westerners. The enlisted men who went
out of their way to follow the advice of the
newspaper were in fact rewarded with experiences
unusual for men who had grown up in an insular
country. Ingrisano, for example, met a Jewish
family in Tientsin who were trying to send their
daughter to Palestine. While visiting with the
family, he met a White Russian who was eager to
"show me his bayonet scars & lashes he had received
from the Communists in his many efforts to escape
across the border." Ingrisano also remembered one
group of German expatriates. "They were ex-
military officers who wore their uniforms at formal
affairs." At one gathering he attended, "it was
like a Hollywood setting. The men in uniform,
stiff, bowing from the waist up, the women in long
flowing gowns, waltzes being played and I remember
being quite fascinated by it all." There was even
a bust of Bismarck. "I don't think they were
aware of anyone else in the city or even in the
world. They lived in a pre World War I period,
despised . . . Hitler, and in their insularity
talked to no one else, believing one day they would
go home to Germany. In their snobbishness they'd
stare right through you if your hair wasn't
cropped, all your medals on right, your sword at
the proper angle and I think they were wearing
spurs even when dancing."[117] Jack A. Wagner, while
serving in the navy, met a Chinese officer who
offered him a colonel's rank in his army near
Chefoo.[118] Many other enlisted men have commented upon visiting the homes of Westerners in
China.

The enlisted men also gathered at locations
other than the red light districts. Enlisted
marines in Shanghai, for example, had NCO and
Private's clubs where, according to Erskine, the
men could go and drink.[119] Battell believed that
the clubs "were finer than any officer's club that
you found in the States."[120] In other cities, the
favorite spot to meet was at a restaurant or bar
operated by a former military man. Glen R. Smith,
for example, remembered the Service Bar run by a
retired soldier by the name of Noble. The former
Fifteenth Infantryman also remembered Foochow
Street, where there was a bowling alley. Other
locations in Tientsin for those who did not care to
drink included confectionaries "mostly run by
Russians."[121] Men of the Asiatic Fleet liked to
gather at a beach-front cafe run by a German and

known variously as "Fritz's" or "The Jew's." For
Peking marine NCOs, a favorite spot was Hempel's, a
combination butcher shop, bar, and hotel. Howell
noted   there   were   sailors'   clubs   at   Ichang
[Yichang], Changsha, and Chungking [Chongqing], and
he considered them "very vital necessities if
anything resembling spirit is to be maintained in
the crews."[122]
    Completely   breaking   the   stereotype   of   the
drunken China hand, some servicemen spent a great
deal of time at the YMCAs scattered throughout
China.   Berkeley recalled that there "was a nice
little Navy YMCA [in Peking] . . . that non-
drinkers liked."[123] The YMCAs were established in
China in an effort by Western social reformers to
fight the problems of urban society in the rapidly
growing Chinese cities.   One of the methods of
accomplishing this was through the establishment of
educational programs at the Y. The programs also
helped the men of the American military by
providing language lessons in Chinese, Spanish, and
Russian.   The Peking establishment in 1937 offered
a "Things Chinese Forum." The American Embassy
Guard News reported that the series gave many tips
on the buying of curios.   There was also some
information on Chinese history. Other discussions
included material on Chinese currency, the history
of the Great Wall, and carpets and carpet-mak-
ing.[124] Some men would spend their days at the
Y and then go to the cabarets at night.[125]
    In   Tientsin,   one   of   the   favorite   off-duty
activities was strolling along the Bund, followed
by walking in Victoria Park. "[T]his park is far
more than a mere collection of trees surrounding a
pond," extolled The Sentinel.[126] Soldiers from all
of the Western powers strolled through the area,
most looking for someone new to meet. Finney
described his meeting with a soldier of the Royal
Scots Guard Regiment and his fascination with
learning the history of that regiment.[127] In addition, as suggested by the regimental newspaper,
there   were   early   movies   within   the   Western
concession for a soldier to attend; these let out
in sufficient time for the soldiers to attend the
nightly band concerts given in the park.[128]
    Other   activities   in   Peking,   according   to
Johnson, included visiting the Canedrome Gardens to
watch dog races and games of jai lai.[129] The Walla
Walla reported in 1933 that Corp. Cecil R. Bates,

Service Company, had played the world chess
champion, a Dr. Alckhine, to a draw in an
exhibition at the Foreign YMCA.[130] The men, in
short, sought out activities that would pass the
off-duty hours, and the comments of many newspapers
and the reminiscences of the men themselves show
that not everyone spent his time in dissipation.
In fact, the men in China sought out the same types
of entertainment as the men of their own age in the
United States. In Shanghai in 1933, for example,
the marines were caught up in the flag-pole sitting
craze sweeping the United States. The Walla Walla
reported that Pfc. John J. Andress had remained
aloft for six hours and forty-four minutes, thereby
setting a new record.[131]

The material that has been presented suggests
that the stereotype of the old China hand's
off-duty hours needs to be reconsidered. The
picture of officers living a life of luxury,
employing a large staff of Chinese servants, and
attending one party after another is correct up to
a point. There were, however, many officers who,
while required by customs of the service to attend
a certain number of social affairs, did not
necessarily go to every function. Many officers
and their families, freed from normal household
drudgery, saw their service in China as a chance to
tour and shop in one of the most exotic locations
in the world.

The picture that most requires revision is that
of the enlisted man's free time. The evidence
clearly shows that many men can be classed as
boors, who were interested only in liquor, prostitutes, and brawling, and who looked forward to
retiring in the Middle Kingdom so that they could
continue this type of lifestyle. Indeed, the two
largest problems faced by the American military in
China were alcohol and venereal disease. On the
other hand, there were a number of men who did not
use all of their free time in the pursuit of vice.
They did their tour of duty and then returned to
the United States. There were also men who wanted
to learn more about China and the Chinese and, to
the extent possible, traveled and tried to
comprehend as much as possible about the country in
which they were serving. In short, the men undertook a variety of off-duty activities, and to
picture them only as drunken louts is too simplistic.[132]

The social life in China for the American
military began to alter in the 1930s as the
Japanese commenced their move in force into China.
The "Japanese presence," according to Gerald C.
Thomas, "spread over everything."[133] As pointed out
in the introduction, the State Department and
others became concerned that a brawl between army
personnel and Japanese troops in the Tientsin area
might spark an international incident. As the
Japanese advanced and tensions increased, families
were periodically evacuated from the Middle
Kingdom. In 1932, the China Station was not open
to wives, due to fighting. Even while fighting was
taking place, American military men seemed to live
in "an atmosphere of unreality."[134] Robert B.
Luckey commented that it "was very difficult in
those days to really get anybody excited in
Peking." The marine officer went on to relate that
he had attended a large dinner party on the roof of
the Peking Hotel on the night the Japanese fought
their way into the city. "They had a pretty good
battle going. . . . And we were sitting up there in
the roof garden of this . . . [hotel] in tuxedos
and having a dinner party while this was going on.
It was sort of old hat in Peking. There was always
somebody shooting or fussing around the place. You
never thought very much of it."[135] Robert E.
Hogaboom also recalled a similar incident in
Shanghai where between "courses we would walk out
on [to a] balcony and watch the burning of Shanghai
and the withdrawal of the Chinese from their
positions as the Japanese drove them out."[136]
Joseph C. Burger, however, realized that after the
fall of Peking, "this was the end of the good life
in Peking, as we knew it."[137]

The recollections of the American military men
serving in China in the 1930s showed that things
were changing to end the "good life." However,
following the lead of their government, the
officers and men continued to remain neutral or
aloof from the fighting between the Japanese and
Chinese. In the best traditions of the old
colonial powers, they tried to carry on their
normal off-duty activities, even as everything
around them was falling apart.

NOTES
    1. William L. Hauser, "The Peacetime Army: Re-
trospect and Prospect," in The United Army in

Peacetime: Essays in Honor of the Bicentennial, 1775-1975, eds. Robert Higham and Carol Brandt (Manhattan, KS: Military Affairs/ Aerospace Historian Publishing, 1975), 207.

2. GEN Graves B. Erskine interview by Benis M. Frank (1970), 129, Marine Corps. Oral History Collection, (MCOH) Marine Corps Historical Center (MCHC), Washington, DC.

3. MGEN Ion M. Bethel interview by Frank (1968), 37, MCOH.

4. RADM William D. Irvin interview by John T. Mason, Jr. (1978), 64-68, Oral History Program, Naval Institute (OHNI), Annapolis, MD.

5. LGEN James P. Berkeley interview by Frank (1969), 102, MCOH.

6. Anthony Ingrisano, China Service Questionnaire (CSQ) to Dennis L. Noble (DLN), 16 July 1984.

7. Glenn Howell, "Log of Glen Howell," XXXIX, p. 10,910, Naval Operational Archives, (NOA) U.S. Naval Historical Center (NHC), Washington, DC.

8. LGEN Robert B. Luckey interview by Frank (1969), 198, MCOH.

9. Larry I. Bland and Sharon R. Ritenour, eds., The Papers of George Catlett Marshall, Vol. I.; "The Soldierly Spirit," December 1880-June 1939 (Baltimore: Johns Hopkins University Press, 1981), 273.

10. Hauser, "Peacetime Army," 207. The horse in army life is also described in: Martin Blumenson, The Patton Papers, 1885-1940 (Boston: Houghton Mifflin, 1972), passim.

11. MGEN William F. Battell interview Frank (1972), 64, MCOH.

12. Robert Hugh Williams, The Old Corps: A Portrait of the U.S. Marine Corps Between the Wars (Annapolis, MD: Naval Institute Press, 1982), 61, 63-65.

13. BGEN Fred D. Beans interview by Frank (1971), 37, MCOH.

14. Bland and Ritenour, Papers of Marshall, I, 286, 293.

15. This officer wishes to remain anonymous. His questionnaire remains in the possession of Dennis L. Noble. Other information on sports is found in the completed CSQs to DLN of: George St. Lawrence, 26 June 1984; Howard L. Povey, 5 July 1984; Glen R. Smith, 23 July 1984; Edward J. Ormiston, 9 August 1984; Laney E. Rutledge, 20 August 1984; GEN

Clifton B. Cates interview by Frank (1967), 81-82, MCOH.

16. The Sentinel (Tientsin, China), 28 January 1921, pp. 2-3.

17. Ibid., 1921-1922, passim.   In 1928, a hunting camp was mentioned, but no location given. The Sentinel, 27 October 1928, p. 15.

18. Legation Guard News (Peking), 15 November 1930, p. 6.

19. Ivan Buster, CSQ to DLN, 27 May 1983.

20. Battell interview, 67.

21. MGEN George H. Cloud interview by Frank (1979), 13, MCOH.

22. The Sentinel, 4 April 1924, p. 5.

23. Ibid., 9 May 1924, 6.

24. Ibid., 12 November 1926, pp. 1207-08.

25. The Walla Walla (Shanghai), 21 June 1930, p. 4.

26. The Walla Walla, 24 June 1933, p. 6; American Embassy Guard News (Peking), 1 October 1936, p. 40, shows a photograph of a sightseeing party to "Manchuco."   Advertisement for sightseeing each Saturday in American Embassy Guard News, 15 March 1937, pp. 2, 20.

27. Bland and Ritenour, Papers of Marshall, I, 293.

28. BGEN Samuel B. Griffith II interview by Frank (1970), 44, MCOH.

29. Quoted in Kemp Tolley, Yangtze Patrol: The U.S. Navy in China (Annapolis, MD: Naval Institute Press, 1971; reprint, 1984), 107-08 (page references are to reprint edition).   Other information on travel may be found in the completed CSQs to DLN of the following: Floyde O. Schilling, 14 July 1984; John T. Salistean, 15 July 1984; Chauncey S. Abram, 26 August 1984; Harry K. Hayden, 2 August 1984; John C. Ponick, 27 June 1983; Jack E. Paine, 16 July 1984; Frank H. Farley, 1 August 1984; Harry A. Taylor, 11 August 1984; Paul Newman, 13 August 1984; Vern L. Dorsey, 10 August 1984; Albert Tidwell, 14 July 1984; Lyle E. Keyes, 20 July 1984; Lloyd M. Mustin, 2 April 1985.

30. Robert J. Plummer, CSQ to DLN, 22 July 1984.

31. The Sentinel, 13 May 1921, p. 4; 5 January 1923, p. 5; 18 January 1924, p. 3.

32. Ibid., 14 December 1923.

33. Ibid., 14 January 1921, p. 3.

34. Ibid., 7 October; 4 November 1921, pp. 5, 6.

35. Ibid., 8 April 1921, p. 10.

36. American Embassy Guard News, 1 January; 1 August 1936, pp. 2, 1.

37. Richard McKenna, "Adventures with Libraries," in New Eyes for Old: Nonfiction Writings by Richard McKenna, eds. Eva Grice McKenna and Shirley Graves Cochrane (Winston-Salem, NC: John F. Blair, 1972) 19-39.

38. "Log of Howell" LXI, p. 11,277.

39. Ibid., p. 2,040.

40. Unless otherwise noted, all material on Chinese money is found in: Kemp Tolley, "Three Piecie and Other Dollars Mex," Shipmate, 28, no. 10 (December 1965): 8-10.

41. Joe W. Stryker, China Ensign (New York: Vantage Press, 1981), 83.

42. The pay of a 1LT, mounted, in 1901, was $1,600. Official U.S. Army Register (Washington: Government Printing Office, 1901), endpapers. By 1937, there was no difference in the pay of a mounted or unmounted officer. Official U.S. Army Register (Washington: Government Printing Office, 1937), endpapers.

43. Ingrisano CSQ; Robert K. Griffith, Jr., Men Wanted for the U.S. Army: America's Experience with an All-Volunteer Army Between the World Wars (Westport, CT: Greenwood Press, 1982), 237-38.

44. Battell interview, 69.

45. MGEN August Larson interview by Frank (1970), 14-15, MCOH.

46. Ingrisano CSQ.

47. Ibid.

48. The Sentinel, 11 February 1921, p. 15.

49. Stryker, China Ensign, 16-19; Tolley, "Three Piecie," 9.

50. Buster CSQ.

51. LGEN Robert O. Bare interview by Frank (1968), 14-15, MCOH.

52. Customs of the Fifteenth Infantry, (Tientsin-Peping, China; Pelyan Press, 192[?]; reprint, Cornwallville, NY: Hope Farm Press, 1959), 16 (page references are to reprint edition).

53. The Sentinel, 24 September 1926, p. 1,041.

54. Battell interview, 69-70.

55. The Sentinel, 24 September 1926, p. 1,045.

56. Battell interview 69.

57. The Sentinel, 24 September 1926, p. 1,045.

58. Donald J. Fox, Jr., CSQ to DLN, 24 August 1984.

59. Bobette Gugliotta, Pigboat 39: An American

Sub Goes to War (Lexington, KY: University of Kentucky Press, 1984), 18.

60. Battell interview, 63.

61. Ibid., 63-64.

62. Customs of the Fifteenth Regiment, 16.

63. Tolley, Yangtze Patrol, 188.

64. Bland and Ritenour, Papers of Marshall, I, 286.

65. Adolf B. Miller, "Diary", 6 November 1927, Papers of Adolf B. Miller, Box 4, P.C. 196, Personal Papers Collection (PPC), MCHC.

66. Battell interview, 64.

67. Erskine interview, 128-129.

68. Ibid., 129.

69. Brooke Astor, A Patchwork Child (New York: Harper & Row, 1962), 48-128.

70. Fox CSQ.

71. Griffith interview, 47-48.

72. Fox CSQ.

73. The Sentinel, 17 August 1927, p. 10.

74. Alberta J. Matthews, CSQ to DLN, 13 September 1984.

75. Miller, "Diary," 28 November 1927.

76. BGEN Russell N. Jordahl interview by Frank (1970), 50, MCOH.

77. Berkeley interview, 103.

78. "Log of Howell," X, 7 April 1921, pp. 2,820-2,821; ibid., XI, 3 June 1921, pp. 3,079-80.

79. Ibid., VIII, 27 September 1920, pp. 2,020-21.

80. Richard McKenna, "Life Aboard the USS Goldstar," in The Left-Handed Monkey Wrench: Stories and Essays by Richard McKenna, ed. Robert Shenk, (Annapolis, MD: Naval Institute Press, 1986), 130.

81. Bland and Ritenour, Papers of Marshall, I, 273.

82. Berkeley interview, 91.

83. Charles G. Finney, The Old China Hands (Garden City, NY: Doubleday, 1961; reprint, Westport, CT: Greenwood Press, 1977), 38 (page references are to reprint edition).

84. The Walla Walla, 5 December 1931, p. 8.

85. Carl M. Tuttle, CSQ to DLN, 6 August 1984.

86. The Sentinel, 9 January 1925, p. 10.

87. Oliver G. Webb, CSQ to DLN, 16 August 1984.

88. Stryker, China Ensign, 30. Howell remarked that the Commanding Officer and doctor aboard a Yangtze River gunboat were "a pair of useless drunks." "Log of Howell," VIII, 25 September 1920,

p. 2013.   Many did not bend to peer pressure, for, as Henry J. Poy put it: "Coca-cola was everywhere to be found," Henry J. Poy Papers, China Repository (CR), NOA.

89. Griffith, Men Wanted, 155.

90. The Sentinel, 18 November 1927.   Also, one article proclaiming marriage of "Pvt. Walter of Co. I. married by Chaplin Bronso," The Sentinel, 25 July 1924, p. 4.

91. "First Sergeant C. C. Dunlap had as his guests Staff Sergeant and Mrs. Stonefield," The Sentinel, 5 December 1924, 9; Griffith, Men Wanted, 155-56.

92. Forrest C. Pogue, George C. Marshall: Education of a General, 1889-1939 (New York: Viking Press, 1963), 240.

93. Erskine interview, 139.

94. Commanding Officer's Diary, 20 July 1928, Papers of VADM Robert C. Giffen, CR, NOA.

95. GEN Paul L. Freeman interview by COL James N. Ellis, (1973), 22, Senior Officer Debriefing Program (SODP), Army War College (AWC), Archives, U.S. Army Military History Institute (A, USAMHI), Carlisle Barracks, PA.

96. BGEN William D. Connor to The Adjutant General, 15 November 1923, with enclosures, folder "China 350.03 to 726.1," Box 1350, Records of the Adjutant General's Office (AGO), Record Group (RG) 407, National Archives, Washington, DC.

97. GEN William H. Arnold interview by COL. Warren R. Stumpe (1975), 56-57, SODP, AWC, A, USAMHI.

98. Ibid., 57; Freeman interview, 23.

99. Arnold interview, 57; Ingrisano CSQ.   Other information on VD may be found in completed CSQs to DLN of the following: John T. Salistean, CSQ: Rutledge CSQ.

100. 1LT Joseph E. Johnson interview by COL Joseph B. Ruth (1977), 33, MCOH.

101. Beans interview, 47.

102. Tolley, Yangtze Patrol, 95.

103. Finney, Old China Hands, 255-56.   McKenna, however, noted that many sailors preferred Japanese women to Chinese.   Richard McKenna, "The Girl in Tatsebi," in Left-Handed Monkey Wrench, 215-60 and passim.   Fernando E. Pedro, CSQ to DLN, 7 June 1984, also supported McKenna's comments.

104. Tolley, Yangtze Patrol, 95.

105. Battell interview, 73.

106. Cloud interview, 14-15.

107. Berkeley interview, 91-92.

108. Tolley, Yangtze Patrol, 96.

109. Ingrisano CSQ; Tuttle CSQ.

110. Laurence C. Hanson, CSQ to DLN, 28 July 1984.

111. Buster CSQ.

112. "In the afternoon, I took about twenty of my gobs for a hike along the beach. We visited a pagoda," "Log of Howell," VIII, 11 September 1920, p. 1974.

113. The Orient (Shanghai), August 1924, pp.6-7.

114. Tuttle CSQ.

115. Poy, passim, CR, NOA.

116. The Sentinel, 5 October 1923, p. 5.

117. Ingrisano CSQ.

118. Jack A. Wagner CSQ to DLN, 11 August 1984.

119. Erskine interview, 132.

120. Battell interview, 72. Some of the enlisted clubs were well established organizations. The NCO Club in Peking had been established in 1916. American Embassy Guard News, 1 July 1936, p. 8.

121. Smith CSQ.

122. "Log of Howell," XLI, 2 February 1926, p. 11,277; Stryker, China Ensign, 32.

123. Berkeley interview, 93.

124. American Embassy Guard News, 15 April 1937, p. 13. With regard to a lecture by Dr. Y. T. Wu, "nationally known Chinese," on the Sino-Japanese "problem" and other lectures at the Y, "the reception by the men had been most gratifying." The Walla Walla, 7 December 1935, p. 17. Other comments on courses in The Walla Walla, 1 November 1930, p. 3, and 9 September 1933, p. 34; American Embassy Guard News, 1 June 1937, p. 4. Other materials on the YMCA may be found in the CSQs to DLN of the following: Edwin C. Schierhorst, 15 July 1984; Arthur G. Gullickson, 18 August 1984; Cloud interview, 13-14. Information on the YMCA in China is also found in: Kenneth Scott Latourette, World Service: A History of the Foreign Work and World Service of the Young Men's Christian Associations of the United Stats and Canada (New York: Association Press, 1957) and Shirley S. Garrett, Social Reformers in Urban China: The Chinese YMCA, 1895-1926 (Cambridge, MA: Harvard University Press, 1970).

125. Tuttle CSQ.

126. The Sentinel, 11 July 1924, p. 11.

127. Finney, Old China Hands, 45-52.

128. The Sentinel, 11 July 1924, p. 11.

129. Johnson interview, 24-25.

130. The Walla Walla, 4 February, 28 October 1933, pp. 7, 13.

131. Ibid., 28 October 1933, p. 13.

132. Cloud's coments on his tour of duty in China during 1927-29 reflects how some men felt: "To me it was very interesting because I had studied some history of the Orient, and this gave me a chance to see something that I was interested in. There was something to do all the time." Cloud interview, 13-14.

133. GEN Gerald C. Thomas interview by Frank (1966), 117, MCOH.

134. Berkeley interview, 59-60.

135. Luckey interview, 77.

136. GEN Robert E. Hogaboom interview by Frank (1970), 126, MCOH.

137. LGEN Joseph C. Burger interview by Frank (1969), 103, MCOH.

5

AMONG THE "HEATHEN CHINEE": AMERICAN SERVICEMEN'S PERCEPTIONS OF CHINA AND THE CHINESE

The desirability of the China Station is firmly entrenched in American military mythology. Many men requested duty in East Asia because of the low cost of living and high money exchange rate, plus easy duty hours. Some intended to retire in the Middle Kingdom. Yet the written and oral reminiscences of China hands are usually silent about the Chinese and their country.

An insight into this paradox comes from an incident related by Charles G. Finney, an army enlisted man who volunteered for the Middle Kingdom in the 1920s. When Finney located a soldier who had served in East Asia and asked him about the duty, the former China hand went to great lengths to describe how easy it was to soldier in the Fifteenth Infantry. There was, for example, no KP, very few fatigue details, and a small amount of guard duty. Finney was perplexed. If the duty was that good, why did the soldier leave? Because, retorted the man, China "ain't a white man's country."[1] This chapter will examine how the American military men and their families viewed China and the Chinese. Particular focus will be given to how three people observed their surroundings, as a way to illustrate the pervasive views of some of the U.S. military in China.

One of the ways to understand a people is to read and write their language. Chinese, being a tonal spoken language and using pictographs (characters) for writing, is not easy for Westerners to learn. Nevertheless, in the 1920s, there was an effort on the part of the Fifteenth Infantry commander to have some of his troops learn at least the rudiments of the language. In 1923, Brig. Gen. William D. Connor requested from the Adjutant General $400 from contingency funds to hire teachers to teach "colloquial Chinese."[2]   The funding was approved, and all officers were required to attend the course. The students were to undertake the training until they were familiar with "the fundamentals of the elements of the Chinese spoken language."[3] Officers, as Charles L. Bolte would recall, were to take lessons for at least "an hour a day," five days a week, for one year, and then examined to see if they were qualified to be awarded the distinctive patch of interpreter.[4] This patch consisted of the Chinese character zhong, which when used with the character guo, represents China. The insignia was worn on the right sleeve of the blouse. It was to be removed, however, upon transfer to another duty station outside of the Middle Kingdom.[5] Paul L. Freeman recalled that his examination consisted of the instructor taking an ordinary Chinese from off the street and then telling the Chinese about bandits attacking a village. Students were then required to "interpret what he was telling us."[6]

Some officers became so interested in their studies that they continued even after completing the mandatory requirements. Lt. Col. George C. Marshall was proud of his abilities to learn the basics quickly. In a 1925 letter, he related that he had come out in the first section after less than one year of instruction, even though his classmates had had at least a seven-month head start.[7]

Newly arrived enlisted men were also required to learn some Chinese. These men, however, were required only to undertake a "selected vocabulary."[8] This amounted to about one session per week until they could recognize some of the tones. The Fifteenth Infantry's newspaper made much to-do about the average soldier's having to know some Chinese in order to be eligible for duty in China. In 1926, after disturbances in the Tientsin area, The Sentinel reported that it had become "very apparent" that non-commissioned officers who came into contact with Chinese soldiers should be able, "in a tactful and definite manner," to make their orders clearly known. To fill this "apparent" need, twenty volunteer enlisted men were selected

to take part in an experimental Chinese language
training program. The Sentinel reported that the
lessons proved an early success. At the Tongshan
Railroad Station, for example, a corporal who was
guarding a bridge reported that his knowledge of
Chinese made the civilian crowds in the area "seem
more friendly" toward the Americans. So that more
enlisted men would enroll in the program, volunteers were rewarded with visits to Peking and other
locations. The men successfully completing the
course were also awarded the zhong badge.[9]

The Fifteenth Infantry's program does seem to
indicate that one service was making an effort to
have officers and selected enlisted men learn at
least the rudiments of Chinese. Of course, the
program was undertaken to make military operations
easier, not for cultural purposes. Furthermore,
most military organizations reflect their
commanding officers' views. Unfortunately, when
Col. Reynolds J. Burt took over the Fifteenth
Infantry in 1931, the language program ground to a
halt. Burt felt Chinese was a "fool language," but
conceded that it would be useful for dealing with
tradesmen.[10]

In 1919, the army began to assign officers to
Peking for formal language courses. At nearly the
same time, a very few navy and marine corps
officers also began to receive assignments for
similar training, which usually meant an intelligence billet. There is no indication that enlisted
men were ever sent to such a formal program. If
rankers wished to learn Chinese, they could attend
classes at the YMCA on their off-duty hours or pick
it up on the streets. Evidence indicates that some
men did in fact undertake courses in the language.[11]

It is interesting to note that, while army
officers and some enlisted men were undertaking
required language training, of the 317 line
officers attached to the Asiatic Fleet, not one had
a Chinese language qualification. There were naval
officers who were listed as fluent in Spanish,
French, and Italian, but none in Chinese.[12]

In general, the officers and men who took
advanced course in Chinese or learned the language
from other sources were the ones who seemed to
appreciate China the most. Put another way, the
more one knew of the language, the less inclined he
seemed to make racist remarks about the Chinese.

An excellent example of this generality is marine officer Samuel B. Griffith II. Griffith attended the formal program in Peking. The marine spent at least six hours a day, five days a week, with a teacher.   At different times in the program, instructor and pupil would go out into a market in Peking for practice. The marine officer felt it took about fifteen months before he "had a hold" of speaking and another five or six months before he could read newspapers. Griffith was quick to point out that in no way was he ready for "classical Chinese" or Chinese philosophy. When asked what he found most interesting about duty in China, the officer replied, "Chinese people." Many years after his service in China, an interviewer remarked to the marine officer that the Chinese were corrupt and cruel, and Griffith responded with a very emphatic: "Oh no! I think that is terribly wrong." After his retirement from the Corps, Griffith received his doctorate from Oxford, with his dissertation being the difficult translation of Sun Tzu's classic work On the Art of War, written between 400-320 B.C.[13]

The regimental newspapers and magazines of the American military in China give one of the best indications of how the majority of Yankees felt about China and the Chinese. In almost every issue of The Sentinel during the early 1920s, the derogatory word "Chink" is used, along with "slant-eye." A good example of how many felt about the Middle Kingdom appears in a 1921 article by Corp. Vance Lyndale to all "griffins" (newly arrived soldiers to the East).   The corporal's first observation was that the griffins would not like China, because it was "not a white man's country." In fact, if the new men actually found a soldier who enjoyed serving in the Middle Kingdom, it would be evident that "there was something queer about him." Lyndale went on to warn the neophytes against liquor and women, both of which were "rotten." But, with enough fortitude, the soldiers would soon be on their way back to "God's country." Lyndale was careful, however, to point out that the Fifteenth Infantry was one of the best regiments in the army.[14]

Was Lyndale expressing the consensus viewpoint of the American military in China? With certain qualifications, it would appear so.   Without knowing more about the corporal, we can note the

year in which he wrote his comments, 1921, and
hypothesize that he was likely one of the soldiers
assigned to China at a time when there were few
volunteers for that station.   Soldiers everywhere
and in all periods of history tend to grouse quite
loudly about being sent to far-off places against
their wishes.   Given unhappiness about his assignment, Lyndale as an individual, would be unlikely
to take the time to learn anything about China and
the Chinese.

Lyndale's comments, however, do represent the
American military man's thoughts during the early
1920s, as revealed through his magazines and
newspapers.   As already noted, The Sentinel is
replete with racist words and bits of doggerel,
such as:

> There's a land far away,
> From the old U.S.A.
> On the shore of the great Yellow sea.
> Its [sic] the home of the Chink,
> And the place I dont [sic] think
> For a guy whats [sic] a white man.
>   See?

> Still there are some guys
> I'll admit its [sic] a surprise,
> Who try and stay more than two years,
> Yet the reason is quite plain,
> I have but to explain,
> There aint [sic] nothing above
>   their ears.[15]

Most importantly, The Sentinel continued to carry
Lyndale's diatribe, or portions of it, in
succeeding issues that were read by new arrivals to
the Fifteenth Infantry.

The reminiscences of many military men serving
in China reinforce Lyndale's view.   Edward J.
Ormiston recalled that his first impressions of the
Chinese were "far from complimentary."   Expressing
the view of a great many Americans, Ormiston felt
that the Orientals lacked moral standards, were
disease-ridden, illiterate, and poverty-stricken.[16]
At the time of his service in the Middle Kingdom,
Benjamin F. Draper did not think the Chinese were
very intelligent.[17]   Jack A. Wagner noted that many
military men felt the people of China were "highly
mercenary."[18]   The Sentinel noted that on payday,

the "cycle of gold it seems, starts in the mines
and ends in the hand of the chinks. We're only one
little station on its way to the slant-eyes."[19]
Albert Tidwell, however, probably best described
what happened to many military men in China.   The
former marine related that when he first arrived in
Peking, he felt like criticizing his fellow marines
for the way they treated the Chinese.   "The
terrible part of this thinking," recalled Tidwell,
"is that within a few months I too was considering
the Chinese as animals and not as fellow humans."[20]
    The differences between East and West were just
too great for most military men to overcome.   This
was especially true regarding the enlisted men, who
tended in general to have less education than their
officers.   The cultural baggage that most servicemen brought to China simply would not allow them
to rise above their stereotypes of China and the
Chinese.   Historian Robert McClellan has detailed
the evolution of America's stereotype of the
"heathen Chinee," stressing the inconsistency
of America's image of China.[21]   Until the early
1900s, the prevalent feelings were anti-Chinese,
due in large part to the resentment of cheap
Chinese labor displacing white workers in the
United States.   This hatred was fueled by missionaries, diplomats, journalists, and travelers who
brought back tales of cruelty, debauchery, and
poverty.   Furthermore, as McClellan argues, America
at this period was in the process of defining its
new identity as a world power.   China,with its
ancient civilization, had the potential to seem as
great or greater than the United States.   To
counter this threat to America's self-image, the
Chinese "had to appear as an inferior, backward,
and uncivilized race."[22]   By 1905, American
attitudes began to change once again.   The United
States, flushed with its victory in the
Spanish-American War, was now more sure of its
place in the world.   The Chinese were still held in
contempt, but American superiority was now
"expressed in more sophisticated ways," ways that
better conformed to a country with worldwide
ambitions.   Most importantly, if China were to be
opened for business and if missionaries were to
save the souls of the "heathen Chinee," a new way
of viewing the residents of the Middle Kingdom was
in order.   If the period prior to 1905 can be
called the age of contempt for China, then the

years from 1905 to 1937 may be dubbed the age of benevolence.[23] It should be recognized that the feelings of Americans toward China did not automatically change in 1905 for even during the period of "benevolence," there were still feelings of contempt.

The inconsistency and swings in perceptions of the Chinese are readily reflected in the comments of those who served in the Middle Kingdom. One army officer in the 1930s wrote that the Chinese were not terrible and, despite stories to the contrary, the average Westerner lived better in China than any other place in the world.[24] Burt, true to form, wrote to his sister that he felt the Chinese were harmless and were child-like in their seeking of praise.[25]

As the 1920s progressed, The Sentinel began to change its viewpoint. In 1925, for example, an editorial noted that the longer one remained in a country, the more one was inclined to see the good points of the country's customs. Furthermore, Lyndale's comments to griffins were dropped and replaced with columns on "things Chinese," which described many of the customs of the Middle Kingdom and gave histories of some of the towns and cities that soldiers were apt to visit. By the 1930s, the regimental newspaper was exhorting its readers to make an effort to travel and see China.[26]

Why this change? A number of reasons, other than those discussed above, can be put forth. General Connor's interest in China, as evidenced by his commitment to have troops learn the Chinese language, perhaps influenced the paper. As soldier-editors were transferred, so too the newspaper's viewpoint changed. It is enlightening to note that some of the most racist remarks appeared in The Sentinel when the chaplain was editor. Lastly, as the Fifteenth Infantry settled in for a long stay in Tientsin, its ranks were filled largely with volunteers, who would likely be less dissatisfied readers. A regimental newspaper will not continually print complaints about the duty if most of the men are satisfied with their station. All of this, however, does not mean that American servicemen lost their racism or began to love duty in China. That strong racism and dislike remained close to the surface is illustrated by a sailor's 1933 letter. "When I leave this place," wrote Ernie Place to his mother in Iowa, "I sure aint

[sic] coming back. I've seen enough of this yeller race to suit me awhile and some."[27]

Contributing to an environment of cultural misunderstanding was the fact that most American military men tended to live in enclaves, especially in the larger cities such as Tientsin, Shanghai, or Peking.   In the concessions or International Settlements, it was difficult to tell in what country one was residing.   Parts of Tsingtao, according to naval officer Henri Smith-Hutton, reminded him of a German city, due to that country's long involvement in the area.[28] The 1924 headlines of The Orient proclaimed that the citizens of Chefoo gave a large reception for the sailors of the American Asiatic Fleet. In the illustration accompanying the article, the only Chinese present are servants; all the "citizens of Chefoo" turn out to have been Westerners.[29] Soldiers, sailors, and marines could spend their entire time in these settlements and never enter the "native city." Thus, the men would not have to learn the language or the customs of the people. Barbara Tuchman has correctly noted that The Sentinel could have been published at any military post in the United States.[30]   Life, in other words, was conducted as if in any Western city.   The sailors of the South China and Yangtze Patrols were the military men most likely to mix with the Chinese, as their ports of call were in more isolated locations.   Even there, however, the men tended to frequent establishments run by Westerners.

In general, the combination of living in enclaves and not speaking the language caused the American military men to view the Chinese as simply a faceless mob and probably not even human.   This may help to explain why many servicemen acted as they did in the Middle Kingdom.   Most of the men and their wives, when interviewed about living in the Orient, commented upon the cheapness of life. Robert O.   Bare, recalled that when he arrived in Tientsin, the street poles were festooned with the severed heads of executed Chinese.[31]   One of the duties of the deck seamen on the Yangtze River gunboats "was to free floating bodies which had become trapped by the gangway."[32] After spelling out a number of examples of the cheapness of life or the strangeness of Oriental justice, however, other Americans would recall that most griffins

would go to great lengths to witness a beheading,
with The Sentinel reporting on one group walking
21 li (7 miles) to see an execution.[33]   Donald
Curtis' wife was struck by a rickshaw puller in a
dispute   over   the   fare   in   Shanghai's   French
Concession.   The woman fell and broke her leg.   For
this "serious crime," the puller was executed by
the French.[34] In other words, Westerners bore as
much responsibility for the cheapness of life as
did   the   Chinese.   The   Sentinel   ,   for   example,
gleefully   reported   a   soldier   laying   a   cigarette
paper   on   a   sleeping   Chinese's   hand   and   then
lighting it "to see if the Coolie would jump."   The
effect,   the   paper   reported,   was   "marvelous."[35]
Naval officer Glenn Howell related an incident of
two drunken sailors confronting a Chinese cobbler,
who had presented a bill to one of the men.   One of
the sailors said, "Why don't you throw that Chink
overboard?"   A   bet   of   two   dollars   was   wagered;
thereupon   the   hapless   Chinese   was   thrown   into   the
river and drowned.[36]   In a culture that venerated
its ancestors, Westerners were also callous about
the dead.   Howell reported that a golf course was
located in a graveyard, with the "greens being made
in . . . [the] spaces between the graves."
Earlier,   the   naval   officer   had   noted   a   Western
tennis court "in the very center of [a] cemetery
with graves all about it."[37]
    The evidence indicates that most military men
simply ignored the Chinese.   There were, however,
two exceptions to this generalization.   The first
deals   with   servants.   In   addition   to   the   "boys"
employed   in   the   barracks,   married   officers   had
servants   in   their   homes   and   also   had   rickshaw
pullers.   In short, a number of Chinese came into
daily personal contact with the American military
men   and   their   families.   For   many   Yankees,   all
their   perceptions   of   the   Chinese   were   based   upon
these servants.   The   oral   histories   and   written
records   of   the   servicemen   and   their   families
convey basically the same image of these menials:
they were obedient but very aloof.   Marine officer
Fred Beans remembered that he did not keep a key to
his own front door; the number one servant would
not permit it. Beans had only to ring the bell, at
any hour of the day or night, and within minutes
the man would be at the door.   No matter how sub-
servient the servant acted, however, the marine
officer felt he considered all Westerners barbar-

ians.[38] The servants could provide some surprises.
In a rage, marine officer Graves B. Erskine
threatened to whip his servant. The man never
flinched or changed his expression recalled the
marine; he just "bowed and said, 'Master, a
gentleman never loses his temper.'"[39]   Most
officers also commented upon the honesty of this
group of Chinese people, but related that theft,
according to Chinese law, was punishable by death.
Marine officer William F. Battell believed that the
people with the hardest life were the rickshaw
pullers. They had to remain available at all
hours. His "boy" received five dollars a month and
claimed to have a wife and seven children to
support. When Battell became sick and was confined
to the hospital, the rickshaw puller stayed by the
wall near the dispensary. The marine officer had
no idea where the man slept or lived.[40] While the
servants may have seemed aloof to Westerners, at
least they appeared human to them as well. This is
reflected in The Sentinel's editorial that decried
the practice of summarily dismissing unworthy
servants. The paper noted that just because these
people had no legal redress, this was not a good
reason to take advantage of them.[41]

Chinese were used for some rather amazing duties
in addition to cleaning and household duties.
In Shanghai, a man identified only as "Friday" had
the sole task of retrieving foul balls during
baseball games.[42] One should, however, not be
quick to criticize military men for these
practices. At a party given by civilian
Westerners, Howell felt something moving under the
table. He asked his hostess what was happening.
The lady, quite matter-of-factly, informed Howell
that as there were no screens in the windows, it
was highly probable that the guest's ankles could
be bitten by insects, so she was having the problem
corrected. The naval officer then peered under the
table and saw a Chinese crawling about, placing the
dinner guests' feet into bags.[43] In short, all
Westerners in China used the Chinese in demeaning
roles and many saw them as not quite human.

The records and reminiscences of the American
military men and their families record little
biographical information about Chinese servants.
But there were a few exceptions. The Fifteenth
Infantry and the marine corps in Peking each had
one Chinese man who appeared to be more than just

ordinary servants. Li San was born in Tientsin in July 1861.   He was first employed by the U.S. Government in 1892 at the American Legation in Peking and, three years later, was transferred to the military attache office, where he remained until 1900.   He "performed especially meritorious service" as a runner between Peking and Tientsin during the Boxer Uprising and worked briefly for Maj. Gen. of Volunteers Adna Chafee, the commander of the American forces during this period.   Li then returned to work for the military attache until 1912, when he was transferred to the Quartermaster Corps at Tientsin. In 1925, The Sentinel noted that it was "hoped by all who know him that he may. . . receive   recognition   of   his   service   by   some retirement." This, however, did not come about as Li died on duty, 29 June 1928, at Tientsin, leaving a widow and two minor children.   The Fifteenth Infantry's band escorted the funeral procession.[44]

To   the   north,   at   Peking,   the   marine   corps employed Chang Bon Shang, also in the Quartermaster Corps.   Chang was born in Tientsin in 1876 and attended Pei Yang College at the age of sixteen. In 1900, he acted as interpreter and purchasing agent at Tientsin.   He arrived in Peking with the American forces during the Boxer Uprising and was employed by the army until 1905 and thereafter by the marine corps.   In 1930, one service publication noted that Chang was held in "high esteem" and had a   record   of   "faithful,   capable   and   efficient service." Tidwell recalled that the Chinese man was "practically" the quartermaster for the legation. Chang died on 14 March 1935, and the Legation Guard Annual stated that most leathernecks in the capital thought of him "as more of a Marine than a native of China." The Annual went on to inform its readers that as an honor to Chang, the legation guard's band escorted his funeral.[45]

Preliminary   research   indicates   that   Chinese nationals serving as mess attendants and stewards aboard U.S. Navy ships were assigned service numbers, ranks, and personnel records.   In fact, some of these men retired from the navy without ever leaving the Asiatic Station.   I obtained permission from the U.S. Navy to examine the service records of fourteen Chinese who had served in East Asia during the period 1901-37.   Because of federal privacy law, however, the navy stipulated that no names could be used in any study based upon these records.[46]

This very rough evaluation of the fourteen Chinese serving aboard navy ships reveals that only one man listed a place of birth away from the larger coastal or river port cities. Ten of the men signed aboard in Hong Kong, Canton, or Shanghai. This is not surprising, as the larger ships, such as cruisers, would be in these cities and thus be able to ship more Chinese than a gunboat. One man signed aboard at Tientsin, while another began his career in Yokohoma, Japan, where his sister resided.

The average age at time of enlistment was twenty-five, with the youngest nineteen and the oldest thirty-three years of age. The occupations before enlistment may be inferred from a letter in one service record, which stated that the man had "served faithfully and well" in the capacity of "Boy" in the Hankow Customs Club, but was seeking new employment due to the "reduction of staff and [the] club's poor position."

Some of the new enlistees recorded their reasons for entering the service of the United States. The responses ranged from making the navy a career to bettering themselves and "retirement." The career patterns of the men seem to indicate that most did, in fact, want to remain in the navy. Of the fourteen men sampled, ten retired from the U.S. Navy, one received a bad conduct discharge (for concealing VD), one was not recommended for reenlistment after his first enlistment, one was killed in action during World War II, and one was missing in action and presumed dead. The career of one Chinese national serving in the U.S. Navy will have to represent them all until permission can be obtained to undertake further research on this subject.

The subject was born on 4 April 1877 at Ningpo. He signed aboard the Colorado on 30 September 1907 as a mess attendant third class. By 1 June 1909, he had reached the rank of mess attendant first class. At the end of the same month, he was moved from the enlisted men's mess to begin work as a wardroom steward.

He remained aboard the Colorado until 1911 and then received a series of three consecutive transfers to ships for less than a month each before arriving at his permanent berth aboard the Monadnock, an old double-turreted monitor stationed in the Philippines.   During his approximately four years of service aboard the Colorado, the mess attendant/wardroom steward's evaluations, or marks, for conduct were never lower than "excellent," and his proficiency was rated from "very good" to "excellent."   The reason for the transfer can be found in a letter in the man's service record, which noted that he was "not entitled to entry into the United States" when the ship returned to America, due to the Chinese Exclusion Act.

The wardroom steward served aboard the Monadnock until 1915.   In that year, his rank was changed to cabin steward.   His evaluations continued to be "very good" to "excellent," while his conduct never dropped to below "excellent."

In 1916, the cabin steward was assigned to the U.S. Navy Radio Station, Cavite, Philippine Islands.   He remained at this station until 1922, when he began service on the Yangtze River Patrol. His first assignment was in the flagship of the patrol, the Isabel.   He then served in the gunboat Palos.   On 20 March 1926, the cabin steward, while again serving in the Isabel, entered the Fleet Reserve, prior to being placed permanently on the retired list of the U.S. Navy.   He listed 1110 Bubbling Well Road, Shanghai, as his address in retirement.   At sixty years of age, on 15 November 1937, the retired cabin steward died at his home. His record indicates that he was married and had two children.

The use of Chinese as servants, however, also caused some men to look upon Orientals as less than human.   In fact, this attitude has also been reported by soldiers during the early Vietnam War era who employed locals as servants.   One soldier, for example, recalled that it made some men become "very arrogant," while others became benevolent, trying to learn more about the servant's family, and another group was "Just accepting the situation and enjoying the fact that they had somebody who was going to take care of all their Army duties."[47]

The very small segment of Americans who saw the Chinese as human had difficulties in continuing their friendships.   There were few public places for Westerners to entertain Chinese friends.   No Chinese, for example, were allowed in Western clubs except as servants.   This was not just an American rule, for, as marine officer James P. Berkeley reported, the British in Peking every year repainted a sign in their club that read: "LEST WE FORGET," which referred to the Boxer Uprising.[48] It is unfortunate that the military people who did try to understand the people of the Middle Kingdom left us so few written or oral records.

Most men serving in the Middle Kingdom also did not understand the political events that were swirling about them. Years after serving as an enlisted China hand, Richard McKenna, who wrote arguably the best novel of the navy in China, noted that he had not been aware of the political events happening along the Yangtze River during his China tenure.[49] Naval officer Henri Smith-Hutton recalled that most junior naval officers also had very little idea what was transpiring in China.[50] Articles in service newspapers indicate that most men were more interested in when restrictions on their passes would be lifted rather than in what was happening during times of unrest.[51] This lack of knowledge, however, was not altogether the fault of the various military commands. By the middle of the 1920s, regimental newspapers began to publish articles on what was happening in the Middle Kingdom. The Sentinel, for instance, ran a column by Maj. Joseph Stilwell on events in China. The army and marine corps scheduled lectures on events in their areas. Brig. Gen. Smedley D. Butler, commander of the Third Marine Brigade, in 1928 gave a speech to the marines on their mission in the Celestial Kingdom. This, of course, does not imply that the men actually read the information or listened attentively to the lectures. In 1925, The Sentinel reported that its circulation reached 60 percent of the Fifteenth Infantry. Whether this readership chose to read Stilwell's information or flipped to the sports or company gossip pages is unknown. The men on the river patrols had less chance of determining what was taking place around them, due to their isolation. These sailors had to depend on English-language newspapers or their commanding officers for information.[52]

Not only could American military men not fathom the Chinese culture; they also could not understand their military thinking. In general, servicemen either ignored the fighting taking place around them because, as one marine in 1932 noted, China had been fighting for at least twenty years, or they looked askance upon the quality of the Chinese troops and equipment.[53]   "We didn't have much respect for . . . Chinese soldiers," recalled marine officer George H. Cloud.[54] As the years progressed, however, some Western officers began to revise their opinions. Beans felt that the Chinese could make very good soldiers if properly led.[55] (One, of course, can say this about the troops of any country.) Marine officer Edward A. Craig noted that the Chinese were very good with trench mortars, which they used frequently.[56] William J. Scheyer recalled that "we could hardly believe the news" that Chinese forces had made a very stubborn defense against the Japanese attacking Chapei, a suburb of Shanghai.[57]

Even while giving these forces credit for their defense, Western officers still could not understand some of their actions. Beans noted that after the resistance at Chapei, the Chinese streamed through the International Settlement in Shanghai. The remaining rear guard was captured by the Japanese forces. In the vicinity of Soochow Creek, the Chinese would "throw their rifles down, and kneel right down and let the Japanese shoot them in the back of the head."[58] Robert E. Hogaboom recalled looking down from the roof of the Foohung Flour Mill and watching the fate of the Chinese troops. "As soon as [the Japanese] could capture [a Chinese soldier] they would bayonet him or have him lean over and . . . an officer would chop his head off with his sword, or they would shoot them right on the spot."[59] Soochow Creek at this point is approximately twenty yards wide, and contemporary photographs show the waterway literally clogged with bodies. Most American officers witnessing this killing could not understand why the Chinese did not try to escape.

Even though the American military men could not fathom the Chinese either culturally or militarily, the evidence suggests that they were more in sympathy with the Chinese than with the Japanese. This did, however, present a problem. Scheyer wrote that while his fellow marines' sympathy was with the Chinese in the current fighting, they wondered if an overwhelming victory against the Japanese might "boomerang" against Westerners. The well-known thoughts on extraterritoriality could cause "a jubilant army" to quickly train their attention on Americans. "[W]e might have been, and perhaps still are, sitting on a very dangerous powder keg," wrote Scheyer.[60]

Radioman First Class Henry J. Poy, a first-generation Chinese-American who served in China in the early 1920s. Photograph taken 1923-24. (Courtesy of U.S. Navy Historical Photogaph Center, NH 91394.)

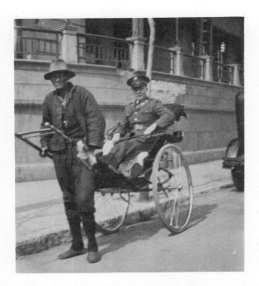

The soldiers of the Fifteenth Infantry in Tientsin wore tailor-made uniforms, and even privates carried swagger sticks. (Courtesy of Anthony Ingrisano)

Sgt. John T. White of the Mounted U.S. Marine Corps Detachment, Peking, China, 1931. The pack animal is carrying a machine-gun tripod. (Photograph courtesy of Clem D. Russell)

One of the favorite gathering places for the sailors of the Asiatic Fleet in Chefoo. (Photograph courtesy of Oliver G. Webb)

A Chinese sailor known only as "Guam" is typical of the sailors on the China Station in the period 1930-33. (Photograph courtesy of Oliver G. Webb)

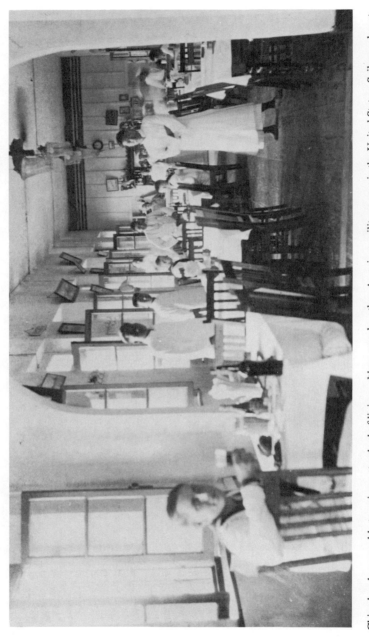

China hands were able to enjoy a standard of living seldom seen by other American military men in the United States. Sailors relax at a beachfront establishment in Chefoo in the early 1920s. (Photograph courtesy of Oliver G. Webb)

Fifteenth Infantry troops ferry equipment across a river, probably near Tientsin, ca. 1935-36. One of the problems facing U.S. troops in China was the lack of good roads and bridges. This and the fact that much of the countryside was highly cultivated prevented much-needed maneuvers. (Photograph courtesy of Arthur G. Gullickson)

Troops of the Fifteenth Infantry receive a salute from Chinese soldiers. The Chinese unit has been identified as the Nineteenth Route Army, known as the "Long Knives" for the *da bao* (beheading sword) they carried. (Photograph courtesy of Arthur G. Gullickson)

Some Fifteenth Infantry commanders stressed marching. Troops make their way through the countryside, probably near Tientsin, ca. 1935-36. (Photograph courtesy of Arthur G. Gullickson)

Troops wrestle with a wagon mired in the mud. (Photograph courtesy of Arthur G. Gullickson)

Harold R. Isaacs has written that our "emotions about the Chinese have ranged between sympathy and rejection, parental benevolence and parental exasperation, affection and hostility, love and a fear close to hate."[61] This love-hate relationship is excellently illustrated in the journals of naval officer Glenn Howell.

Howell, who has been extensively quoted throughout this study, was a prolific diarist. From his graduation from the naval academy in 1911 until his medical retirement in 1932, the officer made long entries in his journals. His observations fill over 135 thickly bound volumes. In addition, Howell wrote a number of articles concerning service in China for the prestigious U.S. Naval Institute Proceedings. Howell served three tours of duty in China, the first in 1916, the second as commanding officer of the Yangtze River gunboat Palos in 1920-22, and the last in 1925-27, in the Isabel, the flagship of the Commander of the Yangtze River Patrol.

Many of Howell's entries seem to indicate that he was a keen observer of the passing scene and enjoyed serving in the Middle Kingdom. In 1916, he wrote in his journal that he came to East Asia with the preconceived idea that the Chinese were a calm, impassive people. Instead, in Shanghai, he found an "active, eager, vivacious, and in the main, happy [people.] They are gregarious and I have never seen the family life adhered to so closely." In 1922, while serving in the Palos, there are references to Howell's arising early to watch in fascination the "stir of the crowds." As a sailor, however, the young officer particularly enjoyed observing life aboard the junks on the Yangtze River, which he found "always different, always the same, always interesting. [It] presents a moving picture of China and the Yangtze, reel after reel."[62]

When serving as skipper of the Palos, unlike many of his brother officers on the Yangtze Patrol, Howell made an effort to go out into the countryside and, because of this effort, was considered an expert on the river. He at one time organized an overland expedition in Szechuan [Sichuan] Province, from Heng-ch'ou [Hengchou] to P'ing-shek [Pingchen]. His observations of the people and sights are delightful. He saw the beauty of the land, in many cases "as if an artist

had begun a picture in the intention of sketching."
He found, as the sailors-turned-explorers continued
further inland, the people growing more and more
curious, for they apparently had seen very few
Westerners. Howell's comments on the Chinese,
however, were probably his best. He observed, for
example, a family gathering for a meal at one of
the villages:

> [T]he wrinkled, old grandmother who kept
> an alert eye upon the cooking but was not
> too much occupied to miss anything that
> was going on in her little world; the shy,
> quaint, small mother, with her baby unwink-
> ing [?] in her arm, its vivid red cap
> standing out as a blob of color; the little
> cheeseye [child] hiding behind his grand-
> mother and peeping out upon us; two hens
> pecking away at the ground; a pig grunt-
> ing comfortably near the fire; three ducks
> waddling about the place; two work dogs
> barking at the strangers; the man of the
> house dignifiedly at one side, inspecting
> us with expressionless eyes, smoking his
> long pipe with an occasional puff. 63

Three months after his overland expedition,
Howell spent a week at a Taoist Temple at Yolo-shan
[Yueyang]. He found the setting relaxing and
delighted in finding old objects in the area. He
located, for example, a Buddha in a cave behind a
temple and noted that the region had an "inexhaust-
ible supply of surprises, if one but has the
patience to seek them out." The naval officer also
devoted time at the temple to writing a play and
reading Chinese history.64

Howell's descriptions of China are worth
recording here. In 1921, he observed that the
country was overrun with soldiers. The people
desired peace, but until some man strong enough
arose there would be "this everlasting scrapping up
and down the land." In 1925, he felt that China
was on the threshold of great changes. At Hankow,
he wrote that it was no wonder that the poor of
China hated Westerners,

> who make it possible for thousands of them
> to exist [in poverty.] We, with our com-
> fortable food, our warm clothes, our

> leisure, our golfing, our riding while they
> pull, our overseeing while they work. The
> negro slave in the South before the War had
> an infinitely better time of it."[65]

From the preceding, Howell appears to have been
very attuned to China and the Chinese. And yet, the
man who could see why the poor of the Middle Kingdom would hate Westerners could also pen, one month
later, that the Chinese "are a lazy people. . . .
The moment a Chinaman gains sufficient money to
support him[self] he ceases to labor with his
hands."   Christianity was not "for these
exasperating people."   The Chinese, according to
Howell, were not capable of appreciating any of the
world's great religions.   "A joss or two, dimly
recognized and dimly and spasmodically worshiped is
apparently about the limits of their intelligence."
The naval officer also saw nothing wrong in beating
a rickshaw puller who shoved a white woman in a
fare dispute. In short, while Howell was, indeed,
above the average American military man in his
feelings about China and the Chinese, he could not
escape the cultural baggage he brought with him to
the Middle Kingdom.   The observations of the naval
officer are a revealing example of the love-hate
relationship of the West with China.[66]

If Howell was unusual for military officers in
China, then Henry J. Poy, an enlisted sailor, is
the best example of an anomaly among the men in the
ranks serving in the Middle Kingdom.   Poy was a
first-generation   Chinese-American,   born   in
Portland, Oregon, in 1902.   He had experienced the
strong prejudice against Orientals that was prevalent on the West Coast at the beginning of this
century.   During his high school years, he learned
Morse code and could operate wireless equipment.
At the age of sixteen, he lied about his age to
enlist in the navy.   The recruiting officer, once
he found that Poy was serious about entering the
service,   cautioned   him   about   the   hardships   of
living   in   cramped   quarters   aboard   ship   with
"intolerant shipmates."   When the recruiter found
that   the   young   man   could   operate   wireless
equipment, he signed him aboard.[67]

Poy served at a number of stations and arrived
in China in 1923 as an electrician's mate (radioman)   second   class,   a   senior   non-commissioned

officer's rank. This was unusual. The navy of the
1920s was a white one, with very few minorities.
In 1923, for example, there were 6,356 minority
personnel, 165 of them were Chinese and Chinese-
Americans, serving as enlisted men in the navy,
while whites numbered some 75,899.[68] Furthermore,
most of the Chinese who did serve in the navy were
servants of officers. Poy was, indeed, an anomaly.
The radioman's seniority kept many of the whites
from blatantly calling him "chink"; instead they
dubbed him "Confucius." Poy later recalled that at
least the "slur was of a little higher classifi-
cation."[69]

The young sailor tried to see as much of his
father's homeland as possible. On a trip to Peking,
he met a Chinese-American he had known in Portland
before the man returned to China to become an
officer in the Chinese army. Throughout his stay
in the Middle Kingdom, he was besieged by curious
Orientals and Occidentals. One group would ask if
he was really Chinese, while the other would
inquire if he was really in the U.S. Navy. Once,
while serving in the South China Sea Patrol, Poy
was granted a seventy-two hour leave to visit his
father's village. No sooner had he arrived than
there was a warning of a possible bandit attack,
and the sailor had to take his turn manning a guard
post. During the return journey, the ship he was
traveling in was attacked by pirates, and the
sailor managed to escape being captured or killed
by hiding in the coal storage hold and blackening
his face with coal dust.

As Poy's stay in the Middle Kingdom lengthened,
he began to be bothered by some of the sights he
observed. In 1924, for example, while serving in
the gunboat Pampanga, the radioman watched a group
of Chinese army recruits being drilled by a
corporal. The Chinese non-commissioned officer
began to become exasperated with some of the
recruits. The squad was marched to the riverbank,
where one man was ordered to break ranks and kneel.
Thereupon, the corporal drew his pistol and shot
the recruit in the back of the neck. "He [then]
kicked his body into the fast moving river." By
the time Poy had one year remaining in the Middle
Kingdom, the sailor would recall that he had become
accustomed to the traditions practiced in rural
China. He wrote that he no longer "wept at public
executions" and had become "hardened to the cruel-

ties meted out to the peasants." Poy felt that the people of Hunan, Hopei [Hebi], and Szechuan Provinces were "50 to 100 years behind" those living in the coastal areas.   In his written recollections of the period, even though he noted becoming "inured" to the unfathomable behavior of the Chinese people, there is an undercurrent of either shock or sorrow at being unable to quite grasp what he is observing in his father's country. His comments indicate a desire to return to the United States.

Perhaps one of the reasons for Poy's disillusionment is that his father's description was of the ideal China, and reality was simply too much for the young sailor. If, after one year, Poy--who could speak one dialect of Chinese and whose father had come from China--could feel shocked and anxious to return to the United States, then it would be unrealistic to expect other military personnel to react to China in a more sensitive fashion. In any event, one can perhaps better understand why many Americans could not grasp what they observed in China by reviewing the comments of this unusual sailor.

The thought of coming into a strange land, with no friends, must have made many young soldiers, sailors, and marines somewhat apprehensive and nervous. How then would a young woman, with two children, feel about entering China in the 1930s? Helen H. Chapel, wife of marine Lt. Charles E. Chapel, arrived in Shanghai with her family in 1933. When she first debarked into the swirling city, she was most "timorous" about typhoons, bandits, pirates, and disease. The Chapels lived in a temporary apartment until they found more permanent quarters in the French Concession, across from the French Army barracks.[70]

Chapel was at first afraid to venture out of her apartment, not because of danger, but because she was afraid of becoming lost in the bewildering maze of streets. She was surprised that Shanghai "is so very English and French" that she had difficulty in realizing that she was in China. The sight of beggars bothered her greatly and she noted that if one began to take an interest in "native life," one quickly beheld a person with elephantiasis and was quickly dissuaded from any further observation. However, she did report that Chinese architecture was interesting. Within three months, however, the

however, the young wife was writing that she was
not noticing the beggar and other things that formerly distressed her, although she was still put
off by the slow pace of Shanghai. In another three
months, Chapel was coming close to saying she loved
China and, in fact, rather enjoyed the smells of
the city, could ignore the dirt, and hardly noticed
the Chinese. When able to make a journey out into
the countryside, she wrote to her mother that it
reminded her of being in Illinois or Iowa.

Like the military men in China, Chapel's views
on the Chinese are interesting to note. Chapel
wrote her mother that she had never thought the
Chinese were capable of appreciating nature, until
one day she observed a group of coolies watching a
bird in a tree. Nearing the end of her stay she
was able to write that every place you live is
basically the same, with only minor variations. She
now felt that the Chinese were no different than
anyone else. Chapel now admitted she loved China,
respected the Chinese, and felt Westerners could
learn something from the older Chinese civilization. As far as Chapel was concerned, living
in Shanghai was the same as living in any major
city in the United States. Finally, when meeting
a new couple just arriving in Shanghai, she
indicated her complete transformation. The wife
of the new couple was nervous and scared to death.
Chapel wrote that this no longer made sense to her
and she felt safer in Shanghai than in the United
States. Helen Chapel's daughter, years later, was
to write that her mother's friends were mostly
marine officers' wives, while her father was the
one who mixed with the Chinese the most. Of the
three Americans we have observed, however, Chapel
seems, according to the available evidence, the one
who appreciated China and the Chinese the most.
Her accounts, once she became accustomed to the
country, do not contain the racist remarks found in
Howell's journals. There is no hint in her letters
of why this change came about, other than the
comments that she spent long hours at the window
observing the passing scene. One can speculate
that Chapel, perhaps, had a mind that was capable
of maturing the longer she remained in the Middle
Kingdom. Chapel was in China during a period of
low exchange rates, and there are constant comments
about the difficulties in making ends meet. Thus,
unlike many Americans in the country, money does

not seem to have been a factor in her love of the Middle Kingdom. Most of Chapel's letters that have been preserved were to her mother, and she would presumably tend not to put too many shocking statements in them. Thus, we may not have a completely accurate view of the young woman's perceptions of life in East Asia. On balance, however, it does appear that Chapel proved The Sentinel's observation that the longer one lives in a country, the more one appreciates it, to which should be added: provided that one has a mind capable of understanding what one is observing. Helen Chapel seems to have been a rare individual capable of understanding.

It would be wrong for the reader to believe that everyone who served in the Middle Kingdom hated China and the Chinese. If this were so, then, obviously, there would have been few volunteers for duty in East Asia. While there were many comments against the country in The Sentinel, the paper in 1928 also ran a contest in which soldiers submitted essays on "why I like China."[71] As pointed out elsewhere in this study, there were three broad groups of American servicemen in China: the largest contained those who simply put in their time, visited various sights, and returned to the United States after their tours of duty. To be sure, they enjoyed sightseeing and the high money exchange rate. Touring and more funds for off-duty hours, however, could be had in other countries. This group of men usually paid no attention to the Chinese, other than thinking of them as a strange and exotic people, and tended to see them as a faceless mob, a backdrop, so to speak. Paradoxically, most of the men who remained in China after their retirement or discharge belonged to this group. The retirees knew they could stretch their meager retirement stipends further there and still live in enclaves that were basically like the West. In short, there was no need for them to be anything but Americans. The second and third categories were in the minority. One group hated China and the Chinese and was extremely vocal about expressing its viewpoint. The last and smallest group of men serving in China included those who tried to understand the culture and people of the Middle Kingdom. Only a few of these men remained in China after retirement or the end of their service contracts. Many of the men, such as

Griffith, left to further their careers.

An examination of the views of American military men and their families on China shows that most did not understand the country and its people. The two largest reasons for this inability to comprehend the Middle Kingdom were the cultural baggage that most Americans brought to East Asia and the inability to speak the Chinese language.   Most military men looked upon the residents of the Celestial Kingdom as "stoical, fatalistic, with a kismetic twist coursing through their blood," and as "the despair of those who try to understand them."   In short, they were "incomprehensible."[72] In the lifetimes of many of the men who served in China, the attitudes of their countrymen toward the Chinese had swung from hatred to benevolence, and it is no wonder that many servicemen could not sort out their feelings about this far-off land and its people.   Military tour limitations and fluctu- ating assignments within China were secondary factors.   Naval officer Smith-Hutton correctly pointed out that because the sailors of the Asiatic Fleet spent so little time in each port, it was "impossible" to make friends with the Chinese. Others have also noted that two or three years in a country are not enough to learn about a culture.[73] It was, however, the mindset and inability to speak the language that caused the greatest difficulties. A lack of comprehension produced a lack of contact. As one naval officer put it, "we generally followed the British system of not associating with the 'natives,' unfortunately."[74]

NOTES

1. Charles G. Finney, The Old China Hands (Garden City, NY: Doubleday, 1961; reprint, West- port, CT: Greenwood Press, 1977), 17 (page refer- ences are to reprint edition).

2. W. D. Connor to The Adjutant General of the Army, file 350.03 AFC, folder "Countries--American Forces in China, 350.03 to 726.1," Box 1350, Record Group (RG) 407, Records of the Adjutant General's Office (AGO), National Archives, Washington, DC.

3. The Sentinel (Tientsin, China), 18 March 1927, p. 4.

4. GEN Charles L. Bolte interview by Arthur Zoebelin, Senior Officer Debriefing Program (SODP), Army War College (AWC), 1971-1972, Archives, U.S. Army Military History Institute (A, USAMHI),

Carlisle, PA.

5. GEN Paul L. Freeman interview by COL James N. Ellis, 29 and 30 November 1973, pp. 34-35, Paul L. Freeman Papers, SODP, AWC, A, USAMHI; Bolte interview, 36.

6. Bolte interview, 34; Freeman interview, 34-35.

7. Larry I. Bland and Sharon R. Ritenour, eds., The Papers of George Catlett Marshall; Vol. I, "The Soldierly Spirit," December 1880-June 1939 (Baltimore: Johns Hopkins University Press, 1981), 274-75); Bolte interview, 36.

8. The Sentinel, 2 December 1927, pp. 16, 24, 26.

9. Ibid., 23 April 1926, p. 433; 30 November 1929, pp. 1-2, 4.

10. As quoted in, Roy K. Flint, "The United States Army on the Pacific Frontier, 1899-1939," in The United States Military and the Far East: Proceedings of the Ninth Military History Symposium, United States Air Force Academy, 1-3- October 1980, ed. Joe C. Dixon (Washington: Government Printing Office, 1980), 149.

11. Freeman interview, 36; John N. Hart, The Making of an Army "Old China Hand": A Memoir of Colonel David D. Barrett (Berkeley: Institute of East Asian Studies, 1985), 2; The Walla Walla (Shanghai), 16 September 1933, p. 10, lists language courses at the Navy YMCA in Shanghai. Besides Chinese, Russian and Spanish were also offered. The Legation Guard Annual, 1935, 37, lists sixty-four students of Chinese language in Peking.

12. Register of the Commissioned and Warrant Officers of the United States Navy, 1923 (Washington: Government Printing Officer to 1923), passim.

13. BGEN Samuel B. Griffith II interview by Benis M. Frank (1970), 41-43, Oral History Collection (MCOH), Marine Corps Historical Center (MCHC), Washington, DC. The dates I have used are from: Samuel B. Griffith, Sun Tzu The Art of War (New York: Oxford University Press, 1963), 11.

14. The Sentinel, 22 April 1921, p. 1.

15. Ibid., 26 August 1921, p. 3.

16. Edward J. Ormiston, China Service Questionnaire (CSQ) to Dennis L. Noble (DLN), 10 August 1984.

17. Benjamin F. Draper, CSQ to DLN, 11 August 1984.

18. Jack A. Wagner, CSQ to DLN, 11 August 1984.

19. The Sentinel, 7 October 1921, p. 12.

20. Albert Tidwell, CSQ to DLN, 14 July 1984.

21. Robert McClellan, The Heathen Chinee: A Study of American Attitudes Towards China, 1890-1905 (Columbus: Ohio State University Press, 1971), 250.

22. Ibid., 248.

23. Ibid., 253. I have used Harold R. Isaac's chronology for the various ages of American perceptions of the Chinese. The various ages are the following:
1) The Age of Respect (Eighteenth Century)
2) The Age of Contempt (1840-1905)
3) The Age of Benevolence (1905-1937)
4) The Age of Admiration (1937-1944)
5) The Age of Disenchantment (1944-1949)
6) The Age of Hostility (1949-   )
Harold R. Isaacs, Scratches on Our Minds: American Images of China and India (New York: John Day, 1958), 71.

24. Paul Caraway to Forrest Caraway, 5 December 1935, "Personal Letters, 1935-1938"; Caraway to [mother], 5 May 1938, ibid., Paul W. Caraway Papers, A, USAMHI.

25. Burt to [sister], 25 December 1933, "Personal Correspondence," Reynolds J. Burt Papers, A, USAMHI.

26. The Sentinel, 16 January 1925, p. 5; The Sentinel, 1930s, passim.; The Walla Walla also ran similar articles on Chinese matters. For example, "The Chinese Funeral Procession," 19 December 1936, pp. 21-22.

27. Ernie Place to Mr. and Mrs. D.C. Place, [parents], 6 August 1933, "Miscellaneous Folder #2," Kemp Tolley Papers, China Repository (CR), Naval Operational Archives (NOA), Naval Historical Center (NHC), Washington, DC.

28. Captain Henri Smith-Hutton interview by John T. Mason, Jr. (1976), 130, Oral History Program, U.S. Naval Institute (OHNI), Annapolis, MD.

29. The Orient (Shanghai), 18 August 1924, pp. 1, 6, 7.

30. Barbara W. Tuchman, Stilwell and the American Experience in China, 1911-1945 (New York: Macmillan, 1970), 98.

31. LGEN Robert O. Bare interview by Frank, (1968), 16, MCOH.

32. Papers of Henry J. Poy, CR, NOA; Mrs. Roy C.

Smith, Jr., interview by John T. Mason, Jr. (1986), 162-64, OHNI.

33. The Sentinel, 18 April 1924, p. 6.

34. BGEN Donald Curtis interview by Frank (1970), 39-40, MCOH.

35. The Sentinel, 25 February 1925, p. 14.

36. "The Log of Glenn Howell," XXXIX (1925), 10,857, NOA.

37. Ibid., XIII (1920), 1,853; ibid., XXXIX (1925), 10,804.

38. MGEN Fred D. Beans interview by Frank (1971), 38, MCOH.

39. GEN Graves B. Erskine interview by Frank (1970), 159-60, MCOH.

40. MGEN William F. Battell interview by Frank (1971), 67-68, MCOH.

41. The Sentinel, 26 September 1924, p. 5.

42. The Walla Walla, 13 September 1930, p. 5.

43. Papers of Glenn Howell, CR, NOA.

44. The Sentinel, 19 June 1925, p. 3, 30 June 1928, pp. 5, 27.

45. Legation Guard Annual, 1930, 54; Legation Guard Annual, 1935, 40, 42; Tidwell CSQ.

46. All service records are located at The National Military Personnel Records Center, St. Louis, MO.

47. Al Santoli, Everything We Had: An Oral History of the Vietnam War by Thirty-three American Soldiers Who Fought It (New York: Random House, 1981), 7-8.

48. LGEN James P. Berkeley interview by Frank (1971), 103, MCOH. Ormiston reported that he changed his mind about the Chinese as he spent more time in China. Ormiston CSQ.

49. Eva Grice McKenna and Shirley Graves Cochrane, eds., New Eyes for Old: Nonfiction Writings by Richard McKenna (Winston-Salem, NC: John F. Blair, 1972), 8-10.

50. Smith-Hutton interview, 28.

51. Legation Guard Annual, 1931, 21; The Walla Walla, 12 March 1932, p. 17; The Sentinel, 21 November 1924, p. 8.

52. Adolf B. Miller,"Diary," 4 February 1928, Papers of Adolf B. Miller, Box 2, P.C. 196, Personal Papers Collection (PPC), MCHC; The Sentinel, 17 April 1925, p. 4; 17 December 1926, 1,344; November 1927, passim.

53. William J. Scheyer, "Diary," 4, Papers of William J. Scheyer, P.C. 115, PPC, MCHC.

54. MGEN George H. Cloud interview by Frank (1970), 42, MCOH.

55. Beans interview, 29.

56. LGEN Edward A. Craig interview by Frank (1968), 54, MCOH.

57. Scheyer, "Diary," 7.

58. Beans interview, 30.

59. LGEN Robert E. Hogaboom interview by Frank (1970), 127, MCOH.

60. Scheyer, "Diary," 15.

61. Isaacs, Scratches on Our Mind, 64.

62. "Log of Howell", II (1916), 414-15; XI (1921), 3,311-12; XIII (1921), 3,922-23; XLI (1926), 1,050.

63. Ibid., XIII (1921), passim.; IX (1921), 2,430; IX (1921), 2,367-68.

64. Ibid., X (1921), 2,831-32.

65. Ibid., IX (1921), 2,423-24; XXXIX (1925), 10,998; XL (1925), 11,132.

66. Ibid., XLI (1926), 11,248; XL (1925), 11,140-41; XXXIX (1925), 10,857.

67. Papers of Henry J. Poy, 21 November 1984, CR, NOA. Finney also relates an incident involving a Chinese-American who served with the Fifteenth Infantry in the 1920s. Finney, Old China Hands, 85-97.

68. Frederick S. Harrod, Manning the New Navy: The Development of a Modern Naval Enlisted Force, 1899-1940 (Westport, CT: Greenwood Press, 1978), 183.

69. Unless otherwise noted, all materials on Poy are in: the typewritten reminiscences of Henry J. Poy, undated and unpaged, Henry J. Poy Papers, CR, NOA.

70. Unless otherwised noted, all material on Chapel is located in: Helen H. Chapel Collection, Accession number 840214, PPC, MCHC.

71. The Sentinel, 23 December 1928, pp. 12, 29.

72. The Walla Walla, 22 August 1931, pp. 18.

73. Smith-Hutton interview, 30. Others who made comments on not having enough time to learn about the Chinese were: Beans interview, 29; Erskine Erskine inteview, 160; MGEN William A. Worton interview by Frank (1967), 165, MCOH.

74. This officer wishes to remain anonymous. His questionnaire remains in the possession of Dennis L. Noble.

6

GOING ASIATIC: SERVICEMEN WHO REMAINED IN CHINA

In the first three decades of the twentieth century, the phrase "he has gone Asiatic" was a common
part of the military lexicon.   The term had two
broad connotations, neither was altogether flat-
tering.   A serviceman in East Asia who had eccentric ideas or plans was said to have gone Asiatic.
(It should be noted, that while the phrase was
apparently derived from service in the Middle
Kingdom, it was eventually applied to anyone in
the entire military establishment who was somewhat
odd.)   The largest use of the term, however, dealt
with those men who decided to remain in China.
Former sailor George St. Lawrence recalled a shipmate,   Boatswain's   Mate   Leo   Bauman,   who   was
nicknamed "Chino Ah Hee."   The boatswain's mate had
spent at least fourteen years in China, and "his
only fear was receiving orders to the U.S." Bauman
dressed in traditional Chinese clothing whenever
possible and spoke excellent Chinese.   "He paused
long moments when speaking English as if he [had
forgotten] the language."[1]   In 1931, a leatherneck
stationed in Peking, while packing for his return
to the United States, dejectedly remarked: "Home,
hell,   this   my   home,   I'm   going   to   a   foreign
country."[2]   The   above   two   men   are   excellent
examples of servicemen who would have been labeled
as   "going   Asiatic."   Many   Westerners   did   not
consider   it   entirely   proper   to   accept   Chinese
culture.   Those men who wished to remain in East
Asia were looked upon as somewhat odd.   To ration-
alize this decision, some Westerners implied that
only drunken retired military men would ever choose

to remain in China.   This viewpoint, in large measure, is the one that has persisted.   Most oral tales and written fiction of the military in the Middle Kingdom have servicemen spending long years on the China Station, retiring, and either opening a bar or living a life of dissipation. This myth of service life needs some reexamination.

As word began to filter from post to post and throughout the fleet that service in China meant short duty days where even a private could have a servant and exotic delights for the taking, more and more men began to volunteer for duty in East Asia.   One way to remain in the Middle Kingdom was by voluntarily extending a tour.   From 2 February 1923 to 23 November 1923, thirty-one men either extended or reenlisted to remain with the Fifteenth Infantry.[3]   There were other ways that a man could remain on the China Station.   Kemp Tolley recalled that a few dollars slipped to a chief yeoman could keep a sailor in the Asiatic Fleet, if the chief was adept at his paperwork.[4]

The army made much of the Fifteen Infantry being composed of volunteers.   Military mythology has held that, in general, personnel serving in China were long-service men.   At first blush, a regiment of experienced soldiers may seem to be desirable. A longer reflection, however, will show that such an organization can be very weak, especially if it does not include adequate training.   Beginning with Brig. Gen. William D. Connor, commanders began to worry that the Fifteenth was, in fact, becoming a command of old and out-of-shape soldiers.   Charles G. Finney recalled that in 1927, the non-commissioned officers of the regiment had developed a system of helping men retire in China.   A sergeant would know a fellow non-com in the United States who had two to three years remaining before retiring with thirty years of service.   The man would be told of the pleasures of serving and living in China.   Then, an unhappy younger sergeant could be found who did not care for duty with the Fifteenth.   A mutual transfer would be arranged for both men to move in grade.   The newcomer would finish out his last few years, then talk a master or first sergeant to step down for a day, thus allowing him to retire at near top pay and take up with other retired sergeants in the Tientsin area.[5]

Brig. Gen. Joseph C. Castner felt that something needed to be done to stop the regiment from becoming a resting place for older non-commissioned officers. In a 1927 letter to the Adjutant General, Castner stated that allowing long tours of duty in China was "a serious error on the part of the War Department." In order to prove this rather strong statement, the general ordered ninety-nine long-tour servicemen to undergo extensive physical examinations. The checkups revealed sixty-six as "defective," with twenty-four of them "recommended" to return to the United States. Castner felt that soldiers sought long China tours in order to "continue cohabiting with low caste Chinese, Japanese, and Korean or Russian women, and to indulge freely in intoxicants and narcotics." Even before receiving a reply from Washington, the general noted that he had already suspended granting extensions to long-tour men and requested the Adjutant General's help in keeping the men from returning to China by circulating notices to recruiting officers that certain classes of men were no longer desired on the China Station. On 24 February 1927, the suggestion was implemented. Men who had served in East Asia would not be considered for reassignment there for a three year period.[6] Yet, despite the desire of the War Department and the regimental commander to pare down long-tour China service men, there were still ways to circumvent regulations. In 1933, for example, Col. Reynolds J. Burt complained to the Adjutant General that "many old reenlisted men and men who have served before in China" were still being ordered to East Asia. Thus, even when the army attempted to reduce the number of long-tour China service men, it was not completely successful.[7] The marine corps conducted a similar plan to weed out the old China hands, with similar results.[8]

The drive to have effective, combat-ready troops is understandable. There was, however, another factor influencing some commanders to oppose long-tour servicemen remaining in China. Castner's 1927 communication succinctly spelled out a very strong concern. The general noted that many of the servicemen marry "low caste [Oriental] women . . . lowering the prestige of all Americans in the eyes of the orientals and everybody else."[9] In other words, most enlisted men who chose to retire in China must have gone completely Asiatic to consider marrying a woman from East Asia. This attitude was not too surprising, given the tendency of officers of that day to see enlisted men as little more than grown-up children, as well as the prevailing mind-set among many that Caucasians were the superior race.

Some enlisted men harbored attitudes similar to their leaders' and looked askance upon marriage to a Chinese. They often concluded that anyone who desired either to remain in the Middle Kingdom--with some exceptions that will be detailed later--or to marry an Oriental had to be completely Asiatic. This attitude led to some strange and amusing fears on the part of many men serving in East Asia. An undercurrent of worry runs through the few diaries of those who served in the Middle Kingdom that they might themselves be going Asiatic. In relating this uneasiness, one must understand that for most American military men in China, even those with college educations, what we would now call "culture shock" was too great for most to comprehend. In fact, it was the rare individual who desired to understand the country where he was living. Added to this was the mindset of the period that Asians were inferior. There-fore, if a soldier, sailor, or marine began to state that he wished to remain in China, then, according to the preceding beliefs, there was cause to worry that he might have slipped over the edge of sanity.

Another worry was that, the longer one remained in China, the better the chance that one would become much like the Chinese, who were viewed as deceitful and corrupt. As Howell put it, he would be glad when his tour was finished, for he "didn't [care] to become a confirmed Easterner." Part of becoming a "confirmed Easterner," as many saw it, was to yield to the temptation of making illegal money. Most military men in China were familiar with the system known as "squeeze." Navymen on the Yangtze River, for example, saw merchants charge the navy for, say, one hundred pounds of coal, but deliver only ninety-nine pounds. The merchant then would sell the other pound for an additional profit. This type of transaction seemed hideous to Westerners of the period, and "squeeze" was used as proof of the devious ways of the Chinese. Yet Westerners in China were equally corrupt. Howell, for example, recorded in his diary that he was once offered "ten thousand dollars" if he would not search the gunboat he commanded for opium on her scheduled trip to Shanghai.   He refused, and a search of the <u>Palos</u> revealed that the drug had, in fact, been secreted aboard. The officer immediately launched an investigation.   A chief boatswain's mate had not resisted the chance to make a large sum of money.   The stress of the undertaking eventually proved too much for the chief, and he was returned to the United States for psychiatric examination.   Interestingly enough, the crew had learned of the hidden drugs before Howell and had, on their own, thrown most of the contraband overboard.[10]

Were the men who decided to remain in China drunkards and wastrels, as Castner and other officers felt?   There is no doubt that this in fact describes many.   There is also evidence to support another view, however.   Earlier in this work, a number of reasons were put forth about the difficulties of researching enlisted men. If researching active-duty men is a difficult undertaking, then obtaining information on retired enlisted men is doubly hard.   Once the men left the active list, they seem to have disappeared completely.   Only a few have been brought half-way into the light of history by brief mentions by former China hands and the reminiscences of officers.   In both cases, however, we must be careful with these observations, as they may reflect only the stereotype of the retired China hand.   One other caveat must be placed upon the discussion of those men who decided to remain in China.   Strangely missing from the mythology of the military men in the Middle Kingdom is the fact that many servicemen who remained were not retired, but had left the armed forces before their thirty years.   Some, in fact, obtained special discharges or bought their way out of the military in order to remain in China.   In short, not every former serviceman in the Middle Kingdom was a retiree, which weakens the argument that only drunken long-term servicemen would care to remain in East Asia.   Some men stayed in the Orient for a more "respectable" motive than drunkenness and inertia--to enter into an accepted business venture.   Throughout the United States' contact with East Asia, there has always been the dream of riches from the China market.   In fact, the dream persists into current times.   If a military man stated that he was remaining in East Asia to enter into business, this would have been understood

better by the Occidentals living in China. The
reaction would have been much different if the man
stated that he simply liked the Orient and wished
to remain there. In the following discussion of
why servicemen remained in China, I have included
both those who retired and those who simply took
their discharges to live in the Middle Kingdom.
Since both types have been used interchangeably to
make up the mythology of former military men in
China, it is best to discuss both groups.
Furthermore, I believe that both groups, in the
end, remained in East Asia for similar reasons.

The reasons that some men decided to remain in
China are diverse. Former marine Corp. David Adix
stated that he would enter into business in
Shanghai. Virgil Findley and his wife also decided
that in 1930 a business career in the bustling city
of Shanghai offered a good opportunity. Pfc. C.
A. Belief, a former editor of the Fourth Marines
news magazine, The Walla Walla, received a special
discharge to take up a position on the Mercury
Press in Shanghai. Still another marine with a
journalistic bent, John E. Lusignan, joined the
advertising staff of the China Press in 1932.
Ex-Pvt. P. J. Campbell joined another ex-marine on
the staff of radio station XGKO in Shanghai. Floyd
Franklin Glass, a navy chief printer (a rating that
took many years to reach) decided to end his naval
career and received a special discharge in order to
start The Orient, a newspaper for rankers on the
China Station.[11]

A few enlisted men were successful enough
entrepreneurs to have been mentioned in the
recollections of those who served in China, and we
can thus glimpse some of these otherwise forgotten
men. One was an ex-soldier by the name of Jimmy
James, who left the Fifteenth Infantry shortly
after World War I. He tried a number of positions,
including U.S. Assistant Deputy Marshall in
Shanghai in 1923. The following year, he began to
sell sandwiches to sailors when the fleet was at
Chefoo. When the Asiatic Fleet moved to Manila in
winter, James would move back to Shanghai.
Eventually, he set up a restaurant located next to
the YMCA on Szechwan Road in Shanghai that catered
to American servicemen. His business was so
successful that he opened a chain of eating establishments. Many old China hands who served in
Shanghai recalled with great nostalgia the times

they spent in the ex-soldier's restaurants.[12]

Marine enlisted man Frank Gowan became successful in Peking by a slightly different method than James. Gowan also took his discharge in China, but married into the German family of Richard and Anna Hempel. The family had a thriving hotel, butcher shop, and restaurant in the capital city. Because of the son-in-law's former association with the corps, Hempel's became a favorite watering place for non-commissioned marines. Gowan established the tradition of the "Knights of the Round Table," whereby if one could drink a liter of beer in one quaff, one's name would be placed on a silver label affixed to a round table. In any event, Gowan was able to pursue a successful career in Peking.[13]

Not all of the men who remained in China were as well remembered as James or Gowan. Most were simply small shopowners, bartenders, or worked for some large organization. In 1926, Howell noted that he had met a man by the name of Wokinsin who was the agent for Standard Oil Company. Wokinsin had first come to China in 1919 as a chief yeoman in the Asiatic Fleet. A chief commissary steward, known only as "Jingles," had retired and ran a restaurant in Hong Kong. Another chief commissary steward ran a bakery and gave out baked goods to former gunboat sailors. Garry L. Murphy recalled that one of his retired navy friends obtained a "position as a U.S. Marshall." A former soldier ran a dry-cleaning establishment in Tientsin. Tolley recalled a former chief who ran an ice plant in Chungking.[14]

True to mythology, many of the men did open bars that catered to Western military men. In fact, along the Yangtze River ports, many of these bars were run by an ex-navy man, and when he died or quit, the establishment would be taken over by another ex-sailor. The operation of these drinking establishments that depended upon sailors or other military men was not considered an approved type of business by most of the Western society that lived in China.

There were, of course, some retired men who chose not to work. Finney detailed what he knew about a man he called Msgt. George Smith. Smith was born in 1872 and had enlisted in 1893. He had been involved in combat operations during the Boxer Uprising and, later, during the Punitive Expedition into Mexico in 1916. He spent a number of years in various posts, returned to the Fifteenth Infantry in 1920, and retired three years later. Finney found that Smith broke the stereotype of the hard-drinking sergeant. The former non-commissioned officer enjoyed books, and the young soldier would spend many evenings with him discussing the works that they had read.[15]

Finney, in describing the lives of retired Fifteenth Infantrymen, noted that many of the men settled down with Chinese women to become "old married men." Some "even went through marriage ceremonies."[16] Former navy enlisted man C. W. Lavine recalled a navy chief petty officer who had married a Chinese woman and then returned to the United States. After receiving his retirement from the service, the chief returned to his wife and opened up "Bud's Place," a bar that was a favorite of the Monocacy's crew in Hangkow.[17]

Marine officer Fred Beans recalled that "a lot of Marine officers . . . were planning to retire to Tientsin or Peking."[18] Current research, however, has uncovered only four recorded instances of U.S. military officers remaining in China. Howell noted in his journal that he knew of a former "poor naval officer" who was let go in 1914. The man went to law school and decided to practice in Shanghai. By 1926, he was "a successful lawyer with a good income."[19] The Sentinel, reported that in 1922, Lt. John D. Moore, a veterinarian, was leaving the army after seven years of service to take up practice in Tientsin.[20] Donald R. Fox, Jr., recalled a former navy dentist practicing in Shanghai, and Glen R. Smith remembered an officer who lived in Peking.[21] While there were undoubt-edly more officers who either returned to the Middle Kingdom or left the service and remained in China, their proportionate numbers were never as high as those of the enlisted men. Again, this is not too surprising. As mentioned earlier, for an officer to remain in one location for a long period could cause harm to his career. Furthermore, most officers who served in China were already married with established families. It would have taken a great deal of fortitude to give up the security of a career to remain in China. Most importantly, however, many officers saw themselves as either middle-class or upper-middle-class, and to remain in the Middle Kingdom would be living below what they felt was their station in life.[22]

Why did enlisted men choose to remain in China and be labeled Asiatic? Most of the rankers during this period--from 1901 to 1937--were poorly educated and, in many cases, came from poor families. Even if they retired from the military in the upper non-commissioned ranks, the amount of money they received would not be enough to live comfortably in the United States. Where else could an enlisted man, with only a few hundred dollars in pension, live as well as in China? Finney has noted that in 1927, retired pay for senior non-commissioned officers was around four hundred Chinese dollars a month. The men would give their Chinese women perhaps one hundred Chinese dollars a month for an allowance to run their apartments. This small amount "represented wealth, when one considers that the average coolie in Tientsin. . . grossed less than eighteen dollars American a year."[23] Thus, living in East Asia offered a chance for financial security that they could not find in their homeland.

For the men who left the service before retirement, their inducement to remain in China was very close to that of those who retired. There was very little chance for them to be able to rise above blue collar status in America. China, however, seemed to them the place to break out of their economic stratum. Some men took advantage of this opportunity and carved out comfortable niches for themselves; others squandered their chance and succumbed to dissipation. No matter which route these enlisted men traveled, it is interesting to note that, so far as it can now be determined, none of them lived in the hinterlands or took Chinese citizenship. The men may have lived in the Chinese section of an international settlement, but they never really left the security of a Western settlement. As pointed out earlier, living in a foreign concession was not unlike living in the West. Many of the enlisted men, however, were never assimilated even into the Western society in the settlements. Those who chose to operate bars, or not work at all, remained on the outside of this culture-within-a-culture. Thus, there seems to have been a complicated culture-within-a-culture-within-a-culture in the Middle Kingdom. Again, this is not really too surprising when one recognizes that the American military, generally, has always been considered a society of its own outside of mainstream America, and this was simply carried over into China.

One other connotation of the term "going Asiatic" needs comment, and that deals with eccentric behavior. When one studies the actions of some of the leaders of the military establishment in China, one is struck with what can best be called the strangeness of decision-making. An excellent example is the plan by Brig. Gen. Smedley D. Butler. There was always the realization among marine officers that, should a major battle be encountered, the leathernecks would not be able to use the roads, since they would be clogged by fleeing civilians. In order to provide clear access for the troops, one plan was formulated to have a horse-drawn wagon loaded with money proceed up a road, with currency dribbling out of the cart. The crowds would flock in the direction of the withdrawing vehicle, while the leathernecks would proceed unhindered in the opposite direction.[24]

The marines had been sent to China amidst a large amount of publicity about the imminent danger of the "yellow peril" to the Western concessions. When the expeditionary force landed in Tientsin, Finney and other soldiers marveled at how efficiently the leathernecks were able to land and quickly set up defensive positions. Soon after arrival, Butler inspected the Fifteenth Infantry's honor guard and was impressed by their smartness. He returned to his headquarters and called a meeting of his officers. Years later, marine officer Joseph C. Burger recalled that Butler's first orders to his officers were "to collect all bayonets and have them nickel plated [and] shine all eyelets on the packs. . . .[I]t sort of burst the balloon about being a big expeditionary force."[25]

In a 1927 letter to the Commandant of the Marine Corps, Butler wrote that he wanted to spruce up the marines in order to compete with the British troops in the area. He assured the Commandant that "no outfit of Marines were ever licked yet," and he intended to be victorious in waging this war of spit and polish.[26] Butler's obsession with showmanship became so legendary that, during an air show when a marine fighter aircraft lost both wings, the spectators applauded the pilot as he floated to earth in his parachute--they thought it was simply a part of the exhibition. "Trust Smedley," said one woman, "to put on a fine show."[27]

Butler, however, was not the only officer to have strange ideas or eccentric ways of operating. According to navy officer George Van Deurs, Adm. Charles V. McVey's only interest was "the proper personal honors and his golf score."[28] Army Col. Burt, of the Fifteenth Infantry, who has been described as "an old fuddy duddy," had a fetish for his troops looking spruce at inspections and ceremonies. Burt claimed to have written a march entitled "Kings of the Highway." The music, of course, was required at every function of the regiment. The band quickly grew weary of playing the piece, and when Burt departed China, the band played the song as his ship pulled away and "then threw the music into the water." The colonel, on another occasion, became visibly shocked that the post exchange would sell condoms, a strange attitude for a man who worried about the VD rate of the regiment. Burt's successor, Col. G. A. Lynch, was so caught up in the New Deal that a local house of ill repute posted a sign in its window that proclaimed: "NRA, we do our part."[29]

One of the navy's more colorful officers serving in China was Earl Winfield Spencer, first husband of Wallace Warfield who would become the Duchess of Windsor. Spencer had an appetite for cigars, liquor, and adventure. The naval officer eventually died from a stab wound. As the commander of the small gunboat Pampanga on the South China Patrol, he would undertake rather unusual missions. Once, when trying to determine the future intentions of some pirates, he took his radioman, Henry J. Poy, aboard the buccaneers' ship as an interpreter. The two men were armed only with cigars and a weak cover story. The only plan known to Poy was that if the two sailors did not return within a specified time, the gunboat was to come full speed ahead and attack the pirates. Fortunately for Poy and Spencer, they were able to gather the information without any damage, except to the enlisted man's nerves.[30]

Normal operating procedures in some areas of East Asia, especially aboard the gunboats operating on the rivers of China, had a bizarre nature. James P. Clay remembered "potato piloting" on the Pearl River [Zhu Jiang] during foul weather. A sailor was placed in the bow to throw potatoes as far as possible: "When no splash was heard, you were too close to the beach." The _Mindanao_, a gunboat that drew only seven feet of water, used a man in the bow with a bamboo pole instead of a lead line to take soundings.[31]

Each of the officers discussed above must have seemed somewhat Asiatic. Whether these men were affected by duty in China is difficult to assess. Butler, for example, was always attracted to anything "flashy"; that is, he looked for anything that would catch the eye of his superiors and, of course, further his own interests.[32] Furthermore, not all of his ideas were as preposterous as the money scheme. Being unconventional could, in fact, be an advantage in China. The river gunboats, for example, were required to operate in areas without guidance and with very small crews. Not every situation, contrary to the beliefs of some senior officers, can be covered by naval regulations, and an officer who could think for himself could be an asset. Some of the officers were probably no more eccentric than others back in the United States. In the States, these men could be tucked away in isolated posts or auxiliary ships. In China, however, there was no place to hide them and they were much more visible. There is no current evidence that the War Department or the Navy Department deliberately chose officers who thought unconventionally for service in East Asia.

The men who went Asiatic and remained in China were, in general, enlisted men. Not all of those who chose to live in the Middle Kingdom were retired military men. In fact, there were probably more who simply finished their enlistment, took their discharge, and did not return home. Although myth has branded these men with a drunken image, the reasons they remained ranged from wanting to start a business to a desire to continue a life of dissipation at the lowest possible cost. Even if they could not verbalize the underlying reasons for not returning to their homeland, the common factor was that they realized that there was very little chance to succeed at home and that China at least offered a glimmer of hope for some type of success. Furthermore, on a practical note, the men who did retire in China from the military were able to live on at a much higher level than was possible in the United States. Some of these men, as Howell correctly noted, continued to live neither "in society or its borders." Perhaps, in the final analysis, this is what many of them desired; after all, they had never really been a part of main-stream America. If this was their goal they succeeded admirably. Most of the old retired China hands have slipped behind the veil of time into complete anonymity.[33]

NOTES

1. George St. Lawrence, China Service Question-naire (CSQ) to Dennis L. Noble (DLN), 6 June 1984.

2. The Walla Walla (Shanghai), 5 December 1931, p. 1.

3. The Sentinel (Tientsin, China), 7 January 1921, p. 1, 22 August 1924, p. 3, 8 February 1936, p. 1. In 1922, the tour of duty on destroyers was eighteen months, but by 1934 line officers with the rank of commander and above could expect two-and-a-half years on station. A marine would serve the same amount of time. Fleet Review, 13, no.1 (January 1922): 15; "Roster of United States Asiatic Fleet and Stations," 1 October 1934, Record Group (RG) 80, General Records of the Department of the Navy, National Archives, Washington, DC. Data are derived from The Sentinel, 2 February 1923, to 23 November 1923, passim.

4. Letter, Kemp Tolley to Dennis L. Noble, 20 February 1987.

5. Charles G. Finney, The Old China Hands (Garden City, NY: Doubleday, 1961; reprint, Westport, CT: Greenwood Press, 1977), 250 (page references are to reprint edition).

6. J. C. Castner to Adjutant General, 17 January 1927, "Countries File, China", Box 483, RG 407, Records of the Adjutant General's Office (AGO), National Archives. The 27 February 1927 letter is included as an enclosure to the file with Castner's 7 January 1927 communication.

7. R. J. Burt to Adjutant General, 12 October 1933, Countries File, China, Box 483, RG 407. In a 29 November 1933 memorandum to the AGO, J. M. Cummins, Acting Assistant Chief of Staff, noted that perhaps Burt was exaggerating in his complaint. Cummins noted that only four "old reenlisted men" had been sent to Tientsin and "obviously," this number "would not have any serious effect on the efficiency of the 15th Infantry." The memorandum is part of enclosure to

Burt's 12 October 1933 letter.

8. "I remember when I got out there, there was a movement going on . . . I can remember Jerry Thomas . . . Erskine and . . . Vandegrift talking in the office and saying, 'We've got to start weeding out these guys [who have been in Peking too long].'" LGEN Robert B. Luckey interview by Benis M. Frank (1973), 80-81, Oral History Program (MCOH), U.S. Marine Corps Historical Center (MCHC), Washington, DC.

9. Castner to Adjutant General, 17 January 1927, Countries File, China, Box 483, RG 407.

10. RADM George Van Deurs interview by CDR Etta-Belle Kitchen (1974), 241-42, Oral History Program, Naval Institute (OHNI), Annapolis, MD; "The Log of Glenn Howell," VIII, 6 September 1920, p. 1963, 13 September 1920, p. 1976, 9 November 1920, pp. 2,150-55; ibid. X, 7 April 1921, pp. 2,821-22, Naval Operational Archives (NOA), U.S. Naval Historical Center (NHC), Washington, DC. The opium incident is also reported in: Glenn Howell, "Opium Obligato," U.S. Naval Institute Proceedings, 64 (December 1938): 1,729-35. Some interesting cases involving military men who fell prey to the chance for easy money are found in: MGEN Omar T. Pfeiffer interview by MAJ Lloyd E. Tatem (1968), MCOH.

11. The Walla Walla, 16 August 1930, p. 5, 16 April, 30 September, 10 December, 1932, p. 5 in each; The Orient (Shanghai), July 1924, p. 10. Military men, of course, have not ceased to remain in the Orient, and many of the reasons for remaining away from the United States are still the same as for the old China hands. A popular work on the subject is: Mike Sager, "Thailand's Home for Wayward Vets," Rolling Stone, (10 May 1984), pp. 27-28, 33-34, 36-37, 72.

12. Kemp Tolley Papers, "Miscellaneous", China Repository (CR), NOA.

13. Clem D. Russell, CSQ to DLN, 5 July 1984; 1LT Joseph E. Johnson interview by COL Joseph B. Ruth (1977), 50-51, MCOH.

14. "Log of Howell," XLI, 7 February 1926, p. 11,311; William R. Hardcastle, CSQ to DLN, 5 September 1984; Lawrence VanBrookhoven, CSQ to DLN, 2 July 1984; Garry L. Murphy, CSQ to DLN, 28 June 1984; Glen R. Smith, CSQ to DLN, 23 July 1984; Tolley CSQ.

15. Finney, in general, chose not to use the correct names of the enlisted men he wrote about

and instead used composite descriptions.   Finney
stated that he last communicated with Smith in 1938
and did not know the ultimate fate of the ex-soldier. Finney, Old China Hands, 252-57.

16. Ibid., 255.
17. Papers of C. W. Lavine, CR, NOA.
18. BGEN Fred D. Beans interview by MAJ Thomas
E. Donnelly (1971), 80, MCOH.
19. Howell, "Log of Howell," XLIII, 7 July 1926,
p. 11,550.
20. The Sentinel, 8 December 1922, p. 5.   Moore
died in Tientsin in 1935. The Sentinel, 7 December
1935.
21. "Colonel Love, US Army retired lived in
Peking and was a student of ancient Chinese art."
Smith CSQ; Donald R. Fox, Jr., CSQ to DLN, 21
August 1984.
22. The major exception to this generalization
is Col. David D. Barrett who spent twenty-three
years, in a career that spanned thirty-five years,
in China. John N. Hart, The Making of an Army "Old
China Hand": A Memoir of Colonel David D. Barrett
(Berkeley, CA: Institute of East Asian Studies,
1985), xi.
23. Finney, Old China Hands, 255.
24. Subject File: 1911-1927, ZK File/Box 799,
Marine Corps 3rd Brigade Under General Smedley D.
Butler, U.S.M.C., RG 45, Naval Records Collection
of the Office of Naval Records and Library,
National Archives.
25. LGEN Joseph C. Burger interview by Frank
(1969), 33, MCOH. On nickel plating see: GEN
Vernon E. Megee interview by Frank (1967), 49-53,
MCOH.
26. Brig. Gen. Smedley D. Butler to Maj. Gen.
Cmdt. J. A. Lejeune, 22 April-5 May 1927, Smedley
D. Butler Papers, P.C. 54, Personal Papers Collec-
tion (PPC), MCHC.
27. Robert Sherrod, History of Marine Corps
Aviation in War II (Washington DC: Combat Forces
Press, 1952), 28.
28. Van Deurs interview, 50.
29. GEN Charles Bolte interview by Arthur J.
Zoebelein (1971), 40, 67, Senior Officers
Debriefing Program, (SODP) Army War College, (AWC)
Archives, U.S. Army Military History Institute (A,
USMI), Carlisle Barracks, PA.
30. Papers of Henry J. Poy, CR, NOA; "West River
Pirates," China Gunboatman (Spring [19]86): 6.

31. James P. Clay, "Pearl River Log: A Different Navy, A Different World," U.S. Naval Institute _Proceedings_, 115, no.   12 (December 1970), 60, 63.   Kemp Tolley is currently editing a newsletter on the South China Patrol, _The China Gunboatman_, which is an excellent source of short information on the patrol.

32. For material on Butler's love of showmanship, see: Pfeiffer interview, 85-86; GEN Vernon E. Megee interview by Benis M. Frank (1967), 49, MCOH, MCHC.

33. Letters were sent to each of the divisions that dealt with retired personnel of the armed forces, requesting information on how many men had retired in China during the period 1901 to 1937. Each service responded with a negative answer to this inquiry.   Furthermore, Dr.   Stephen E. Bower and Dr. Marilyn A. Kindred, historians of the U.S. Army Soldier Support Center, Fort Benjamin Harrison, Indiana, stated that "they knew of no one that had or was looking for this type of information."   Letter, Truman R. Strobridge, Historian, Joint Chiefs of Staff, to Dennis L. Noble, 8 April 1988.

7

LAND THE LANDING PARTY: INCIDENTS REQUIRING A SHOW OF FORCE

One of the myths of the China Station is that of landing parties rushing ashore to rescue missionaries from the "yellow peril." Most of the servicemen on the China Station perpetuated the story of military men bravely performing rescue missions, only to be rejected by those they were rescuing. A glance at the record, however, indicates that this point of view needs to be examined in more detail. On the one hand, there is some reason to question the accepted myth. On the other, the record also shows that the United States kept her armed forces in China busy in operations requiring a show of force throughout their years in the Middle Kingdom. The marine corps, for example, records a total of at least twenty-eight landings from 1905 to 1934.[1] The 1920s saw the largest use of troops. China was swept with revolution and warlords. The efforts of Chiang Kai-shek to reunite the country caused further strife. Indeed, the period was one of change and dramatic confrontations. Richard McKenna, with his novelist's eye for tension, chose the 1920s as the period for his work The Sand Pebbles, rather than the 1930s when he actually served in East Asia. The 1920s are also one of the few periods in Sino-American relations closely examined by American military historians and other writers. Bernard Cole, Kenneth W. Condit, Edwin T. Turnbladh, and Kemp Tolley have all more than adequately covered the military activities during this time frame, especially along the Yangtze River.[2] The information available thus allows us either to confirm or dispel the myth of landings under fire.   Rather than attempt to cover every incident of possible combat, only a few operations representative of what the soldiers, sailors, and marines faced in China will be discussed.   Because missionaries are generally central to the stories of servicemen on rescue assignments, this chapter will also discuss how these emissaries of God were viewed by the men of the American military.

The sailors of the navy who were most likely to be involved in landing operations entailing risk were those serving on one of the river patrols. This is not to say the men serving in the larger ships of the Asiatic Fleet did not face dangerous situations.   Jack A. Wagner, for example, recalled a landing at Chefoo in which the sailors of the Finch were marched up a narrow street directly into machine-gun fire, "but the Chinese gunners did not have tracers and did not know their fire was going over our head."[3]   Nevertheless, the men serving on the river gunboats were in the isolated locations where most missionaries were serving and thus were most likely to be called upon for assistance. Indeed, one of the symbols of this period is the ubiquitous gunboat.   Contrary to myth, very few of the situations in which American troops were landed actually required the firing of weapons.   This is illustrated by an incident that took place in Hunan Province in June 1920.

In the fall of 1917, Gen. Wu P'ei-fu's forces entered Hunan, via Yochow [Yueyang], and drove back the troops he encountered.   Shortly thereafter, Gen. Chang Ching-yao [Zhang Jingyao] was appointed military and civil governor.   Three years later, Wu began to pull his troops out of the province.   There ensued a struggle between Wu and Chang over whose troops would remain, with Chang claiming some divisions from Wu's army.   In the meanwhile, troops from the south, under Gen. Tan Yen-kai [Tan Yangai], began to advance as the northern troops began their withdrawal.   In the manner of most warlord retreats and advances, the hapless towns in their path were thoroughly pillaged.   Astride the path of Chang and Tan was a college of the Reformed Church of the United States at Lakeside, near Yochow.[4]

On 13 June 1920, the looting of nearby Yochow began in earnest.   On the same day, a squad of eight men, later identified as belonging to Chang's

Seventh Division, approached the mission compound. Rev. William A. Reimert, the acting president of the college, and George Bachman, another missionary, met the soldiers at the gate. When they found that the men wanted food, the missionaries agreed to their request and engaged them in "friendly conversation." The soldiers then said that they would like to enter the compound. This request was denied by the missionaries. The soldiers no longer requested but now demanded entry. Again they were refused. The squad leader then issued orders, and the soldiers divided into groups on each side of the entry gate. In almost the same instant, a volley was fired through the gate, instantly killing Reimert, while Bachman managed to dive to safety. The soldiers then forced the Chinese gatekeeper to open the entryway, and the two squads entered, firing "promiscuously" at anyone in sight. The entire staff quickly sought cover, as the gunfire continued for several hours. Bachman, however, managed to get a message off to the mission at Yochow requesting help. After tiring of shooting, the soldiers then looted the houses of the president and other staff members, and then withdrew sometime during the night. Early the next day, the women and children of the college began to escape to Chengling [Jiangling].

Meanwhile, the mission at Yochow in turn sent a letter to the governor of the province and to the Chinese military commanders of the brigade in the vicinity. On 14 June, a Chinese officer and twenty-one men arrived and established posts around the college. Later in the same day, another officer and men arrived, inquiring if the mission needed any further protection. A few hours later, yet another group of soldiers arrived. The missionaries were by now fearful that each new group arriving might find something wrong with the other and start fighting among themselves, with the Westerners caught in the middle.

The next day, the original guard was withdrawn and replaced by four lieutenants and ninety-six men. A major soon arrived with information that most of the troops would soon be retreating, but he was attempting to make arrangements with the advancing army for troops to relieve the present guard.

While this was taking place, information about trouble near the college finally filtered to the

American forces.   On 15 June, the gunboat Quiros
got underway from Changsha and arrived at Lakeside.
Immediately upon arrival, a landing force was put
ashore to guard the college.   As more information
became available, the American gunboat Villabos was
also dispatched to the area.   When the full nature
of the event became known, the destroyer Upshur
sped to the scene and landed forty additional
sailors. Other Western nations also sent gunboats
to the Lakeside area.   Eventually, once the area
was felt to be in the "reliable" hands of a southern Chinese general, all the landing parties were
recalled and the ships weighed anchor.

The incident at Lakeside is typical of the
actions undertaken by gunboats and other landing
parties of the navy during this period.   To be
sure, there were actions, such as at Nanking in
1927, where forces were under fire and had as much
action as any novelist would desire.[5]   In the
main, however, the presence of a gunboat and its
landing party were enough to deter any untoward
actions.   This is not to deny that armed landing
forces faced some real danger each time they went
ashore.   Indeed, in most instances, the sailors
encountered large, angry crowds greatly outnumber-
ing themselves.   This type of situation is never
pleasant.

Sailors, however, faced more gunfire directed at
them while aboard their ships than ashore.   The
logs of navy craft plying the Yangtze River are
replete with incidents of shots fired at them and
of return fire.   The log of the destroyer John D.
Ford is typical: "repeatedly fired upon by machine
guns. . .; returned fire with machine guns, rifles,
and seven 4" shrapnel [rounds]; no casualties
sustained by material or personnel; casualties
among enemy unknown."[6]   The fire at the ships was
both directed and random.   The ships, as a symbol
of Western power, were a convenient target for
those who wished to fight this power.   The vessels
were also large targets for the random firing of
roving bandits.

The sailors, soldiers, and marines had some
advantages that helped compensate for their fewer
numbers.   Most of the warlord leaders and Chiang's
troops realized that any firing upon the Americans
would bring the combined forces of the West down
upon them.   Indeed, during the incident at Lakeside, the commanding officer of the British gunboat
Bee, promised to support the other gunboats with

"every gun and man available."[7]

Another factor helping the soldiers, sailors, and marines in difficult situations was the mindset of the Americans. American military personnel felt that they were superior to the Chinese. While they may have had a few moments' thought as to the wide disparity in numbers between them and the Chinese, there was no doubt in their minds that they could handle any incident between whites and Orientals. The sight of confident, armed troops, no matter how small a group, does produce a psychological advantage over large crowds, as many demonstrators in contemporary times have found.

The small gunboats plying China's rivers also had a reputation for meeting situations in rather unorthodox ways. Lt. Comdr. Earl W. Spencer, commanding the gunboat _Pampanga_ on the South China Patrol, offered an excellent example of methods that were not in the navy regulations manual. Spencer was colorful enough, but he was able to accomplish some of his missions because of an unlikely crewman--an enlisted man by the name of Henry J. Poy. The tactics Spencer employed are illustrated by an incident that took place on the West River [Xi Jiang] near Canton in 1927.[8]

The Standard Oil Company reported that one of its junks had been pirated 250 miles up the West River. The _Pampanga_ received instructions from the South China Patrol commander to proceed up the river and to attempt to locate the craft. When the small gunboat reached the suspected area, Spencer decided to use Poy in a shoreside spy mission to locate the junk. A small boat was outfitted with a machine-gun and a group of armed uniformed sailors were to escort the radioman, who was dressed as a worker. The sailors were to proceed up a tributary of the West River to near where the pirates were believed to be in hiding.

The boat reached its assigned location and the radioman-turned-undercover-agent was put ashore after learning how to signal for help in case of an emergency. Poy had first to fight his way through tall grass with all the strength in his "140-pound frame." He then came upon a security guard who took the disguised sailor to the main camp, which turned out to be in a cave. With a very skeptical group of pirates eyeing him, Poy spun out his cover story: one of the crewmen aboard the junk was member of his family. The wife of the missing man was very sick and needed him at home. Could the pirates at least inform him as to the whereabouts of the junk? The leader of the brigands informed Poy that the craft had left for unknown ports upriver. The man then carefully searched Poy, taking whatever money he had on him, but then allowed him to depart.

Sixty years later, the former radioman recalled that as he nervously made his way back to the beach for his pickup, he kept expecting to be shot. Poy reached the beach and signaled for the boat. Suddenly, someone shouted, "Mei-kuo ren [Americans]," which caused the sailor to run to the boat, but no shots were fired. Once aboard the dory, Poy finally relaxed, because behind the cover of the "machine gun squad I had no more fear." The record is strangely silent about the ultimate fate of the junk.

The Fifteenth Infantry's period of greatest testing came during the years from roughly 1924 through 1927. The area around Tientsin became a focal point in the fighting of three opposing warlord armies. Lt. Col. George C. Marshall had no more than arrived at his new duty station at Tientsin than he was thrown into active service. Throughout his nearly three years with the Fifteenth Infantry, Marshall's letters would mention the "sound of the guns booming." The best description of the situation facing the soldiers was penned by Marshall: "We are either just out of near trouble with the Chinese or trouble is hovering near us."9

What Marshall and the regiment were in the midst of was the ebb and flow of the continual battles of the warlords. In 1924, Chang Tso-lin [Zhang Zuo-lin], Wu P'ei-fu, and Feng Yu-hsiang were wrestling for control of what today is Hopei Province. Chang was the warlord of Manchuria, Feng (also called the Christian General) commanded Shansi [Shaanxi] Province, and Wu had Honan. Wu also felt he was the commander-in-chief of the army and navy of China. In 1924, Wu began the process of taking over Manchuria, and Feng agreed to cooperate with him in his conquest. Wu was to have one army at Shanhaikwan to start the attack, while Feng's men moved through Jehol [Liaoning] Province and another of Wu's armies started west of Shanhaikwan. The three-pronged drive would, according to Wu, settle the affairs of Chang.10

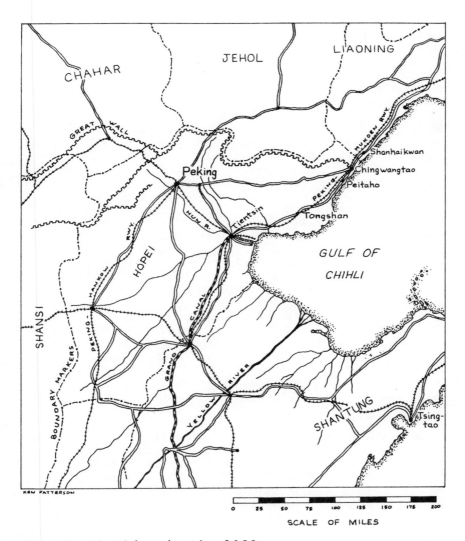

Map. North China in the 1920s.
Note: Geographical locations are given in the Wade-Giles system in use at the time.
Source: Ken Patterson

A glance at the map of North China reveals that Tientsin, with its railroads and nearby seaports, was bound to be caught up in the machinations of the warlords. Thus, most of the Western residents of the city were uneasy as the troops began their movements.   On 23 October 1924, Wu was at Shanhaikwan, ready to launch his attack into Manchuria, when he learned that the Christian General had made other arrangements. Feng instead marched into the now militarily abandoned Peking and proclaimed himself the senior man in North China. Wu's second army, west of Shahaikwan, refused to attack Chang unless something were settled about this new development. Wu now faced Chang's strong and efficient army alone. In a vicious engagement, Wu's troops were completely routed. The retreating army then collided with Feng's troops west of Tientsin, and this finished any fighting spirit left in the collapsing army. Wu managed to reach Taku and escaped aboard a ship.   His troops, however, were not so fortunate.[11]

The three armies tore at each other. Chang's and Feng's men fought Wu's army, after which they fought each other.   In short, as one former Fifteenth Infantryman put it: "King Chaos reigned."[12]   Nearby this melee, sat the city of Tientsin, rich with food, clothing, and other items, beckoning both defeated and victorious troops. To meet the expected invasion,the international forces stationed in the city established a series of posts around it. Their orders were to prevent the armed soldiers, no matter which army, from entering Tientsin.

The Fifteenth Infantry's area of responsibility stretched some seven miles, covering canals, dikes, a branch of the rail line, and assorted bridges and roads. Four outguards, or posts, were established. These posts were also stocked with food caches of rice, cabbage, and tea. The idea was to stop the warlord soldiers and inform them that they could not pass into the city with their arms. If they wished to give up their arms, they would be given food and allowed to proceed--in other words, food for guns. Further, food would be given if the troops elected to proceed around the city. Scattered between the outguards and the city were small lookout posts manned by a corporal and two privates.   They were to monitor the soldiers proceeding into the city. Meanwhile, the main body of the regiment was kept in its barracks as a reserve, ready to move out if one of the outposts needed assistance. The scattering of the outposts kept Marshall, an inveterate horseback rider, constantly in the saddle. At one time, he claimed to have ridden at least twenty-five miles a day on his rounds, which he considered "good fun and instructive."[13]

Each of the outguards was, for the time and place, adequately equipped. Post number 2, manned by Company E, for example, was under the command of a senior sergeant, who had at his disposal two squads of men, two Browning Automatic Rifles, one heavy Browning water-cooled machine-gun, twenty-one Springfield rifles (said to have been one of the best infantry weapons in the world) and five Colt .45 automatic pistols. All in all, this amounted to a formidable amount of firepower. There was, however, a catch: the sergeant had the only live rounds, and these were for his pistol--the remainder of the outpost's complement was provided with blank ammunition. Headquarters was worried that someone might become too excited and fire without orders, thus plunging the United States into a large-scale fight with the warlords. The troops were to use a combination of bluff and bribery to divert the rag-tag soldiers they might encounter.[14]

Bluffing could cause some tense moments. Marshall related that "many of the officers carried out their missions . . . with guns or knives pointed at their stomachs."[15] In one case, for example, Capt. William B. Tuttle commanded a truck with nine enlisted men. Tuttle was to investigate the report of a large group of warlord soldiers entering the American defense zone. As the truck advanced along a road-dike, at least five thousand warlord troops were seen advancing over the field. Tuttle halted the truck, ordered his men to remain with the vehicle, and began walking out to meet the Chinese. When they observed the truck, the warlord soldiers fixed bayonets and continued toward the spot where Tuttle stood. In Chinese, Tuttle shouted a command to halt, which the troops, surprisingly, obeyed. While the soldiers on each side nervously watched, with the Americans perhaps a bit more worried, the American captain parlayed in Chinese with his opposite number. After a long period of wrangling, the warlord soldiers withdrew.[16]

Similarly, Matthew B. Ridgway received orders to take as many men as needed and, with "bluff, expostulation or entreaty," turn aside some twelve thousand of Chang's troops. The officer thereupon picked two men and shadowed the Chinese all day on horseback.[17] It was Tuttle, however, who earned the distinction of being immortalized by the regiment's unofficial poet. "Tuttulius at the Dike" honors the captain for the above situation and others where his coolness did prevent possible disasters.

. . .

"Sound the Alert, Saphonius
And do not lose your head.
If you and I should blunder
We're all as good as dead.
But on the Dike an Army
May well be stopped by three
Now who will stand on either hand
And keep the Dike with me?"

Then outspake Koch Sargeutius.
Of German stock was he;
"Sir, I will stand on thy right
    hand.
And keep the Dike with thee."
Then outspake stout Perrilius
A corporal proud was he,
"I will abide on thy left side
And keep the Dike with thee."

. . .

The vanguard of the Chinese horde
Had crossed the Racecourse Road;
Tuttulius gave, "As Skirmishers,
Fix bayonets and load."
The Kuominchun gazed scornfully
Upon the dauntless band,
And brave Tuttulius was annoyed
To see how promptly they deployed
At one short sharp command."

'Twas then that Bill Tuttulius
Made the play that on the war
For on the sullen Kuominchun
He loosed his Chungua hua-erh.
His tones were well ... [neigh]
    perfect
And filled them with chagrin;

The Army in awed silence stood
While Bill's lips poured forth
   a flood
of purest Mandarin.
     . . .
He used expostulation.
Entreaty, threat and bluff
Until the men from Kalgan
At last cried out, "Enough!
You may keep your prized concessions
Until we come again
Show us the way to Hai Niu Cheng"
And Bill replied, "Tsai Chien."

So Bill returned a hero
To hear his praises sung;
For oft we tell how his Chinese
Turned back the host of Feng.
And when, a few weeks later
George held a Chinese test
To see which ones should graduate
He passed Bill with the rest.[18]

Enlisted men also proved adept at bluffing. At
outpost number 2, commanded by a sergeant, the
American infantrymen were startled to see well-
dressed mounted men approaching. Sitting astride
Manchurian ponies were troopers in dark green
uniforms. Each man had a long lance that rested in
a socket by his stirrup and carried a long da bao,
the Chinese beheading knife, in a scabbard strapped
to his back and unsheathed by reaching over the
left shoulder.   The troops proved to be White
Russian lancers employed by Chang.
The troopers halted in front of the sergeant's
position. They

drew their Mauser pistols, affixed the
grips of them to their wooden holsters
which were shaped like rifle stocks, and
thus made . . . 9mm submachine guns out of
the weapons. They sat their ponies, lances
steadied in left hand, Mausers held in
right hand and rested across the pommel. In
back of each trooper's left ear, the haft
of his beheading knife thrust up.[19]

Even these well-trained and impressive troops were
turned aside.   The Fifteenth Infantry was also

responsible for providing a guard detail, along
with other Western nations, on the Peking-Mukden
train between Tientsin and Peking.   Furthermore,
there was at least one company to guard the rail
center at Tongshan.   Here, at the rail center, in
October 1925, the guard sheltered the employees and
families of the nearby Kailan Mining administration.[20]

Train guard details could prove dangerous. The
journey of October-November 1924 included Lt.
William Johnson and fourteen enlisted men, plus one
officer from each of the international garrisons in
Tientsin.   The first problem encountered centered
on the inabilities of the Japanese and American
officers to communicate with each other.   Eventually, an arrangement was made whereby an interpreter was found.   Then it was discovered that the
French   officer   could   speak   neither   English,
Chinese,   or   Japanese.   The   British   officer,
however, came to the rescue and managed to trans-
late.

At one point in the journey, Johnson spotted two
Chinese   soldiers   leaping   aboard   the   locomotive.
When the train slowed, Johnson vaulted from the
car, ran to the engine, and climbed the ladder.   A
man stood with his back to him blocking Johnson's
way   and,   when   the   man   refused   to   move,   the
lieutenant shoved him.   The   soldier   turned,   and
Johnson found himself staring into the muzzle of a
luger.   The second man in the cab held the crew at
bay with his pistol.   The   American   lieutenant
attempted   to   have   the   engineer   stop,   but   the
railroad man was more inclined to listen to the man
holding the pistol.   Later, Johnson was informed
that the trackside was littered with bodies, but
the officer reflected that his mind was on other
matters and he had not noticed.

The train was eventually stopped at a station,
and the Chinese warlord commander requested entry
into the troop cars while escorted by his personal
bodyguard. Johnson refused, but said that both he
and   the   commander   could   enter   together.   The
American   officer   and   the   warlord   had   no   sooner
begun their tour of the cars when the voice of the
British officer was heard shouting: "Don't fight,
don't fight, hold your ground, my lad!" At almost
the same instant, the strident voice of a private
left to guard the entrance was heard shouting for
the lieutenant.   Both Chinese and American officers

rushed to the entrance, to behold the entire body-guard "with leveled pistols trying to get past Pvt. Reynolds." The warlord called his men to attention and then made a show of shaking hands to indicate friendly relations. The remainder of the journey was somewhat anti-climatic.[21]

The professional performance of the soldiers of the Fifteenth Infantry caused no incidents during the long period of unrest. The work that the men accomplished is commendable; at times, there were hundreds of thousands of troops swirling past the outguards. Close examination of the duties illustrates just how narrow the gap between success and disaster really was. The attitudes of the American troops also exemplify the mindset of the Westerners. That is, the soldiers of the Fifteenth Infantry had so little respect for the Chinese that, although badly outnumbered, they felt that there was very little danger in their assignments.

The work facing marines in Shanghai, Peking, and, for a short period, Tientsin parallels that of the soldiers of the Fifteenth Infantry. Marine officer Edward A. Craig, for example, recalled that at one checkpoint in Shanghai, the leathernecks disarmed so many troops entering the International Settlement that they "had a pile 10 feet high of Mauser automatic pistols . . . [and] thousands of rifles."[22] While no soldier of the Fifteenth was killed, Marine officer Adolf B. Miller recorded in his diary on 19 May 1927 that the Chinese had fired into the leathernecks' camp at Tientsin; nearly six months later, on 1 November 1927, he noted that another "Marine accidentally killed at 2 AM."[23]

In addition to manning posts around Tientsin, Shanghai, and Peking, marines were used as landing forces from the major units of the Asiatic Fleet. Furthermore, in times of extreme unrest, leather-necks were temporarily detailed to gunboats and American commercial ships on the Yangtze River. The armed guards aboard commercial ships were used quite often. In 1934, for example, one newspaper reported that from December 1933 to May 1934, there had been thirty-two details aboard ships.[24] Mar-ines were also called out to help ship captains. Miller recorded on 20 May 1927 that the ship President Lincoln had "sent an S.O.S. for a company of marines . . . [because she] had a mutiny."[25]

There were also some unusual missions performed by the leathernecks. James P. Berkeley related that the legation in Peking received a call from the American Board Mission to help bring in the children from a school some fifteen miles north of the city. Berkeley was given the detail and assembled a platoon of marines and six trucks. Machine-guns were mounted on the vehicles and large American flags were attached. The small convoy took "off for the hinterland." They passed through a relative no man's land between Japanese and Chinese troops. The entire journey was made in this highly charged atmosphere.

The convoy finally arrived at the mission, only to have the person in charge inform the rescuers that the children had already left. As an after-thought, the missionary stated that "since you are here with all those trucks, would you mind taking this silver and these rugs back to the American Board Mission in town?" Berkeley, many years later, wryly recalled: "So we rescued the missionaries' rugs and silver, anyway!"[26]

Marine officer William Worton experienced a perplexing incident. Worton was detailed by the American Minister to ride to the headquarters of a Chinese general to investigate the killing of two farmers. The leatherneck, using the most polite Chinese that he could muster, attempted to explain the nature of his mission to the general: "He listened and listened and said nothing." Finally, tea was brought in, signaling the end of the interview. After finishing tea, Worton prepared to depart. "I bowed very politely from the waist, bringing my hands together in the old custom." The general escorted the marine to the front door and then, in perfect English, said, "Sometime when you're not so busy, ride over here again and maybe we can split a bottle of whiskey together." Worton, completely taken aback, asked why the general had allowed him to struggle with the Chinese language "for three hours" when he spoke such good English? The warlord replied: "Major, congratulations to your teacher. I haven't heard such polite terms in Chinese since my grandfather's day. I just enjoyed every minute of it." The general informed the marine that he had "attended Purdue University."[27]

The primary mission of the American forces in China was the protection of American interests and lives. Peter Karsten has argued that naval of-ficers, however, felt that the protection of busi-ness interests should be the largest duty of the

navy.[28]   Indeed, many of the former China hands
felt that they were in the Middle Kingdom to
protect Standard Oil's interest.   Former Fifteenth
Infantryman Anthony Ingrisano recalled that his
post during the Sino-Japanese War was at a machine-
gun near an American oil installation.   "We used to
say we were there to protect the oil interests."[29]
Nevertheless, protecting American lives in China
was one of the two stated reasons for stationing
military forces in China.   In the majority of
cases, the people the servicemen were called upon
to protect were missionaries.   The dependency of
these people upon military force led, strangely, to
very strong tensions between the two groups.

It is enlightening to read the reminiscences of
former China hands about the people they were to
protect, especially among the naval personnel who
were most likely to perform rescue operations.
William Sims informed a friend in 1901 that he felt
very strongly against missionaries.[30]   Worton felt
that the majority of American missionaries in
Peking were "a sorry lot."   They were anti-military
and did not care to mix with service people.[31]

There was a veritable hierarchy of likes and
dislikes among the military concerning missionaries.   Usually, Catholics were accepted because
they were well-educated.   Medical personnel were
never frowned upon.   The groups that did engender
extreme hostility were those that would now be
labeled fundamentalist.[32]   Navy officer Glenn
Howell wrote that he did not think missionaries
should be in China.   Like most military men, Howell
did acknowledge good works by medical personnel,
but, he said, "deliver me from these narrow
upcountry missionaries!   Their creed they believe
not because they have ever thought it out, but by
sheer repetition."   Howell felt that the best way
to save China was to "open Chinese minds" with
sensible education, which included the three R's,
and to "develop their bodies at the same time . . .
and to season with some good wholesome religion."
Then the navy officer really hit the heart of what
he perceived was the cause of the questioning of
Western religion by the Chinese.

> [L]et some freak with spectacles and no
> common sense, squaredtoed shoes that
> squeak get at [the Chinese] and tell him
> that his parents lied to him, that there

ain't no joss, that there is a being on
high. named God who sits on a throne and
deals out justice . . .with a mob scene
of angels twanging away at harps, that
[God's] mercy is only for those who believe a certain narrow creed, that ninety-
nine percent of the world must go . . .
straight to hell, that only the remaining
one percent can hope to obtain the
mercy--all of this stuff is received by
the Chinese with bland faces.[33]

Missionary crusading zeal and inflexible morali-
ty helped to fuel the animosity. Berkeley recalled
that the Peking hotel had naked mermaids painted on
the wall when it was first built. The "missionaries
made them put bathing suits on the mermaids!"[34] One
Yangtze Patrol officer recalled that when touring a
temple at Yochow with his captain and a missionary,
both officers removed their hats and swords when
entering the edifice. For this action, the
missionary informed the Commander of the Yangtze
Patrol that the two officers had shown respect to
heathen idols. The officer's most damning memory
of the missionaries happened during the heat of a
July afternoon near the Wuhan area. The naval
officer was familiarizing his landing force petty
officers with prearranged escape routes for the
various missions. He planned to arrive at a large
mission, "the size of a small college," at noon,
so that they could rest in the shade. Upon reaching the site, however, they encountered eight-foot
walls "topped with broken glass" and a refusal to
allow the men inside. Only reluctantly were the
sailors given even a drink of water. The officer
then moved his detail about a mile down the trail
to the shade of a tree. An elderly Chinese farmer
came over and invited the men to sit on benches
under his fruit trees. Once the Americans had
settled in the shade, the farmer brought tea. The
officer reflected on the difference of the "hospitality between a wealthy American mission . . . in
a large compound of allegedly Christian[s] . . .
and an elderly Chinese farmer to whom the loss of a
single crop would be a disaster!"[35]
It should be recognized that the military's
criticism of the missionaries of China during this
time period has been echoed in modern scholarship.
Some historians have written scathing comments
about the missionaries. Nathaniel Peffer, for

instance, observed that some missionaries "were barely literate," and they never attempted to learn about China's philosophy and religion.[36]

The friction between missionaries and those who chose the profession of arms may, on reflection, be seen as a natural thing--after all, their callings were at opposite poles. Furthermore, many of the men filling the ranks of the armed forces were not what missionaries would consider "good" people--they drank and womanized. By the same token, some military men would probably see something strange in those who did not care to drink. It can also be recognized that, if the missionaries were seen favoring the military, it would appear to some Chinese that they approved of the symbol of the unequal treaties. This was one of the great conundrums facing those who tried to spread Christianity in China. If they supported the gunboats, they might be despised by the Chinese. On the other hand, in times of revolution and unrest, when large groups of undisciplined soldiers wandered the countryside, could they take the chance of expecting protection from anyone but the Western military forces? Did they wish to risk putting themselves at the mercy of the courts of China? An objective view of the missionaries' situation shows that, indeed, they were in the middle of an insoluble problem. This problem was never successfully brought to a satisfactory solution during the period under study. Instead, the military continued to supply protection while the two groups eyed each other warily. In short, both were trapped by the frequently stereotyped way that each perceived the other. They could never reach an accord.

Missionaries were not the only ones to receive censure from the military men in China. Many gunboats were dispatched to a troubled area upon receipt of information from the American Consul. Some naval officers began to doubt the veracity of the dispatches. The commanding officer of the Ashville, for example, reported to the Commander of the Asiatic Fleet that in all the locations to which he had rushed expecting an incident, he found upon arrival that the "American Consul . . . said 'Well the grave crisis has passed but there remains strong possibilities of trouble and I think ASH-VILLE should remain here for sometime.'"[37]

The primary mission of the U.S. military in

China was the protection of American lives and property. In the period from 1901 to 1937, a number of incidents in the Middle Kingdom caused soldiers, sailors, and marines to conduct active operations to fulfill this assignment. However, the U.S. and equipment in the country were never adequate to the task. In December 1926, for instance, American heavy weapons in Tientsin, Tongshan, and Peking amounted to sixty-five machine guns, six 37mm mortars, fifteen 3-inch Stokes mortars, fifty-two automatic rifles, and six 3-inch landing guns.[38] Marine Brig. Gen. Smedley D. Butler, in his normal blunt style, stated the seemingly obvious: that there were not sufficient armed men in the United States, "let alone here in China . . .[to] protect the lives and property of Americans living away in the bushes."[39] What helped to save the American forces from disaster was the mindset of Westerners and the fact that Chinese leaders knew that any major resistance would bring the wrath of the West down upon them and perhaps invite additional partitioning of their country. Americans saw themselves as far above the Chinese and, while sometimes reflecting on the disparity of numbers, knew that they could defeat any Oriental. Former marine Albert Tidwell's comment best sums up this attitude: "I thought the world was afraid of a squad of Marines armed with pop guns."[40] This is not to disparage the military achievements of the servicemen in China. Hopelessly outnumbered and sent by a government that did not wish to have any incidents that might drag it deeper into Chinese affairs, they were given an almost impossible task. That they performed it without major loss of life is a testimony to their professionalism and training. Most situations that required a show of force were conducted under tense conditions. When the tension was broken with gunfire, as at Nanking in 1927, American forces performed credibly.[41] Furthermore, the presence of United States troops could and did prevent killing and looting. Villagers near Tientsin, for example, presented the Fifteenth Infantry with a memorial arch in thanks for protection from the sure pillage of the warlords during 1924.[42] In sum, while the myth that most landing parties were under fire while protecting missionaries is false, the soldiers, sailors, and marines performed credibly under trying conditions when called upon to present a show of force in China.

NOTES

1. Harry Allanson Ellsworth, One Hundred Eighty Landings of the United States Marines, 1800-1934 (Washington: History and Museum Division, Headquarters, U.S. Marine Corps, 1934; reprint, 1974, 39-44 (page references are to reprint edition).

2. Bernard Cole, Gunboats and Marines: The United States Navy in China, 1925-1928 (Newark: University of Delaware Press, 1983); Kenneth W. Condit and Edwin T. Turnbladh, Hold High The Torch: A History of the 4th Marines (Washington: History Branch, Headquarters, U.S. Marine Corps, 1960); Kemp Tolley, Yangtze Patrol: The U.S. Navy in China (Annapolis, MD: Naval Institute Press, 1972; reprint, 1984).

3. Jack A. Wagner, China Service Questionnaire (CSQ) to Dennis L. Noble (DLN), 11 August 1984.

4. All material on the Lakeside incident is found in: Secretary of the Navy to Secretary of State, 14 August 1920, with enclosures, Subject Files, 1911-1927, Folder "Conditions there from 1917-1920," WA-7 Conditions in 1916-1922, Record Group (RG)45, Naval Records Collection of the Office of Naval Records and Library (NRC), National Archives, Washington, DC; Commanding Officer, U.S.S. Quiros to Secretary of the Navy, 21 June 1920, with enclosures, Subject Files, 1911-1927, ibid.; Logbook of the U.S.S. Upshur, RG 24, Records of the Bureau of Naval Personnel (RNP), National Archives; Logbook of the U.S.S. Quiros, ibid.

5. For information on the navy's role in the Nanking Incident, see: Roy C. Smith, Jr., "Nanking, 24 March 1927," U.S. Naval Institute Proceedings, 54 (January 1928): 1-21.   Smith was commanding officer of the U.S.S.   Noa, the unit that opened fire at Nanking.   Edward Hoyt, The Lonely Ships: The Life and Death of the U.S. Asiatic Fleet (New York: David McKay, 1976), 101-11; Tolley, Yangtze Patrol, 144-63.

6. Logbook of U.S.S. John D. Ford, 29 March 1927, RG 24.

7. Commander-in-Chief Asiatic Fleet to The Chief of Naval Operations, 1 July 1920, RG 45.

8. All material, unless otherwise noted on Spencer, Poy, and Poy's mission, is located in "West River Pirates," Chinaboatman (Spring [19]

86): 6-8; Papers of Henry J. Poy, China Repository (CR), Naval Operational Archives (NOA), Navy Historical Center (NHC), Washington, DC.

9. Larry I. Bland and Sharon R. Ritenour, eds., The Papers of George Catlett Marshall, Vol. 1; "The Soldierly Spirit," December 1880-June 1939 (Baltimore: Johns Hopkins University Press, 1981), 283, 294.

10. Charles G. Finney, The Old China Hands (Garden City, NY: Doubleday, 1961; reprint, Westport, CT: Greenwood Press, 1977), 100-02 (page references are to the reprint edition); Forrest C. Pogue, George C. Marshall: Education of a General: 1880-1939 (New York: Viking Press, 1963), 230-34.

11. Finney, Old China Hands, 102.

12. Ibid.

13. Ibid., 103; Bland and Ritenour, Papers of Marshall, I, 284; Pogue, George Marshall, 232-34, 237-39.

14. Finney, Old China Hands, 104-05.   It is believed that the name of man in charge was William Hambreck, who, according to Pogue, "turned aside considerable bodies of armed Chinese troops." Pogue, George Marshall, 239.

15. Bland and Ritenour, Papers of Marshall, I, 270.

16. Pogue, George Marshall, 239.

17. Barbara Tuchman, Stilwell and the American Experience in China, 1911-1945 (New York: Macmillan, 1970), 101; Francis F. Vaughn interview by LTC James Sheppard and LTC Jack Hixson (1977), 50, Papers of Francis F. Vaughn, Archives, U.S. Army Military History Institute (A, USAMHI), Carlisle Barracks, PA.

18. The epic poem was written by Major E. F. Harding and has eighteen stanzas. The Sentinel (Tientsin, China), 13 May 1927, pp. 16-17.

19. Finney, Old China Hands, 124-25.   The troop was later killed, their heads "festooned" on a telephone pole, when Nationalist troops caught up with the retreating lancers. Ibid., 148-49.

20. "The Defense of Tongshan," in L. L. Williams, ed., 15th Infantry Annual: May 4, 1924-May 4, 1925 (Tientsin, China: The Tientsin Press, 1925 [?]), 126-27.

21. "A Trip on the Allied Train," in Williams, 15th Infantry Annual, 135-41; The Sentinel, 12 May 1922, pp. 2-3.

22. LGEN Edward A. Craig interview by Benis M.

Frank (1968), 54, Marine Corps Oral History Program (MCOH), U.S.   Marine   Corps   Historical   Center (MCHC), Washington, DC.

24. Adolf B. Miller, "Diary," 19 May, 1 November 1927, Box 4, P.C. 196, The Papers of Adolf B. Miller, Personal Papers Collection (PPC), MCHC.

24. The Chevron (Shanghai), 23 May 1934, p. 1.

25. Miller, "Diary," 20 May 1927.

26. LGEN James P. Berkeley interview by Frank (1971), 89-90, MCOH.

27. MGEN William A. Worton interview by Frank (1967), 167-68, MCOH.

28. Peter Karsten, The Naval Aristocracy: The Golden Age of Annapolis and the Emergence of Modern American Navalism (New York: Free Press, 1972), 385.   As pointed out in the introduction, however, by the middle to late 1920s, the American military for all practical purposes, were in China, to protect American lives, with property being considered only if protecting it was considered no risk.

29. Anthony Ingrisano, CSQ to DLN, 25 July 1984.

30. William S. Sims to Pee Gee, 21 August 1901, "Personal   Correspondence,   July--November   1901," Papers of William S.   Simms, Manuscript Division, Library of Congress, Washington, DC.

31. Worton interview, 96.

32. This officer wishes to remain anonymous. His questionnaire remains in the possession of Dennis L. Noble.

33. "The Log of Glenn Howell," IX (1920), pp. 2,461-67, NOA.

34. Berkeley interview, 78.

35. This officer wishes to remain anonymous. His questionnaire remains in the possession of Dennis L. Noble.

36. Nathaniel Peffer, The Far East: A Modern History (Ann Arbor: University of Michigan Press, 1958), 114.   The standard work on missionaries in China is: Kenneth Scott Latourette, A History of Christian Missions in China (London: Society for Promoting Christian Knowledge, 1929). Another very useful work is: Paul A. Varig, Missionaries, Chinese, and Diplomats: The American Protestant Missionary Movement in China, 1890-1952 (Princeton: Princeton University Press, 1958).

37. J.O.   Richardson   to   Commander-in-Chief, Asiatic Fleet, February 1, 1923, "Reports of Conditions There for January--March 1923," WA-7 China Conditions, RG 45.

38. "Strength of Allied Forces in China in December 1, 1926," Box 628, RG 45.

39. Subject File: 1911-1927, "ZK" File/Box 799, Marine Corps 3rd Brigade Under General Smedley D. Butler, USMC, RG 45.

40. Albert Tidwell, CSQ to DLN, 14 July 1984.

41. The best overview of combat operations along the Yangtze River is in Tolley, Yangtze Patrol, passim. Two navy enlisted men received the Navy Cross for their performances under fire at Nanking.

42. The Sentinel, 1 May 1925, pp. 4-5; Pogue, George Marshall, 127-28.

8

TAPS: CONCLUSION

By 1937, the lifestyle of the old China hands was rapidly disappearing. Ahead lay the bombing of the _Panay_ and the withdrawal of the Fifteenth Infantry from China, as well as most of the Fourth Marines from Shanghai. The American military men who had not left China by 7 December 1941 faced long years of imprisonment by the Japanese. The army's departure from Tientsin in 1938 spelled the end of the old China Station. Even though the military returned to East Asia after World War II, the Communist ascendancy in 1949 caused a complete withdrawal of American troops from China.

As shown in this study, there were three broad classes of viewpoints about duty in China. A very small number hated everything about the country and its people. Another small group enjoyed the duty and wished either to learn as much as possible about the country or to remain after leaving the service. Lastly, the great majority of men simply did their duty and were glad to return to the Western world. This majority saw their surroundings as strange and a bit exotic, but they did not care to spend the rest of their lives in the East.

Why then has the myth of the China Station as desired by all military men survived for so long? The simplest explanation is covered by an old military saying: "The best duty station is your last duty station." In other words, as the years progress, memory dulls the bad times and one recalls only the enjoyable moments. Marine officer Graves B. Erskine also offered another sound reason for the staying power of the myth: what made the duty so attractive were the social, or off-duty, aspects of the service. In later years, old soldiers, salts, and leathernecks would regale younger men about how even privates had servants to take care of the drudgery of garrison duty. If one of the younger men would dare to put forth the question as to why someone would leave such good duty, the answer would probably have been: "It ain't a white man's country."[1]   In sum, the China Station was a place for a vacation, with perhaps a chance for a small fillip of adventure in putting down some inferior local natives, before returning to the real military.

In many ways, the American military wasted its China experience. U.S. military personnel should have learned as much about China as possible, in order to recognize incorrect estimates of its leaders and events later on.   The evidence shows that only sporadically did this take place.   Brig. Gen. William D. Connor's insistence, in the early 1920s, that his officers and selected enlisted men learn the rudiments of Chinese was a positive step in the right direction. However, while Connor was conducting his commendable program, the Asiatic Fleet had no such requirement, even though some of its units operated in areas of isolation where knowledge of the language would have been useful. The general's program came to an abrupt halt when Col. Reynolds J. Burt, who felt that Chinese was a "fool language," took command of the Fifteenth Infantry.[2] Burt did not wish even to leave the compound and mix among the local Chinese, nor did he care to go into the field on maneuvers.

The armed forces could not pursue a program of learning about the country or moving out of their enclaves. Throughout the entire period under study, except for World War I, the military was a volunteer organization.   During good economic times, it had a very small number of men from whom to choose. Furthermore, during this period, military men were held in low esteem.   Thus, until the Great Depression, the U.S. military could not be too choosy about the type of recruit it obtained. Moreover, the small number of men available made it impossible to staff the China Station adequately. As shown in this study, until at least the 1930s, the enlisted man serving in China was generally from the lower class and had a poor education.   To put farm boys from the Midwest or slum-dwellers from urban areas suddenly into a culture far removed from any of their previous experiences and expect them to understand what they were observing was expecting too much. This fact makes Connor's language program even more amazing. The correspondence of some of the Fifteenth Infantry's commanders indicates that they realized that China duty needed a special type of soldier. Again, the times prevented the realization of this goal. The military establishment, then, was forced to put its personnel into enclaves and hope for the best. With the type of people serving in its ranks and the small numbers available, it is little wonder that very few understood China and that most wished to return to more familiar surroundings. Given the above, one of the interesting aspects about the military in China is that even a minority of the men chose to remain in China. As I have argued, many if not most of the men who did wish to remain believed that the Orient offered them a chance to break out of their economic stratum.

The military, largely against its wishes, was ordered to provide protection for the dreams of an American empire in China. The armed forces, like the civilian population of the time, saw little incongruity in having a few thousand troops to stem the efforts of millions of Chinese--after all, was not the West superior? The study of the military in China is an examination of how a very diverse group of men--of all educational levels--reacted to living in a culture that was completely foreign to anything within their previous experiences. The China Station also offers an excellent chance to view how the American military reacted to its role as a colonial occupying force. If a generalization must be made about this reaction, it is that unless the troops had vigorous leaders--and in most cases they did not--the men quickly slipped into a life of dissipation and were not fit for combat. There are, of course, exceptions to all generalizations. Many fine officers and men served on the China Station. Future General of the Army George C. Marshall, for example, was at Tientsin, while at least six future Commandants of the Marine Corps served in East Asia. In the periods of unrest that racked China, especially during the middle to late 1920s, many military men served with distinction in situations of great danger. In the final analysis,

however, the U.S. military in China offers the
student of American military history the chance to
learn about the social context of the overseas
station, not about large issues of tactical
doctrine or strategy. Benjamin Franklin Cooling,
however, has noted "Men, not things, still make
war." It is important to understand how the men
who filled the ranks in peacetime lived so that we
may better grasp how they behaved in war.[3]

NOTES
1. Charles G. Finney, The Old China Hands,
(Garden City, NY: Doubleday, 1961; reprint,
Westport, CT: Greenwood Press, 1971), 30. (page
reference is to the reprint edition)
2. As quoted in Roy K. Flint, "The United States
Army on the Pacific Frontier, 1899-1939," in The
American Military and the Far East: Proceedings of
the Ninth Military History Symposium, United States
Air Force Academy, 1-3 October 1980, ed. Joe C.
Dixon (Washington: Government Printing Office,
1980), 149.
3. Benjamin Franklin Cooling, "Toward a More
Usable Past: A Modest Plea for a New Typology of
Military History," Military Affairs, 52, no. 1
(January 1988): 31.

SELECTED BIBLIOGRAPHY

PRIMARY SOURCES

Government Archives
National Archives, Washington DC:
  General Correspondence of the Navy Department. Record Group 24.
  Naval Records Collection of the Office of Naval Records and Library. Record Group 45.
  Office of the Secretary of the Navy. Record Group 80.
  Records of the Adjutant General's Office, 1780-1917. Record Group 94.
  Records of the Adjutant General's Office, 1917-. Record Group 407.
  Records of the Bureau of Naval Personnel. Record Group 24.
  Records of the Chief of Naval Operations. Record Group 38.
  Records of the Office of the Inspector General. Record Group 159.
  Records of the United States Regular Army Mobile Units, 1821-1942. Record Group 391.
Washington Federal Records Center, Suitland, MD.:
  Marine Corps General Records. Record Group 127.

Personal Manuscript Collections
Archives, U.S. Army Military History Institute, Carlisle Barracks, PA:
  William S. Biddle Papers
  Charles L. Bolte Papers
  Reynolds J. Burt Papers
  Paul W. Caraway Papers

Alvan Gillem, Jr. Papers
Edward Elliott MacMorland Papers
Charles D. Rhodes Papers
Matthew B. Ridgway Papers
Andrew C. Tychsen Papers
George V. Underwood Papers
World War I Survey: Robert Smith Questionnaire
Ivan D. Yeaton Papers
China Repository, Naval Operational Archives, U.S.
Naval Historical Center, Washington DC.:
William T. Bingham Papers
Lawrence P. Bischoff Papers
V. Brown Papers
Ernest Caha Papers
Robert C. Giffen Papers
(Mrs.) Forest Hampton Papers
Glenn F. Howell Papers
Earl H. Kincaid Papers
Herman W. Koch Papers
C. W. Lavine Papers
Frederick W. McLaughlin Papers
Leslie Meyers Papers
Miscellaneous Collection
Robert P. Molten Papers
Granville A. Moore Papers
James F. Moriarty Papers
Albert A. Poirer Papers
Henry J. Poy Papers
Charles R. Price Papers
Albrt L. Prosser Papers
Albert E. Schrader Papers
Thomas H. Seeman Papers
A. S. Smith Papers
Cephas A. Smith Papers
Roy C. Smith II Papers
Sam Sokobin Papers
Kemp Tolley Papers
John D. Wilson Papers
Searle Woods Papers
Manuscript Division, Library of Congress, Washing-
ton, DC.:
Mark Lambert Bristol Papers
William Sowden Sims Papers
Naval Operational Archives, U.S. Naval Historical
Center, Washington, DC.:
Log of Glenn Howell
Personal Papers Collection, U.S. Marine Corps His-
torical Center, Washington, DC.:
H. A. Bailey Papers (accession number 810298 CC)

R.C. Berkeley Papers (P.C. 45)
William T. Bingham Papers (accession number
 8414928)
Robert Blake Papers (P.C. 1093)
James C. Breckinridge Papers (P.C. 48)
Smedley D. Butler Papers (P.C. 54)
Helen H. Chapel (accession number 840214)
Robert E. Hogaboom Papers (P.C. 186)
George William Kase Papers (P.C. 85)
Henry Leonard Papers (P.C. 147)
Louis McCarty Little Papers (P.C. 143)
Adolph B. Miller Papers (P.C. 96)
J. F. Moriarty Papers (P.C. 607)
Archie B. Reed Papers (P.C. 110)
William J. Scheyer Papers (P.C. 115)
Carl S. Schmidt Papers (accession number 790284)
Alexander A. Vandergrift Papers (P.C. 465)
Clayton B. Vogel Papers (P.C. 2)
Thomas E. Williams Papers (accession number
 800560)
Special Collections, Nimitz Library, U.S. Naval
Academy, Annapolis, MD.:
Charles S. Stevenson Papers

Oral History
Oral History Program, U.S. Marine Corps, U.S.
Marine Corps Historical Center, Washington, DC.:
LGEN Robert Osborne Bare. Interview by Benis M.
 Frank, 1968.
MGEN William F. Battell. Interview by MAJ Thomas
 E. Donnelly, 1971.
BGEN Fred Dale Beans. Interview by MAJ Thomas E.
 Donnelly, 1971.
LGEN James Phillips Berkeley. Interview by Benis
 M. Frank, 1971.
MGEN Ion Maywood Bethel. Interview by Benis M.
 Frank, 1968.
LGEN Joseph Charles Burger. Interview by Benis
 M. Frank, 1969.
GEN Clifton Bledsoe Cates. Interview by Benis
 M. Frank, 1967.
MGEN George Harlon Cloud. Interview by MAJ
 Thomas E. Donnelly, 1970.
LGEN Edward Arthur Craig. Interview by MAJ
 Lloyd E. Tatem, 1968.
BGEN Donald Curtis. Interview by Benis M. Frank,
 1970.
BGEN James Patrick Sinnot Devereux. Interview
 by Benis M. Frank, 1970.

GEN Graves Blanchard Erskine. Interview by Benis M. Frank, 1970.

LCL Walter Scott Gasper. Interview by Benis M. Frank, 1975.

BGEN Samuel Blair Griffith II. Interview by Benis M. Frank, 1970.

MGEN John Neely Hart. Interview by MAJ Thomas E. Donnelly, 1970.

GEN Robert Edward Hogaboom. Interview by Benis M. Frank, 1970.

BGEN Bankson Taylor Holcomb, Jr. Interview by LCL Richard D. Alexander, 1970.

GEN Thomas Holcomb. Interview by MAJ Robert E. Barde, 1959.

1LT Joseph Everett Johnson. Interview by COL Joseph B. Ruth, 1977.

MGEN General Louis Reeder Jones. Interview by MAJ Thomas Donnelly, 1970.

BGEN Russell Nelton Jordahl. Interview by Benis M. Frank, 1973.

LGEN Victor Harold Krulak. Interview by Benis M. Frank, 1970.

MGEN Wood Barbee Kyle. Interview by Benis M. Frank, 1969.

MGEN August Larson. Interview by MAJ Thomas E. Donnelly, 1970.

LGEN Frederick E. Leek. Interview by Benis M. Frank, 1978.

LGEN Robert B. Lucky. Interview by Benis M. Frank, 1973.

GEN Vernon Edgar Megee. Interview by Benis M. Frank, 1967.

MGEN David Rowan Nimmer. Interview by MAJ Thomas E. Donnelly, 1970.

MGEN Omar Titus Pfeiffer. Interview by MAJ Lloyd E. Tatem, 1968.

GEN Ray Albert Robinson. Interview by Benis M. Frank, 1968.

GEN Lemuel Cornick Shepherd, Jr. Interview by Benis M. Frank, 1967.

GEN Gerald C. Thomas. Interview by Benis M. Frank, 1973.

LGEN James Latham Underhill. Interview by Benis M. Frank, 1968.

LGEN William Jennings Wallace. Interview by Benis M. Frank, 1967.

LGEN Thomas Andrews Wornham. Interview by Benis M. Frank, 1968.

MGEN William Arthur Worton. Interview by Benis

M. Frank, 1967.
Oral   History   Program,   U.S.   Naval   Institute.
Annapolis, MD.:
> VADM John L. (Jack) Chew.   Interview by John
> T. Mason, Jr., 1979.
> RADM William D. Irvin.   Interview by John T.
> Mason, Jr., 1980.
> Mrs. March A. Mitscher and Mrs. Roy C. Smith,
> Jr. Interview by John T. Mason, Jr., 1986.
> CAPT Joseph J. Rochefort.   Interview by CDR
> Etta-Belle Kitchen, 1970.
> CAPT Henri Smith-Hutton.   Interview by CAPT Paul
> Ryan, 1976.
> VADM Paul D. Stroop.   Interview by CDR Etta-
> Belle Kitchen, 1970.
> RADM George Van Deurs.   Interview by CDR Etta-
> Belle Kitchen, 1974.
> RADM Charles J. Wheeler.   Interview by CDR
> Etta-Belle Kitchen, 1970.
Senior Officer Oral History Program, Oral History
Branch,   U.S.   Army   Military   History   Institute,
Carlisle Barracks, PA.:
> LGEN William H. Arnold.   Interview by COL Warren
> R. Stumpe, 1972-1974.
> GEN   Charles   Bolte.   Interview   by   Arthur   J.
> Zoebelein, 1972.
> GEN Paul L. Freeman.   Interview by COL James N.
> Ellis, 1973.
> GEN Matthew B. Ridgway.   Interview by COL John
> M. Blair, 1971.
> Francis   F.   Vaughn.   Interview   by   LCL   Jack
> Hixson, 1977.

Completed China Service Questionnaires

(In possession of the author, to be deposited in
the respondant's designated historical collection
of either the U.S. Army, Marine Corps, or Navy.
Branch of service at time of duty in China is shown
after name.   No indication of service after name
indicates wife or child of a serviceman.)
> Chauncy S. Abram (USN)
> William G. Alger (USN)
> Ivan Buster (USMC)
> Peter J. Clemons (USN)
> Clarence E. Coffin (USN)
> James P. Dolan (USMC)
> Vern L. Dorsey (USMC)
> Benjamin F. Draper (USN)
> Robert D. Dwan

Frank F. Farley (USA)
Joseph G. Felber (USA)
Donald R. Fox, Jr.
Arthur G. Gullickson (USA)
Lawrence Charles Hanson (USN)
William R. Hardcastle (USN)
Glen M. Hargrave (USMC)
Harry K. Hayden (USN)
Eugene F. Horrall (USN)
Harry Hurlbert (USN)
Anthony Ingrisano (USA)
Julius Isaacson (USN)
Lyle E. Keyes (USN)
Adam A. Komosa (USA)
Victor Kovaleski (USN)
John L. Lilly (USN)
P. Mangogna (USMC)
Thomas Mason (USA)
Alberta J. Matthews
L.M. Matthews (USN)
William Henry Meyer, Jr. (USN)
Edward W. Mooney (USMC)
Gary L. Murphy (USN)
Lloyd M. Mustin (USN)
Paul Newman (USN)
Edward J. Ormiston (USA)
Fred Osborn (USMC)
Jack E. Paine (USMC)
Fernando E. Pedro (USN)
Herbert Phillips (USN)
Robert J. Plummer (USA)
John C. Ponick (USMC)
Howard L. Povey (USN)
John Reber (USMC)
Harry Roberts (USN)
Clem D. Russell (USMC)
Laney E. Rutledge (USA)
Mary Lilly Sage
John T. Salistean (USN)
Paul S. Schatzle (USN)
Edwin C.Schierhorst (USA)
Floyde O. Schilling (USMC)
Glen R. Smith (USA)
Malcolm F. Stimmers (USN)
George St. Lawrence (USN)
Harry A. Taylor (USMC)
Albert Tidwell (USMC)
Kemp Tolley (USN)
Horace Edward Tuckett (USN)

Carl M. Tuttle (USN)
William S. Tyler (USN)
Lawrence Van Brookhaven (USN)
Jack A. Wagner (USN)
Oliver G. Webb (USN)

Newspapers
American Embassy Guard News (in U.S. Marine
Corps Historical Center)
The Chevron (in U.S. Marine Corps Historical
Center)
The Legation Guard News (in U.S. Marine Corps
Historical Center)
New York Times
North China Herald
The Orient
The Sentinel
The Walla Walla (in U.S. Marine Corps Historical
Center)

Other
American Legation Guard Annual, 1934. Peiping:
Peiping Chronicle, 1934.
American Embassy Guard Annual, 1935. Peiping:
Peiping Chronicle, 1935.
Annual Reports of Fleets and Task Forces of the
U.S. Navy, 1920-1941, M971/Roll 12; Asiatic
Fleet Reports, 1923-1929 (Microfilm Publication
of the National Archives.)
Annual Reports of the Navy Department for the
years 1901-1937. Washington: Government Print-
ing Office, 1901-1937.
Legation Guard Annual [1930-1931]. Peking:
Standard Press, 1930-1931.
Navy Directory [for the years 1901 to 1937].
Washington: Government Printing Office, 1901-
1937.
Official Army Register [for 1901-1937]. Wash-
ington: Government Printing Office, 1901-1937.
Register of the Commissioned Officers of the
Navy and Marine Corps [for the years 1901-1937].
Washington: Government Printing Office, 1901-
1937.
U.S. Department of State. Papers Relating to
the Foreign Relations of the United States
[1901-1937]. Washington: Government Printing
Office, 1901-1937.
U.S. Department of War. Annual Reports [for the
years 1901-1937]. Washington: Government Print-

ing Office, 1901-1937.
Williams, L. L., ed. <u>15th Infantry Annual: May
4, 1924-May 4, 1925.</u> Tientsin, China:
Tientsin Press, 1925 [?].

SECONDARY SOURCES

Unpublished Works

Chadbourne, Charles C. II.   "Sailors and Diplomats:
U.S. Naval Operations in China, 1865-1877." Ph.D.
diss., University of Washington, 1976.
Nolan, William Francis.   "America's Participation
in the Military Defense of Shanghai, 1931-1941."
Ph.D. diss., Saint Louis University, 1978.
Rosenberg, David A. "History of the Yangtze Patrol:
A Study in American Imperialism." Thesis for de-
partmental honors in history.   American Universi-
ty, 1969.   Copy in the Navy Department Library,
Washington, DC.
Thomas, Charles W. "The United States Army Troops
in China, 1912-1937."   History term paper, Stanford University, June 1937.

Books

Albion, Robert G., William A. Baker, and Benjamin
Woods Labaree. <u>New England and the Sea.</u> Middle-
ton, CT: Wesleyan University Press, 1972.
Alden, Carroll Storrs. <u>Lawrence Kearny: Sailor
Diplomat.</u> Princeton: Princeton University Press,
1936.
Astor, Brooke. <u>A Patchwork Child.</u>   New York:
Harper & Row, 1962.
Bemis, Samuel Flagg. <u>A Diplomatic History of the
United States.</u> 5th ed. New York: Holt, Rinehart,
and Winston. 1965.
Bland, Larry I. and Sharon R. Ritenour, eds. <u>The
Papers of George Catlett Marshall</u> Vol. I; "<u>The
Soldierly Spirit,</u>" December 1880-June 19<u>39.</u>
Baltimore: Johns Hopkins University Press, 1981.
Blankfort, Michael. <u>The Big Yankee: The Life of
Carlson of the Raiders.</u>   Boston: Little, Brown,
1947.
Borg, Dorthy. <u>American Policy and the Chinese
Revolution, 1925-1928.</u> New York: Macmillan, 1947.
_____ . <u>The United States and the Far East-
ern Crisis of 1933-1938:   From the Manchurian
Incident Through the Initial Stage of the Unde-
clared Sino-Japanese War.</u> Cambridge: Harvard
University Press, 1965.

Bose, Newmain S. American Attitude and Policy to the Nationalist Movement in China: 1911-1921. Atlantic Highlands, NJ: Humanities Press, 1970.

Braisted, William Reynolds. The United States Navy in the Pacific, 1897-1909. Austin: University of Texas Press, 1958.

_____. The United States Navy in the Pacific, 1909-1922. Austin: University of Texas Press, 1971.

Chang, Hsin-pao. Commissioner Lin and the Opium War. New York: Norton, 1970.

Cole, Bernard D. Gunboats and Marines: The United States Navy in China, 1925-1928. Newark: University of Delaware Press, 1982.

Condit, Kenneth W. and Edwin T. Turnbladh. Hold High the Torch: A History of the 4th Marines. Washington: History Branch, Headquarters, U.S. Marine Corps, 1960.

Cooling, Benjamin Franklin. Benjamin Franklin Tracy: Father of the Modern American Fighting Navy. Hamden, CT: Archon Books, 1973.

Davis, George T. A Navy Second to None: The Development of Modern Naval Policy. Westport, CT: Greenwood Press, 1971.

Dennett, Tyler. Americans in Eastern Asia: A Critical Study of the Policy of the United States With References to China, Japan, and Korea in the 19th Century. New York: Barnes and Noble, 1941.

Dulles, Foster. The Old China Trade. Boston: Houghton Mifflin, 1930.

Ellsworth, Harry Allanson. One Hundred Eighty Landings of the United States Marines, 1800-1934. Washington: History and Museums Division, Headquarters, U.S. Marine Corps. 1934; reprint, 1974.

Everett, Robinson O. Military Justice in the Armed Forces of the United States. Harrisburg, PA: Military Service Publishing, 1956.

Fairbank, John King. Trade and Diplomacy on the China Coast: The Opening of the Treaty Ports, 1842-1854. Palo Alto: Stanford University Press, 1969.

_____. Chinese-American Interactions: A Historical Summary. New Brunswick NJ: Rutgers University Press, 1975.

_____., ed. The Cambridge History of China. Vol. X, Late Ch'ing, 1800-1911. Part 1. New York: Cambridge University Press, 1978.

_____., ed. The Cambridge History of China. Vol. XI, Late Ch'ing, 1800-1911. Part 2. New

York: Cambridge University Press, 1978.

_____. The United States and China. 4th ed.
Cambridge: Harvard University Press, 1979.

Fay, Peter Ward. The Opium War, 1840-1842: Barbarians in the Celestial Empire in the Early Part
of the Nineteenth Century and the War By Which
They Forced Her Gates Ajar. Chapel Hill: University of North Carolina Press, 1975.

Finney, Charles G. The Old China Hands. Garden
City, NY: Doubleday, 1961; reprint, Westport, CT:
Greenwood Press, 1973.

Fleming, Peter. The Seige at Peking. New York:
Harper and Brothers, 1959.

Flint, Roy K. "The United States Army on the
Pacific Frontier, 1898-1939." In The American
Military and the Far East: Proceedings of the
Ninth Military History Symposium, United States
Air Force Academy, 1-3 October 1980. ed. Joe C.
Dixon, 139-59. Washington: Government Printing
Office, 1980.

Garrett, Shirley S. Social Reformers in Urban
China: The Chinese Y.M.C.A., 1985-1926. Cambridge:
Harvard University Press, 1970.

Goodwin, C. Ropeyarns From the Old Navy.
Washington: Naval Historical Society, 1931.

Griffith, Robert K., Jr. Men Wanted for the U.S.
Army: America's Experience With An All Volunteer
Army Between the World Wars. Westport, CT: Green-
wood Press, 1982.

Griffith, Samuel B., II. Sun Tzu The Art of War.
New York: Oxford University Press. 1963.

_____. The Battle for Guadalcanal. New York:
Nautical and Aviation Publishing Company, 1963.

Guliotta, Bobette. Pigboat 39: An American Sub
Goes to War. Lexington: University of Kentucky
Press, 1984.

Hagen, Kenneth J. American Gunboat Diplomacy and
the Old Navy, 1877-1889. Westport, CT: Greenwood
Press, 1973.

_____, ed. In Peace and War. Westport, CT:
Greenwood Press, 1978.

Harrod, Frederick S. Manning the New Navy: The
Development of a Modern Naval Enlisted Force,
1899- 1940. Westport, CT: Greenwood Press, 1978.

Hart, John N. The Making of an Army "Old China
Hand" A Memoir of Colonel David D. Barrett.
Berkeley, CA: Institute of East Asian Studies,
1985.

Hauser, William L. "The Peacetime Army: Retrospect

and Prospect." In The United States Army in Peacetime: Essays in Honor of the Bicentennial, 1775-
1975, eds. Robin Higham and Carol Brandt, 207-29.
Manhattan, KS: Military Affairs/Aerospace Historian Publishing, 1975.

Heinl, Robert D. Soldiers of the Sea.   Annapolis,
MD: Naval Institute Press, 1962.

Henson, Curtis T., Jr.   Commissioners and Commo-
dores: The East India Squadron and American
Diplomacy in China. University: University of
Alabama Press, 1982.

Herrick, Walter R., Jr. The American Naval Revolution.   Baton Rouge: Louisana State University
Press, 1966.

Holley, I. B., Jr.   General John M. Palmer, Citizen
Soldiers, and the Army of a Democracy.   Westport,
CT: Greenwood Press, 1982.

Holt, Edgar. The Opium Wars in China. London:
Dufors, 1964.

Hoyt, Edward. The Lonely Ships: The Life and Death
of the U.S. Asiatic Fleet. New York: David McKay,
1976.

Hsu, Immanuel.   The Rise of Modern China.   3rd ed.
New York: Oxford University Press, 1983.

Hurd, David.   The Arrow War: An Anglo-Chinese
Confusion, 1857-1861. New York: Macmillan, 1968.

Isaacs, Harold R. Scratches on our Minds: American
Images of China and India.   New York: John Day,
1958.

Johnson, Robert E. Thence Round Cape Horn: The
Story of the United States Naval Forces on Pacific
Station.   Annapolis, MD: Naval Institute Press,
1963.

_____. Far China Station: The U.S. Navy in
Asian Waters, 1800-1898.   Annapolis, MD: Naval
Institute Press, 1979.

Jones, Edward Sprague.   "The Old China Regiment."
In Customs of the Fifteenth U.S. Infantry, A Fac-
simile Reproduction, 1-10.   Tientsin: Pelyang
Press, 192(?); reprint, Cornwallville, NY: Hope
Farm Press, 1959.

Jones, James.   From Here to Eternity.   New York:
Charles Scribner's, 1954.

_____. World War II.   New York: Grosset &
Dunlap, 1975.

Jordan, Donald A.   The Northern Expedition.   Hono-
lulu: University Press of Hawaii, 1976.

Karsten, Peter. The Naval Aristocracy: The Gold-
en Age of Annapolis and the Emergence of Modern

Navalism. New York: Free Press, 1972.

Kemble, C. Robert. The Image of the Army Officer in America: Background for Current Views. Westport, CT: Greenwood Press, 1973.

Kierman, Frank A., Jr. "Ironies of Chinese-American Military Conflict." In The American Military in the Far East: Proceedings of the Ninth Military History Symposium, United States Air Force Academy, 1-3 October 1980. Joe C. Dixon, 183-98. Washington: Government Printing Office, 1980.

Killigrew, John W. The Impact of the Great Depression on the Army. New York: Garland Publishing 1979.

Knox, Dudley W. A History of the United States Navy. New York: Putnam, 1948.

LaFeber, Walter. The New Empire: An Interpretation of American Expansion, 1860-1897. Ithaca: Cornell University Press, 1963.

Lary, Diana. Warlord Soldiers: Chinese Common Soldiers, 1911-1937. Cambridge: Cambridge University Press, 1985.

Latourette, Kenneth Scott. A History of Christian Missions in China. London: Society for Promoting Christian Knowledge, 1929.

Lederer, William J. All the Ships At Sea. New York: William Sloane Associates, 1950.

Lockwood, Charles A. Down to the Sea in Subs. New York: W. W. Norton, 1967.

Maclay, Edgar Stanton. Reminiscences of the Old Navy: From the Journals and Private Papers of Captain Edward Trenchard and Rear Admiral Stephen Decatur Trenchard. New York: Putnam, 1898.

McClellan, Robert. The Heathen Chinee: A Study of American Attitudes Towards China, 1890-1905. Columbus: Ohio State University Press, 1971

McCormick, Thomas J. China Market: America's Quest for Informal Empire, 1893-1901. Chicago: Quadrangle Books, 1967.

McKenna, Eva Grice, and Shirley Graves Cochrane, eds. New Eyes for Old: Nonfiction Writings by Richard McKenna. Winston-Salem, NC: John F. Blair, 1972.

McKenna, Richard. The Sand Pebbles. New York: Harper & Row, 1962.

Millett, Allan R. Semper Fidelis: The History of the United States Marine Corps. New York: Macmillian, 1980.

Myrer, Anton. Once An Eagle. New York: Holt, Rinehart, and Winston, 1968.

O'Connor, Richard. Spirit Soldiers: A Historical Narrative of The Boxer Rebellion. New York: Putnam, 1973.

Offutt, Milton. The Protection of Citizens Abroad by the Armed Forces of the United States. Baltimore: Johns Hopkins University Press, 1928.

Paulin, Charles O. Diplomatic Negotiations of American Naval Officers, 1778-1883. Baltimore: Johns Hopkins University Press, 1912.

Peffer, Nathaniel. The Far East: A Modern History Ann Arbor: University of Michigan Press, 1958.

Pogue, Forrest C., with the editorial assistance of George Harrison. George C. Marshall: Education of a General: 1880-1939. New York: Viking Press, 1963.

Rodman, Hugh. Yarns of a Kentucky Admiral. Indianapolis: Bobbs-Merrill Company, 1927.

Ropp, Theodore. "Introduction--Armies in Peacetime." In The United States Army in Peacetime: Essays in Honor of the Bicentennial, 1775-1975. eds. Robin Higham and Carol Brandt, 1-19. Manhattan, KS: Military Affairs/Aerospace Historian Publishing, 1975.

Santoli, Al. Everything We Had: An Oral History of the Vietnam War by Thirty-three American Soldiers Who Fought It. New York: Random House, 1981.

Sawyer, Frederick L. Sons of Gunboats. Annapolis, MD: Naval Institute Press, 1946.

Schmidt, Hans. Maverick Marine: General Smedley D. Butler and the Contradictions of American Military History. Lexington: University of Kentucky Press, 1987.

Seager, Robert II. Alfred Thayer Mahan. Annapolis, MD: Naval Institute Press, 1977.

Shenk, Robert, ed. The Left-Handed Monkey Wrench: Stories and Essays by Richard McKenna. Annapolis, MD: Naval Institute Press, 1986.

Sheridan, James E. Chinese Warlord: The Career of Feng Yu-hsian. Palo Alto: Stanford University Press, 1966.

_____. China in Disintegration. New York: Free Press, 1968.

Sherrod, Robert. History of Marine Corps Aviation in World War II. Washington: Combat Forces Press, 1952.

Shoup, David M. The Marines in China, 1927-1928: The China Expedition which turned out to be The China Exhibition: A Contemporaneous   Journal by

David M. Shoup, USMC. Hamden, CT: Archon Books, 1987.

Sprout, Harold and Margaret Sprout. The Rise of American Naval Power, 1776-1918. Princeton: Princeton University Press, 1939.

Sterling, Yates, Jr. Sea Duty. New York: Putnam, 1939.

Stryker, Joe W. China Ensign. New York: Vantage Press, 1981.

Stumpf, C. Aloysious. On a Cruise With the U.S. Pacific Fleet to the Orient: An Account of the American Bluejacket Afloat and Ashore. Boston: Roxburgh Publishing, 1915.

Swisher, Earl. China's Management of the American Barbarians: A Study of Sino-American Relations, 1841- 1861, with Documents. New York: Octagon Books, 1972.

Tan, Chester C. The Boxer Catastrophe. New York: Columbia University Press, 1955.

Teng, Ssu-Yu. The Taiping Rebellion and the Western Powers: A Comprehensive Survey. London: Oxford University Press, 1971.

_____. and John King Fairban,, eds. China's Response to the West: A Documentary Survey, 1839-1923. Cambridge: Harvard University Press, 1979.

Thomas, Lowell. Old Gimlet Eye: The Adventures of Smedley D. Butler. New York: Farrar & Rinehart, 1933; reprint, Quantico, VA.: Marine Corps Association, 1981.

Tolley, Kemp. Yangtze Patrol: The U.S. Navy in China. Annapolis, MD: Naval Institute Press, 1972; reprint, 1984.

Tuchman, Barbara W. Stilwell and the American Experience in China, 1911-1945. New York: Macmillan, 1970.

Tuleja, Thaddeus V. Statesmen and Admirals. New York: W. W. Norton, 1963.

Vandegrift, A. A., as told to Robert B. Aspry. Once a Marine: The Memoirs of General A. A. Vandegrift. New York: W. W. Norton , 1964.

Varig, Paul A. Missionaries, Chinese, and Diplomats: The American Protestant Missionary Movement in China, 1890-1952. Princeton: Princeton University Press, 1958.

Weigley, Russell F. History of the United States Army. New York: Macmillan, 1967.

Wheeler, Gerald E. Prelude to Pearl Harbor: The United States Navy and the Far East, 1921-1931. Columbia: University of Missouri Press, 1963.

White, John A. The United States Marines in North China. Millbrae, CA: John A. White, 1974.

Wiley, Henry A. An Admiral From Texas. Garden City, NY: Doubleday, Doran, 1934.

Williams, Robert Hugh. The Old Corps: A Portrait of the U.S. Marine Corps Between the Wars. Annapolis, MD: Naval Institute Press, 1982.

Williams, William A. The Roots of the Modern American Empire: A Study of Growth and Shaping of Social Consciousness in a Marketplace Society. New York: Random House, 1969.

Willock, Roger. Lone Star Marine: A Biography of the Late John W. Thomason, Jr., U.S.M.C. Princeton: Published by the author, 1961.

Periodicals

Agnew, James B.   "Coalition Warfare--Relieving the Peking Legations, 1900." Military Review, 56 (October 1976): 58-70.

Albion, Robert Greenhalgh. "Distant Stations." U.S. Naval Institute Proceedings, 80 (March 1954): 265-73.

Bellah, J. W.   "The Grand Manner of Josiah Tattnall." Shipmate, 28 (December 1965): 4-7.

Bisson, T. A. "The United States and the Far East: A Survey of the Relations of the United States With China and Japan, September 1, 1930 to September 1, 1931." Pacific Affairs, 5 (January 1932): 66-81.

Brown, W. F. "Fiat Justitia, Ruat Caeleum, Chinese Style." U.S. Naval Institute Proceedings, 64 (November 1938): 1585-88.

Bruce, Bryson. "River Gunboats for Yangtze Service." Far Eastern Review, 24 (December 1928): 128-34.

Butler, Smedley D. "American Marines in China." Annals of the American Academy, 164 (July 1929): 128-34.

Carlson, Evans F. "Legal Bases for the Use of Foreign Armed Forces in China." U.S. Naval Institute Proceedings, 62 (November 1936): 1546-49.

Clay, James P. "Pearl River Log: A Different Navy, A Different World." U.S. Naval Institute Proceedings, 96 (September 1970): 58-67.

Coffman, Edward M. and Peter F. Herrly. "The American Regular Army Officer Corps Between the World Wars." Armed Forces and Society, 4, no. 1 (November 1977): 55-73.

"Conditions of Service in China." Infantry Journal,

29 (August 1926): 167-74.

Cooling, Benjamin Franklin. "Toward a More Usable Past: A Modest Plea for a New Typology of Military History." Military Affairs, 52, (January 1988): 29-31.

Coontz, Robert E. "The Navy and Business." U.S. Naval Institute Proceedings, 58 (June 1922): 987-1,004.

Cope, Jesse D. "American Troops in China--Their Mission." Infantry Journal, 38 (March-April 1931): 174-77.

Crawford, Danny J. "Two Centuries of Teamwork: U.S. Marines and the Foreign Service." Shipmate, (November 1980): 23-27.

Eyre, James K. "The Civil War and Naval Action in the Far East." U.S. Naval Institute Proceedings, 68 (November 1942): 1543-48.

Frank, Benis M. "Shanghai's 4th Marines: The Glory Days of the Old Corps." Shipmate, (November 1979): 13-18.

Gale, Esson M. "The Yangtze Patrol." U.S. Naval Institute Proceedings, 81 (March 1955): 307-15.

Gardner, K. N. "The Beginning of the Yangtze River Campaign of 1926-1927." U.S. Naval Institute Proceedings, 58 (January 1932): 40-44.

Greene, W. W., Jr. "Shanghai, 1937." Marine Corps Gazette, 34 (November 1965): 62-63.

Gulliver, Louis J. "The Yangtze U.S. Gunboats." U.S. Naval Institute Proceedings, 68 (September 1942): 1285-87.

Hobart, Alice T. "What Happened at Nanking." Harper's Weekly, 155 (July 1927): 129-37.

Howell, Glenn. "The Battle of Wanhsien." U.S. Naval Institute Proceedings, 53 (May 1927): 527-33.

_____. "Operations of the United States Navy on the Yangtze River--September 1926 to June 1927." U.S. Naval Institute Proceedings, 54 (April 1928): 273-86.

_____. "Captain Plant." U.S. Naval Institute Proceedings, 55 (March 1929): 206-08.

_____. "Hwan Tsao." U.S. Naval Institute Proceedings, 64 (August 1938): 1151-55.

_____. "Chungking to Ichang." U.S Naval Institue Proceedings, 65 (September 1938): 1312-16.

_____. "Army-Navy Game: Or, No Rules of the Road." U.S. Naval Institute Proceedings, 64 (October 1938); 1435-38.

_____. "Opium Obligato." U.S. Naval Institute

Proceedings, 4 (December 1938):   1729-35.

_____. "Ascent of the Min." U.S. Naval Institute Proceedings, 65 (May 1939): 709-13.

"Infantry Weapons Qualifications," Infantry Journal, 32, no. 1 (June 1928): 72-73.

Jacobs, V. F. G.   "Port of Call."   U.S. Naval Institute Proceedings, 65 (February 1939): 172-76.

Johnson, Felix L. "Naval Activities on the Yangtze." U.S. Naval Institute Proceedings, 53 (April 1927): 506-14.

Karsten, Peter.   "The 'New' American Military History: A Map of the Territory Explored and Unexplored." American Studies Quarterly, 36 (1984): 389-418.

"Last Review: Mounted Marines in China Disbanded." Time (March 7, 1938): 17.

Lee, J.A.   "Between the Wars in the Far East." U.S. Naval Institute Proceedings, 65 (January 1939): 63-73.

Leventhal, Robert M.   "China Marine." Marine Corps Gazette, 56 (November 1972): 36-42.

Livermore, Seward W.   "American Naval Base Policy in the Far East, 1850-1914." Pacific Historical Review, 13 (March 1944): 113-35.

Manning, G. C. "Yangtze."   U.S. Naval Institute . Proceedings, 60 (February 1934): 221-29.

Merrill, James M. "The Asiatic Squadron: 1835-1907." American Neptune, 29, (Apri; 1969): 106-17.

Metcalf, Clyde H. "The Marines in China." Marine Corps Gazette, 22 (September 1938): 35-37, 53-58.

Morton, Louis, "War Plan ORANGE." World Politics, 11 (January 1959): 221-45.

_____. "Army and Marines on the China Station: A Study in Military and Political Rivalry." Pacific Historical Review, 29 (February 1960): 51-73.

Moskin, J. Robert.   "Tracing the Footsteps of the 4th Marines in Shanghai." Fortitudine: Newsletter of the Marine Corps Historical Program, 16, no. 3 (Winter 1986-1987): 13-16.

"Operations in China, 1926-1927." Marine Corps Gazette, 12 (September 1927): 179-83.

Parrish, Noel F.   "New Responsibilities of Air Force Officers." Air University Review, 23, no. 3 (March-April 1972): 12-25.   Originally published in 1947.

Pfaff, Roy. "Sea Duty on the Yangtze." U.S. Naval Institute Proceedings, 79 (November 1933):

1612-22.

Pineau, Roger.   "U.S.S. Noa at Nanking."   U.S. Naval Institute Proceedings, 81 (November 1955): 1221-28.

"Protection of American Interests."   Marine Corps Gazette, (September 1927): 175-83.

Roberts, F. N.   "The First Battalion, 15th Infantry."   Infantry Journal, 40, no. 4 (April 1927): 364-66.

Roberts, Stephen S.   "The Decline of the Overseas Station Fleets: The United States Navy and the Shanghai Crisis, 1932."   American Neptune, 37 (July 1977): 185-202.

Sager, Mike.   "Thailand's Home for Wayward Vets."   Rolling Stone, (May 10, 1984): 27-28, 33-34, 36-37, 72.

Settle, T. G. W. "Last Cruise of the Palos."   Shipmate, 24 (April 1961): 2-6.

Sheehan, J. M.   "From the Side Lines."   U.S. Naval Institute Proceedings, 65 (January 1939): 33-37.

_____.   "Nanking."   U.S. Naval Institute Proceedings, 69 (September 1943): 1189-95.

_____.   "The Gorges of the Yangtze Kiang." U.S. Naval Institute Proceedings, 69 (November 1943): 1418-26.

Smith, Allen E. "A China Tour." Shipmate, 40 (July-August): 29-30.

Smith, Roy C., Jr.   "Nanking, 24 March 1927."   U.S. Naval Institute Proceedings, 54 (January 1928): 1-21.

Smith-Hutton, H. H. "Lessons Learned at Shanghai in 1932."   U.S.   Naval   Institute   Proceedings,   64 (August 1938): 1167-74.

Sutliff, R. C.   "Duty in a Yangtze Gunboat."   U.S. Naval Institute Proceedings, 61 (July 1935): 981-84.

Tate, E. Mowbray.   "U.S. Gunboats on the Yangtze: History and Political Aspects, 1842-1922." Studies on Asia, 12 (1966): 121-32.

_____.   "Admiral Bell and the New Asiatic Squadron, 1865-1868." American Neptune, 32 (April 1972): 123-35.

Tolley, Kemp.   "YangPat--Shanghai to Chungking."   U.S. Naval Institute Proceedings, 89 (June 1963): 80-89.

_____.   "Three Piecie and Other Dollars Mex."   Shipmate, 28 (July 1965): 8-10.

_____.   "Chinese Huntsman."   Shipmate, 29 (June-July 1966): 12-16.

_____. "The Chameleon." Shipmate, 29 (October 1966): 2-5.

_____. "A Day in the Life of a Chungking Gun-boat." Shipmate, 30 (June-July 1967): 8-12, 17.

"West River Pirates." China Gunboatman, (Spring [19]86): 6-8.

Wharton, Wallace S. "Our Chinese Navy." U.S. Naval Institute Proceedings, 51 (January 1925): 68-82.

"Who's in the Army Now?" Fortune, 12 (September 1935): 39-49, 138.

Winslow, Cameron M. R. "Action on the Yangtze." U.S. Naval Institute Proceedings, 63 (April 1937): 491-94.

INDEX

Adix, David, 176
Andress, John J, 134
Arnold, William H, 129
Arrasmith, James M, 21
Arrow War, 6-8
Asiatic Fleet, 19, 20,
  24, 115, 172, 210.
  See also East India
  Squadron
Astor, Brooke, 123

Bachman, George, 181
Bare, Robert O, arrival
  in China, 118-19;
  views of China, 23
Battell, William F, 85;
  Chinese servants, 152;
  off-duty hours, 111,
  113, 122; views of
  enlisted men, 132;
  views of White Rus-
  sians, 130
Bauman, Leo, 171
Beans, Fred D: Chinese
  servants, 151-52;
  duty, 94; retiring in
  China, 178; views of
  Chinese military, 157
Bee (gunboat), 190-91
Belief, C. A, 271
Berkeley, James P, 110,
  155-56; rescue of

missionaries, 199-200;
  views of duty, 85,
  94-95, 124; views of
  enlisted men, 69, 125,
  133
Bernard, Caroline, 120
Boles, Richard, 61-62
Bolte, Charles L, 52;
  Chinese language
  training, 144; views
  of duty, 92
Boxer Rebellion. See
  Boxer Uprising
Boxer Uprising, 9, 11,
  13
Bristol, Mark L. ADM:
  defense of Tientsin,
  27, 28; views of
  Butler, 27; views of
  athletics, 110
Burger, Joseph C: views
  of duty, 135, 180;
  views of officers, 85
Burt, Reynolds J, (Com-
  mander of Fifteenth
  Infantry): obsession
  for showmanship, 91-
  92; regulations on
  venereal disease, 128-
  29; views about, 181;
  views on language
  training, 145, 210;

views on long ser-
vice men, 173
Butler, Smedly D. Brig.
Gen., 24-27, 45, 52,
103, 156; at Tientsin,
92; obsession for show-
manship, 180-81, 188;
plans, 180; views of
mission in China, 26-
28, 34, 35, 204; views
of Navy command, 25-26

Calhoun, W. J, 20-22,
passim
Campbell, P. J, 176
Canopus, 64
Castner, Joseph C. Brig.
Gen: views of long
service men, 172-73;
views on marching,
87-88; views on
mission, 31
Chaffe, Adna, 19
Chang Ching-yao (Zhang
Jingyas), 188
Chang Tso-lin (Zang
Zuolin), 192, 194
Chapel, Charles E, 162
Chapel, Helen H: views
of China,162, 163-
64; views of Chinese,
162, 163-64
Chaumont, 24
Chiang Kai-shek, 23,
102, 190
China: Ch'ing Dynasty,
1-2; early isolation,
2; opening of treaty
ports, 3-7; trade with
U.S., 4-6. See also
Enlisted men; Officers
Chinese: biographies of,
153-55; employment by
U.S. military, 95-96,
118, 119-120, 151-55;
U.S. military views
of, 146-48, 149-51,
164-65, 191, 199. See
also Enlisted men;

Officers; U.S. Mili-
tary
Clay, James P, 181-82
Cloud, George H: duty,
85; off-duty hours,
113; reason for en-
listment, 63; views of
Chinese military, 156-
57; views of enlisted
men, 69-70; views of
White Russians, 130
Colorado, 154
Connor, William D. Brig.
Gen.: language train-
ing, 144, 210; pro-
posed single army
command, 28-30;
venereal disease regu-
lations, 128; views of
long service men, 172;
views of mission, 31
Constellation, 13
Coolie Trade, 6
Craig, Edward A, 157
Curtis, Donald, 151

Daniels, Josephius, 75
Doe, Jens A, 50
Dorsay, William, 57
Draper, Benjamin F, 147
Drunkenness. See Enlist-
ed men; Officers

East India Squadron: and
Arrow War, 14; and
diplomats, 12, 13; and
merchants, 12; and
missionaries, 12;
Taiping Rebellion, 14-
15; changed to Asiatic
Fleet, 15; effects of
American Civil War on,
15; establishment of,
11; make-up of, 12;
mission of, 11-13;
neutrality of, 14.
See also Asiatic Fleet
Education. See Enlist-
ed men; Officers

Empress of China
  (Ship), 5
Enlisted men: age, 56-
  59, 60; arrival in
  China, 85-85, 92;
  career patterns, 56-
  59, 61-63, 77-79, 177-
  78; civilian views of,
  73; in combat, 187-88,
  190, 197-200; courts-
  martial 64-67, 68, 70,
  71-72; death of, 199;
  drunkenness, 65-66,
  78, 125-27; duties of,
  87-92, 93-95, 100-102,
  143; education, 54,
  58, 69-70, 77-79, 210-
  11; equipment of, 90,
  93, 100, 101, 195;
  family life, 74, 127;
  fighting, 130-31;
  language classes, 133,
  144-45; length of ser-
  vice, 54, 55-56, 57,
  59, 65, 77-79; living
  conditions, 86, 92-93,
  99-100; living with
  Chinese, 129-30, 116;
  living with White
  Russians, 129, 130;
  nationality of, 59-61,
  69; off-duty hours,
  110-111, 112-16, 118,
  130-34; officers view
  of, 63-64, 66-68, 70,
  73-74, 75-77, 79;
  place of enlistment,
  58, 59-61, 77-78;
  quality of, 63-64, 85,
  102-103, 172-73; rea-
  son for enlisting, 55,
  57, 59, 61-63, 68, 77-
  78; reason for request-
  ing China, 55, 61, 62,
  143; researching in-
  formation on, 43-45,
  54-55; retiring in
  China, 171-72, 175-
  78, 179-80, 182-83;

social life, 131-32;
  uniforms, 86-87, 99,
  101, 144; venereal
  disease, 127-29; views
  of China, 143, 156,
  171-72; views of Chi-
  nese, 125, 146-48,
  151, 164-65, 174;
  views of duty, 172,
  201, 204; views of
  foreigners, 131-32;
  views of officers, 70,
  73, 74-77, 84 n.73
Erskine, Graves B: and
  employment of Chinese
  servants, 95-96, 152;
  and social life, 109,
  122-23; views of
  officers, 85, 94
Extraterritoriality,
  4, 7

Felder, Joseph, requests
  China, 53
Feng Yu-hsiang (Feng
  Youxiang), 192, 194
Fifteenth Infantry
  Regiment, 44, 86, 156,
  192, 199 204; areas of
  responsibility, 194-
  95; athletics in, 111;
  control of by State
  Dept., 28; humanitar-
  ian efforts of, 102;
  language requirements
  in, 143-45, 210; lo-
  cation of barracks,
  86; long service men
  in, 172-73; ordered to
  China, 21, 23; mission
  of, 30-31; reasons for
  serving in, 143; re-
  creational activities
  for, 115; regimental
  celebration week ("Can
  Do"), 88-89; reenlist-
  ment rate in, 172;
  rifle marksmanship in,
  89-91; social obliga-

tions in, 119; uni-
forms of, 86-87; use
of Chinese servants
in, 95, 96; venereal
disease regulations
in, 128-29; withdrawal
of, 30, 209
Findley, Virgil, 176
Finney, Charles G:
off-duty hours, 125,
133; living with
Chinese, 178, 179;
reason for enlisting,
55; retirement in
China, 172, 178, 179;
rifle marksmanship,
90; uniforms, 86-87;
views of China, 143
Fourth U.S. Marine
Regiment, 27; duty day
in, 92, 93; location of
barracks, 93; ordered
to China, 24; quality
of regiment, 85
Fox, Donald R, Jr., 123;
retirement in China,
178
Freeman, Paul L:
athletics, 88-89;
duty, 103; language
course, 145; requests
China, 52; uniforms,
87; venereal disease
reports, 128-29; views
of enlisted men, 54

Giffen, Robert C, 108
n.69; plans to combat
venereal disease 127-
28
Glass, Floyd Franklin,
176
Gowan, Frank, 177
Griffith, Samuel B, III:
family life, 123;
views of Chinese, 146;
views of enlisted men
54; travel in China 114
Gunboats, 188, 190. See

also under individual
ship

Hanson, Laurence C,
off-duty hours, 131
Hardcastle, William R:
views of enlisted men,
84 n.73; views of
officers, 74
Hargrave, Glenn M, 68
Harrison, Gordon D, 62
Hart, John N, conditions
in Tientsin, 92-93
Hempel, Anna, 177
Hempel, Richard, 177
Hennrick, Charles, 69
Hill, Charles S, 24
Hogaboom, Robert E: so-
cial life, 135; views
of Chinese military,
157
Horrall, Eugene F, 68
Howell, Glenn, 131; and
Chinese servants, 96;
athletics, 111; re-
tirement in China,
178, 182-83; views of
China, 158-59; views
of Chinese, 151, 158-
60; views of duty, 52,
98; views of enlisted
men, 66-67, 76, 115-
16, 125, 133; views of
foreigners in China,
124; views of gun-
boats, 98-99; views
of missionaries, 201-
202
Howes, Norman B, 57
Hung Hisu-chuan (Hung
Xinchuan), 8
Huron, 63. See also
South Dakota

Ingrisano, Anthony, 130;
athletics, 110-11;
venereal disease in-
spections, 129; views
of foreigners in

China, 132; views of
officers, 75, 76-77
International Settlement
(Shanghai), 23, 24,
157, 199
Irvin, William D:
athletics, 110; reason
for enlisting, 45
Isaacson, Julius, 63
Isabel, 23, 155, 158

James, Jimmy, 176-177
John D. Ford (Ship),
190
Johnson, Joseph E: duty
day, 92; living with
Chinese, 129; off-
duty, 133
Johnson, William,
train guard, 198-99
Jordahl, Russell N, 124

Kearney, Lawrence, 4
Knox, Fred, 21

Larson, August, 117
Lavine, C. W, 178
Ledyard, John, 4-5
Leutz, Eugene H. C, 66
Lucky, Robert B: ath-
letics, 111; off-
duty, 135
Lynch, G. A, 181
Lyndale, Vance, views
of China, 146-47
Lynett, Thomas, 57

MacArthur, Douglas, 47,
73-74
McKenna, Richard, 187;
Chinese servants, 95;
view of China, 156;
views of enlisted men,
69, 125; views of
gunboats, 99, 115
Mahan, Alfred Thayer,
17-18
Marblehead, 97
Marshall, George C, 52,

64, 211; language
abilities, 144; rid-
ing, 112, 113; social
life, 122; unrest in
China, 192, 195; views
of China, 90; views of
drinking, 125
Matthews, Alberta J,
123-24
Miller, Adolf B: disci-
pline, 64; duty, 103;
off-duty, 122, 124
Miller, Ellis Bell,
64-65
Mindanao (gunboat), 182
Missionaries, 188-90;
202-203. See also
Enlisted Men; Officers
Monadnock (gunboat), 155
Monocacy (gunboat), 178
Moore, Cecil C, 62
Moore, John D, 178, 185
n.20
Moriarty, James F,
merchant ship armed
guard, 100-101
Morris, Robert, 5
Murphy, Garry L, 177

Newell, Isaac, 88

Officers: age, 50-51;
arrival in China, 86;
assisting mission-
aries, 188-90; career
patterns, 53-54;
courts-martial, 67-68;
decorations of, 50-51,
52; drunkenness, 126-
27; duties of, 87, 88,
93-95, 96-97, 100-102,
108 n.69, 197-99; edu-
cation, 49-50; family
life, 118-20, 121,
123; in combat, 195-
97, 198-99; language
requirements, 143-44,
145-46, 210; off-duty
hours, 109-110, 111-

14; pay of, 117; place
of enlistment, 45-46,
53-54; quality of, 52-
54, 85, 103, 180-182;
reason for enlisting,
45; reason for re-
questing China, 51-52;
social life, 120-24,
134; uniforms, 87, 99,
121; views of China,
113-114, 135, 156,
158-59, 164-65; views
of Chinese, 146, 149,
150-52, 155-56; 159-
60, 164-65, 173, 210;
views of Chinese mil-
itary, 156-57; views
of diplomats, 203;
views of duty, 52, 85,
204; views of enlisted
men, 66-67, 70, 73-74,
75, 76-77, 173; views
of foreigners, 124;
views of missionaries,
201-202; views of
retiring in China,
178-78; where
acquired, 47-49
Opium trade, 2-3, 6
Opium War, 3-4, 13
Ormiston, Edward J,
mounted troops,
101-102; views of
Chinese, 147, 168 n.48

Palos (gunboat), 95,
102 passim; 131-152
passim; 171-203 pass-
im; 239-245 passim
Pampanga (gunboat), 161,
181, 191
Panay (gunboat), 209
Parker, Daniel, 5
Parrish, Noel F, 73
Peking (Beijin), passim
Penquin, 76, 116
Perry, Matthew C, 12, 14
Pfeiffer, Omar T, 24, 67
Place, Ernie, 149-50

Plummer, Robert J, 114
Pope, Benjamin H, 112
Povey, Howard L, 68
Poy, Henry J, 99, 131;
prejudice against,
160; views of China,
161; views of
Chinese, 181, 191-
92
Pratt, Don, 77

Quiros (gunboat), 190

Reimert, William A, 189
Ridgway, Matthew, 45;
use of bluff, 196;
view of duty, 52

St. Lawrence, George,
171
Scheyer, William J, 157
Schiehorst, Edwin C, 68
Shanghai, passim
Smith, George, 177-78
Smith, Glen, 132
Smith, Robert F: arrival
in China, 85-86; du-
ties, 87; enlistment,
55
Smith-Hutton, Henri, 156
South China Patrol, 97,
181, 191
South Dakota, 63, 64.
See also Huron
Spencer, Earl Winfield,
181, 191
Stevenson, Charles, 53
Stillwell, Joseph:
lectures on China,
156; reason for
enlisting, 45
Stimmers, Malcolm P, 68
Stryker, Joe W: chit
system, 118; officers
drinking, 126; pay
officer, 116
Stribling, Cornelius K,
14
Susquehanna, 12

Taiping Rebellion, 7-9
Tan Yen-Kai (Tan
  Yangai), 188
Tattnal, Josiah, 14
Third Marine Brigade,
  25, 97, 102, 156
Thirty-first Infantry
  Regiment, 30
Thomas, Gerald C, 135
Thomas, Lawrence H, 57
Thomason, John W, Jr.,
  75, 94-95
Tidwell, Albert, 68,
  148, 204
Tientsin (Tianjin),
  passim
Tolley, Kemp: Chinese
  money, 116-117;
  long service men, 172;
  retirement in China,
  177; uniforms, 121;
  White Russians, 130
Tracy, Benjamin, 18-19
Treaty of Nanking, 3
Treaty of the Bogue, 3
Truesdale, Karl, 76
Tuttle, Carl M, 125-26,
  131
Tuttle, William B, 195-
  97
Tzu Hsi (Zi Xi), 11

Umsted, Scott, 114
U.S. Army. See Enlisted
  men; Officers;
  Fifteenth Infantry
  Regiment; Thirty-first
  Infantry Regiment
U.S. Marine Corps. See
  Enlisted men; Fourth
  U.S. Marine Regiment;
  Officers; Third Marine
  Brigade
U.S. military, effects
  of depression on, 68,
  78, 210; See also
  Enlisted men; Fif-
  teenth Infantry;
  Fourth Marine

Regiment; Officers;
  Yangtze Patrol
U.S. Navy. See Asiatic
  Fleet; East India
  Squadron; Enlisted
  Men; Officers; South
  China Patrol; Yangtze
  River Patrol

Van Deurs, George, 97,
  181
Venereal Disease. See
  Enlisted men; Officers
Villabos (gunboat), 190

Wagner, Jack J: incident
  of combat, 188; views
  of Chinese, 147; views
  of foreigners in
  China, 132
Webb, Oliver G, 126
White Russians. See
  Enlisted Men
Wheeler, Charles J, 45,
  63-64
White Lotus Rebellion,
  1-2
Williams, Clarence S,
  ADM, 24, 25, 26
Williams, Robert Hugh:
  polo, 112-13; rifle
  marksmanship, 93
Worton, William A:
  Chinese mission, 200;
  intelligence opera-
  tions, 102
Wu P'ei-fu (Wu Peifu),
  188, 192, 194

Yangtze River Patrol,
  99, 102, 114, 150;
  establishment of 12;
  first flag officer,
  23. See also Enlisted
  men; Officers

About the Author

DENNIS L. NOBLE is a part-time Instructor at Peninsula College. He is the author of numerous journal articles and coedited the book *Wrecks, Rescues, and Investigations: Selected Documents of the U.S. Coast Guard and Its Predecessors.* He is also the coauthor of *Sentinels of the Rocks: From "Graveyard Coast" to National Lakeshore.*